MUSLIMS AND CHANGING INDIA

MUSLIMS
AND
CHANGING INDIA

Dr. Y. B. MATHUR

M.A. (Hist., Pol. Sc.) Ph. D.
University of Delhi.

Foreword by
Dr. TARA CHAND

TRIMURTI PUBLICATIONS PRIVATE LIMITED
NEW DELHI-48

MUSLIMS AND CHANGING INDIA

First Published : 1972

Published by

S.P. KUMRIA,
TRIMURTI PUBLICATIONS PRIVATE LIMITED
W-152, Greater Kailash-I,
New Delhi-48

Printed in India By
KALAMKAR PRAKASHAN (P) LTD.,
New Delhi-1

Sales Office
D-24, Odeon Building,
Connaught Place,
New Delhi-1

Regd. Office
W-152, Greater Kailash-I,
New Delhi-48

To

SRI SATHYA SAI BABA

FOREWORD

"Muslims and Changing India" is a study on the various aspects of the Muslim problem in India especially under British rule. The position of the Muslims in relation to the majority community has been peculiar. In two parts of the country—the north-western region or the region beyond the Sutlaj and the eastern that is Bengal, they constitute majority of the population. In the remaining parts they are a minority. These two regions are at two extremes of the sub-continent. They lie outside the main stream of Muslim influence throughout the history of India. They played a secondary role in the cultural life of the country during the middle ages.

But the conquest of Bengal in the last quarter of the 18th century and of the Punjab in the second half of the 19th century raised their importance. Bengal became the chief Presidency and the venue of British administrative policies and cultural influences. The Punjab assumed the role of border defence and centre of military strategy.

They played an extraordinary part in Indian politics. The British pursuing their ambitions for domination over India discovered very early that the key to success lay in exploiting the divisions in Indian society. Lack of political sense among Indians permitted this policy to succeed.

Mediaeval India was riven by all kinds of differences—religious, regional, racial, social, economic. Unity was scarce, groupings were exiguous. It was easy to appeal to personal ambitions and rouse men against their kith and kin. The British in India took advantage of the situation. The Hindus

and Muslims who were hardly conscious of any political conflict between them, were moved by personal loyalty to the
chief under whom they served irrespective of his religion.
After the conquest they gradually acquired a sense of community and feeling of common interests.

The conquest of Bengal and the establishment of land
revenue systems followed by reforms in judicial administration
and introduction of western education were measures which
struck hard blows on the Muslims. The replacement of the
Muslims from the lucrative posts, the establishment of the
permanent settlement and the substitution of Muslims Civil and
Criminal laws and courts by modern judicial, legal codes and
processes, reduced the Muslim aristocracy to penury. Deep
rooted hatred of the alien government spread.

The opportunities created by the overthrow of the Muslim
government were welcomed by the Hindus. They acquired
Zamindaris, worked the judicial apparatus and cooperated in
the development of educational system.

The Muslims became jealous of the Hindus, while fearing
and hating the British. Against the latter they started cons-
piracies with the intention of overthrowing British rule. The
Muslim aristocratic class was so overawed that they scarcely
dared to rebel. The Muslim learned class who were aggrieved
by the British rule because Muslim education had suffered from
loss of patronage of the Government and the Muslim nobility
and because they resented the attacks of British missionaries
and officers on their religion, unfurled the banner of open
revolt and secret conspiracy.

The Muslim opposition movement continued till the
Mutiny. Then Sir Sayyid Ahmad Khan realized the
hopeless character of the enterprise and the futility of attempting to overthrow British rule. He started the movement
to cooperate with the Government which appeared irre-
placeable. His teaching brought about a breach in Muslim
solidarity. The Muslims became divided into two schools—the
rebels and the loyalists. The latter became advocates of
western education, and seekers of government favours. The

rebels hated western education and continued to organise movements of resistance and freedom. They showed interest in Pan-Islamic ideas and supported Muslim countries who were fighting a losing battle against Christian imperialists especially the British.

The loyalists made anti-Hindu gestures to attract the attention of the rulers who welcomed conflict between the two communities in order to thwart the national movements for reform in the system of governments. With the powerful support of the Government the loyalists succeeded in dividing the country.

The chapters contained in the book discuss different aspects of the Muslim history during British rule. The scholarly articles are the result of wide reading and clear thinking. They throw light upon the policies of British by which a country separated by thousands of miles from India maintained its hold over the Indian sub-continent for nearly two hundred years.

Dr. TARA CHAND

PREFACE

This is a study dealing with British policy towards the Indian Muslims. It is based entirely on the Home Political and Confidential Records of the Government of India which were not accessible to research scholars until recently. With these records readily available, I have felt little need to rely on, or quote from contemporary books which were either written from memory or derived from secondary sources. By consulting instead almost all the documents dealing with Indian Muslims I have been able to examine at first hand in this study the changes effected in the political, social, educational, religious and economic life of the Muslims in Modern India.

An account of the Muslim League has been purposely left out of this study because most of the relevant documents have either been destroyed or are not available in India. Nevertheless the present volume will prove useful in this respect also, in so far as at least some of the chapters in it will persuade historians to reconsider the work of the Muslim League in the light of the new material that has emerged from records about several other Muslim political parties which not only opposed the Muslim League but threatened its very existence.

One main point that emerges from this study may be emphasised here. The study as a whole reveals the British view that, despite the overt support and encouragement given to the Indian Muslims this community had proved itself unable to excel or even compete with the other communities in the country. Muslim backwardness in education, their extra-territorial sympathies or Pan Islamic ideas; their attempts to overthrow British government; their internal dissensions and lastly their support to the Congress—but not to the Muslim League—particularly in the North Western Frontier Province, were probably the factors that led the British to arrive at this conclusion.

Some of these essays were published in *Islamic Review*; (London); *Islamic Culture* (Hyderabad) and *Studies in Islam* (New Delhi) but I have added several others in this book to complete the study of Indian Muslims. I owe a deep debt of gratitude to Dr. Tara Chand, the well known historian, and Dr. A.N. Kaul, Professor of English, University of Delhi for all their help and encouragement. I have also to thank Mr. S.A. Ali, Editor, Indian Institute of Islamic Studies, New Delhi and my wife Dr. Uma Yaduvansh, Lecturer in Political Science, Daulat Ram College, Delhi for editing some of the chapters.

School of Correspondence Courses,   Y.B. MATHUR
University of Delhi
2 June, 1972

Contents

1

Religious Disturbances in India

Throughout the British rule religious disturbances broke out with fury almost every year.[1] These disturbances show that they were invariably confined to the Hindu and Muslim communities and originated on such familiar grounds as the cutting of a peepal tree, the fouling of water supply or an insulting and a provocative couplet. But these were the occasions[2] for outbreak rather than the causes. It would not however be difficult to find out why these disturbances broke out with such frequency. The main and chief cause appears to be the existence of public press which led to rapid dissemination of news throughout India. Telegraph further accelerated the process and led to the organisation of meetings everywhere for discussing the nature of such disturbances. Religious sentiments were early stirred by publication of true and false things. Exactly the same thing had happened

---

[1]For example between 1889-93, seven disturbances broke out in Bombay, 46 in Bengal 9 in N.W.P. and Oudh, 17 in Madras, 1 in Punjab and 3 in Hyderabad. Again between 1923-26 riots broke out at 71 places and were responsible for 3000 injured and 260 deaths.

[2]Note by Mr. A. P. Muddiman dated 28.9.1924. Home Political F. No. 140 of 1925, Sr. Nos. 1-17.

throughout Europe in 1848. The news of the overthrow of monarchy of Louis Phillip had its effect in turning men's thoughts to revolutionary outbreaks in Prussia, Austria, Italy and Russia.[3]

According to the opinion of the masses these disturbances broke out on such issues as cow-killing; playing of music before mosques; the construction and demolition of mosques; coincidence of Hindu and Muslim festivals; obstruction in each other's places of worship and in festivals. But the educated classes attributed these to such causes as the increasing heat of religious, political and race discussion, which could be seen from the struggle for Government posts, the question of separate representation; the proximity of census; the growing irritation of Muslims with Swadeshi and boycott agitation coupled with agrarian and social disturbances; Muslim extra-territorial sympathies, and lastly to the missionary or proselytizing movements.[4] Let us now examine these causes.

Cow-killing

The most disturbing element in the politics of India had been the question of cow-killing. This question assumed a definite shape under the British rule and constituted a menance to the peace of the country.[5] Muslims all along regarded cow sacrifice as a religious right whereas it was repugnant to all Hindus much more to Marwaris and Jains,[6] but the propaganda which they carried on in favour of cow protection societies[7] resulted in religious disturbances in several parts of India. For instance, it was reported in November 1912 that serious Hindu-Muslim disturbances took place at Ajodhya and Fyzabad in the United Provinces over the sacrifice of cows by

---

[3]Government of India's Note dated 6.10.1893. Home Political A proceeding Nos, 169-89 dated November 1893.

[4]Government of India's Note dated 6.10.1893. Home Political Proceeding Nos. 169-89 dt. November, 1893.

[5]Home Political B. Proceeding No. 198 of 1924.

[6]Home Political F. No. 179/1/1926.

[7]Government of India's Note dated 6.10.1893, Home Political A: November 1893, Nos. 169-89:

the Muslims on the occasion of the *Id-uz-Zuha*. Hindu-Muslim feeling on this question had always remained strained in Ajodhya which is one of the most important centres of *Vishnu* worship in northern India, and from 1906 onwards constant potentialities of trouble became more imminent to invite the close attention of local authorities. Trouble began in October 1912 in Fyzabad but the serious riots did not occur till the *Id* in November, when the Hindus attacked the Muslims in Ajodhya and Fyzabad, in the former place killing one and injuring 39 Muslims and in the latter place (where the Muslims gave provocation) killing one Muslim. A company of British soldiers had to be called in at Ajodhya and were compelled to fire on and charge the mob, killing three and wounding six Muslims. Indian cavalry were also called in but not actively employed.[8]

To quote another incident, in October 1916, two serious Hindu-Muslim disturbances occurred in the Patna District on the occasion of *Bakr-Id*. Trouble had been anticipated owing to the attitude of the Hindus, and precautionary measures had been taken, but in one village a mob of some 7,000 to 10,000 Hindus endeavoured to present the performance of the sacrifice in spite of the presence of the District Magistrate with armed police. The mob had to be fired on, and finally the Muslims refrained from performing the sacrifice owing to their fear of the Hindus and the weakness and unreliability of of the police force present on the spot. In another village where careful precautions had been taken, a mob of 4,000 Hindus attempted to loot the village and kill the Muslims inspite of the presence of a military police under a European inspector. This force finally had to fire on them and forced them to retire. These riots were due to deliberate Hindu aggression and were the fore-runners of the serious Hindu-Muslim disturbances[9] which broke out in 1918 in Shahabad and Gaya districts where the predominant Hindus determined to terrorise the Muslims and prevent them from performing the sacrifice. The trouble began in spite of a settlement

---

[8] Home Political B. Proceedings Nos. 12-23 dated August 1217.

[9] Home Police B. Proceeding Nos. 59-61 dated November 1916.

that had already been made between the Hindus and Muslims. Large mobs of Hindus attacked the Muslims, looted their villages wholesale, taking away their cattle and damaging their mosques. They attacked the Muslims a second time in the most determined fashion but were beaten off with casualities by armed police who had been drafted in. Subsequently, the same trouble broke out in other places. Numerous villages were looted and Muslims, male and female, were maltreated and in some cases killed. The regular forces including cavalry, infantry and artillery were drafted into the area and local volunteer forces also cooperated. For a fortnight anarchy prevailed in the affected areas. As late as three weeks later sporadic disturbances were still occurring. These disturbances were of a most serious character and gave great trouble before they were repressed.[10]

The Muslims "pooh-poohed"[11] the suggestion of the Hindus to give up eating beef because that would constitute a flagrant encroachment on their religious rights.[12] They argued that its prohibition would be a staggering blow to thousands of poor Muslims, because they would be unable to purchase mutton which was costlier than beef.[13] In self-defence they always stressed that beef-eating was more widely prevalent among Europeans[14] than the Muslims.

One of the favourite arguments trotted out against cow slaughter was that it was a great drawback to the agricultural development of the country. But there was no truth whatever in this contention, because the supply of bullocks for agricultural purposes never fell short of the demand. Again it was argued that cow-slaughter was in a greater measure responsible for infant mortality but the expounders of this argument conveniently shut their eyes to the fact that Indians had enough of cows, besides numerous dairies, all of which

---

[10]Home Political A. Proceeding No. nil dated 1918.

[11]*Paisa Akhbur* Lahore, dated 26th January 1911 and 22nd February, 1911.

[12]Home Political B. Proceeding No. 198 of 1924.

[13]Ibid.

[14]*Paisa Akhbur*, Lahore dated 26th January 1911.

supplied milk in abundant quantity for the nursing of children.[15]

It is no doubt true that Hindus regarded the cow as the halo of sanctity but it was extremely ridiculous to ask the Muslims to treat her with reverence. If on the one hand the Hindus asked the Muslims to stop cow-sacrifice on the plea that it hurt their feelings, the Muslims on the other hand, pressed the Hindus to abstain from performing their religious ceremonies as were opposed to the teachings of Islam. These arguments only brought the Hindus and Muslims on war path. Conflicts between the two communities continued to occur and hampered the peaceful march of the country.[16]

Music Before Mosques

The Muslims objected to the playing of music before mosques on the ground that it disturbed the devotees in their prayers. Sometimes even during the interval between the prayers they did not allow Hindus to play music before mosques because some persons spent their whole time in saying prayers. They regarded music and songs as things of amusement and refused to allow them before mosques.[17] The Hindus, on the other hand considered it to be their right to play music and argued that in the past, processions accompanied by music always passed by mosques at all hours without any objection from the Muslims. They ruled out the Muslim argument as it caused intolerable hardship on them. Their religious and social customs required these processions to pass through public streets with music.[18] There were several precedents to prove that marriage and other processions passed before mosques while playing music e.g. they particularly made references to the mosque in Nimatullah Ghat where Hindu processions on occasions of immersion of

---

[15]Home Political B. Proceedings No. 198 of 1924.

[16]Ibid.

[17]Home Political Proceeding No. 198 of 1924.

[18]Devi Ranta Sharma, General Secretary, Hindu Mahasabha Delhi to the Secretary to the Govt. of India in the Home Department, Simla dated 20.7.1926. Home Political F. No. 179 of 1926.

gods and goddesses passed with music at all hours of the day and night, but no objection was ever raised by the Muslims. Similarly, Hindu dead bodies were carried with music at all hours of the day and night without any opposition.[19] Disturbances seemed inevitable because neither side was prepared to yield. A few illustrations will bear out the truth of this statement. On 23 December 1890, in Khandesh District, the Muslims were excited by the Hindus passing by their mosque in a procession with music, and caused a disturbance by throwing shoes at them. But on the appearance of the police the rioters dispersed. Fourteen of them were arrested but only twelve were convicted; one was fined Rs. 50, ten Rs. 30 each, and one Rs. 40. Again, in another case, on 14 July 1891, in Ratnagiri District the Hindus played music before a mosque and the Muslims stopped them and threw stones at them. The police called a meeting, at which the leading men of both communities were present when after some discussion both parties agreed to stop playing music while passing each others, places of worship.[20] The decision regarding the Bombay disturbances was different from that which was taken in Bengal in 1865. There it had been the custom for Hindu processions to discontinue their music and dancing while passing the Imambara and the Hindus did not complain of the curtailment of their existing privileges.[21] It would also be interesting to note that from 1924 onwards differences arose in Akola City between the two communities[22] over the claims of Hindu processions to play music when passing mosques. On the occasion of the *Ganpati* procession in September of that year acute friction occurred and the district authorities issued orders forbidding music for that occassion within certain prescribed

---

[19]Statesman dated 18.5.1926. See also Home Political F. No. 179 of 1926.

[20]Home Public Proceeding Nos. 348-49 dated September 1894 from the Govt. of Bombay, No. 4801 dated 9th July 1894 forwarding a statement showing Hindu-Muslim Riots between 1888-93, pp. 21-3.

[21]Hon'ble A. Eden, Secretary to Govt. of Bengal to Secy. to the Govt. of India, Home Department, Fort William dated 17th January 1865. Home Public Proceeding Nos. 99-101 dated 31st January 1865.

[22]Chief Secretary to the Government, Central Provinces to the Commissioner, Berar, No. 598/1790-IV, dated Nagpur, the 25th March, 1925, Home Political F.No. 179 and K.W. of 1926.

limits, but recorded that the orders were not to be regarded as a precedent. It was hoped that the dispute would be settled by agreement before the next year, but the negotiations failed. At the *Ganpati* festival of 1925, there was again a clear danger of violence, and in August, the District Superintendent of Police issued an order under Section 30 of the Police Act requiring all persons desiring to take out their *Ganpati* processions to apply for a license. On 20 August, on such an application being made, the District Superintendent of Police required music to be stopped for a certain distance near each mosque on the proposed road. The Hindus regarded this order as an encroachment on their right and did not take out the *Ganpati* procession in question.[23]

The Muslims had pressed their views on the subject of music to the extent of including among musical instruments *tipri* i.e., plain wooden sticks which are struck together. The district authorities, when faced with the question, decided that the use of *tipri* was permissible and on 28 September, the District Magistrate issued an order under Section 144 of the Criminal Procedure Gode directing the Muslims not to interfere with processions which used these *tipri* on the following day. This order was challenged by a Muslim in the court of the Judicial Commissioner, but the Additional Judicial Commissioner rejected the application for revision and declined to fetter the discretion of the District Magistrate in any way. On 24 October, the procession using *tipri* took place under strong police protection.[24]

Meanwhile the Hindus by means of *Satyagraha* went daily through the form of defying the local authorities in regard to playing of music, while a mutual boycott was practised by the Hindus and Muslims. The district authorities tried to keep the situation in hand by special police arrangements and by issuing orders under the Police Act and Criminal Procedure Code; but on 26 October, the growing ill-feeling resulted in riots, in which several people were hurt. Intense public

---

[23]Ibid, para 2.
[24]Ibid, para 2,

anxiety then prevailed for some days, but gradually subsided. Other occasions of dispute arose from time to time, but any fresh outbreak of violence was successfully prevented. Meanwhile the orders forbidding music near mosques remained in force.[25]

On 17 September, 1925, the *Hindu Sabha* at Akola sent a memorial to the local Government asking that the police orders prohibiting music should be superseded and that the Hindus should recieve full protection when conducting their annual *Ganpati* processions with the appropriate observances past mosques. On 9 November an elected deputation of Muslims presented a memorandum to the effect that no orders should be issued which would tend to destroy the ancient custom of stopping music before mosques. On the same day, the Governor in Council received deputations from both the communities. As a result of the discussion it seemed possible that the dispute might be settled by mutual agreement, and under instructions from Government attempts were made by the district authorities to secure this result, but the negotiations again failed. On 14 March, 1926, the Governor in Council again received the two deputations. The Hindus put in a short additional statement and both parties presented their cases.[26] It was finally ascertained that the parties could not come to an agreement among themselves on the points at issue, while a proposal for a reference of the particular dispute in question to arbitration failed. It remained, therefore, for Government to decide whether the orders passed by the local authorities for the preservation of low and order were based on a correct decision on the conflicting views of the two parties, or whether they required any modification in the light of the case now formally placed before Government by the leaders on each side.[27]

The case for the Hindus, as stated in their memorandum was that in the public worship of *Ganpati*, the Hindu processions,

---

[25]Ibid, para 4.

[26]Ibid, para 5.

[27]Ibid.

while passing recognised public mosques, had always been accustomed to play soft music, and that they limited themselves to soft, instead of loud music in deference to the religious feelings of the Muslims, rather than owing to the validity of any custom or usage. They claimed that in law the worshippers in a mosque cannot compel processionists to intermit their music. They asserted that at the *Ganpati* festival of 1925 the District authorities had received timely intimation of the Hindus claim, and it was their duty to secure the passage of the procession without molestation, not to suppress the rights of the Hindus.[28]

The case stated in the Muslim's memorandum was that *Ganpati* processions were unknown in Berar till about 1907, and were not accompanied by music till about 1923. Their present form, and their popularity among Hindus, were largely due to a feeling of hostility to Muslims. Other Hindu processions used to have little or no music, and music was not regarded as essential to them. The stopping of music before mosques was an old established custom throughout Berar and even in territories which had never been under Muslim rule. Music being *haram* (forbidden) its deliberate performance before mosques not only interrupts prayers, but interferes with the canons of Islam. The memorandum urged that, even if the Hindus had a civil right, it could not override that confirmation of religious usage which was stated in Queen Victoria's Proclamation of 1858; or the clear commandments of Islamic faith; or the treaty by which the administration of Berar was handed over to the British Government; that treaty requiring respect for such privileges as had been conferred on the people by the rulers of Hyderabad from time to time.[29]

The negotiations which the district authorities conducted at Akola revealed other difficulties, not mentioned in the memorandum, which tended to prevent settlement by consent. The parties wanted to provide for other processions, and other mosques, besides those originally in question. They raised a

---

[28] Ibid, para 6.
[29] Ibid, para 7.

special point about persons who lived in houses close to mosques. The Hindus maintained that such persons needed to have music directly outside their houses on certain occasions, that this right had never been disputed, and ought not to be affirmed. The Muslims denied both the existence and the feasibility of such a custom. They defined their claims in regard to the space over which music should be stopped; asking that it should be limited to a point beyond a radius of 40 paces i.e., about 33 yards from the premises of a mosque.[30]

The local Government decided that in the case of disputes of this kind, while a settlement by consent may well be expected to cover the whole field of contention, a decision imposed on conflicting parties by an external authority for executive purposes, though based on general principles, should be limited to the points which definitely require orders. It therefore set out briefly the principles which should govern any decision in disputes of this nature and to show generally the application of these principles to the particular case under consideration.[31]

"In matters of religion Government maintains an attitude of strict neutrality, but while sympathising with the neutral desire of each party to perform their religious obligations without interference or annoyance, Government must, where the demands of religion come in conflict with civil right, aim primarily at upholding the common rights of the individual. The complicated circumstances under which the thoroughfares are used by the public, and especially by processions, may give rise to occasions on which the common right has temporarily to be superseded by the use of the emergency powers of the local authorities. But such emer. gencies do not imply any permanent denial of individual rights.[32] In a general way no civil restriction on the use of a thoroughfare arises from the existence beside it of any

---

[30] Ibid, para 8.

[31] Ibid, para 9.

[32] The rights of the individual, when using a public street are described in various Judicial rulings and in the Privy Council ruling reported in India Law Reports 47, Allahabad, page 155,

place of worship. Government has considered the contention of the Muhammadans that in Berar they are in the enjoyment of special rights involving a limitation of the religious customs of their Hindu fellow citizens and that previous usage is in their favour; Berar having been for a long time under Muhammadan administration. Government cannot uphold this contention until its validity has been established by judicial authority. Ordinarily no person has a right to obstruct others when making lawful use of a public street, and alleged customs which are contrary to the principles of religious impartiality, maintained by Government, cannot be admitted until they are legally established. At the same time Government recognizes that Muhammadans should have the opportunity to perform their religious observances so far as possible undisturbed. For example, in the case of certain mosques, especially those of an old established character, it may be reasonable and right that there should be restrictions on the playing of music by other communities, whether in respect of hour, proximity or volume. Such restrictions which may vary according to the circumstances of time and place must, however, be limited to securing on the part of the public and individuals as much consideration as should be given by men of sense and good feeling without unreasonable sacrifice to a party whose religious susceptibilities would otherwise be unduly offended.[33]

"Government recognizes that orders issued to meet an emergency are not necessarily intended as a permanent solution of the situation, while its present instructions are themselves subject to such more final pronouncement on the respective claims of the parties as may be obtained from the judicial courts by consent or by legislation. The orders passed by the local authorities regarding the *Ganpati* procession of 1925 were effective for the purpose for which they were issued, and Government sees no reason to question their propriety. But the situation has now

---

[33] Ibid, para 10,

altered, and it is possible to consider it in a calmer atmosphere. Government has no intention of usurping the functions of the local authorities by formulating instructions on matters of detail. It considers that arrangements should be made to allow the *Ganpati* processions to pass to their destination without being compelled to break of their music beyond what may be considered necessary to give effect to the principles already stated. Orders issued with these objects and based on the principles enunciated will receive Government support.[34]

"Government deeply regrets that the uncompromising attitude of the parties has rendered impossible a settlement of this dispute by mutual agreement. It recognizes that the definition of the attitude of the executive in regard to disputes of this nature, which has now been given, contains no permanent solution of the conflict of views which underlies the situation, and that such a solution can only be arrived at either by the substitution for the present attitude of antagonism of a spirit of conciliation and good will, or by such a reference to the courts of law or such legislation as shall definitely and finally determine the specific rights of each party in respect of the claims which they represent. Government appeals to both parties to sink their animosities and to work together for the common good."[35]

Construction and Demolition of Mosques

Several disturbances broke out in India owing to construction and demolition of mosques. On 16 May, 1891, it was reported from Calcutta that a Hindu who had recently purchased certain land brought a suit in ejectment against the occupier of land, a Muslim, after having duly served him with a notice to quit. The Muslim alleged that, with the aid of public subscription, he had, about 25 years previously erected on this land a small building, consisting of mud and brick walls with a thatched roof, which had since its erection been known

---

[34] Ibid, para 11.

[35] Ibid, para 12,

and used as a mosque. He claimed that he had erected the mosque with the knowledge of the previous owner of the land, also a Hindu. The Sub-judge of the 24 Parganas decided, that the building was not of a substantial character, and that no implicit permission for its erection as a mosque had been given by the previous landlord, and that the dependant was merely a tenant at will. He accordingly decreed the suit in the plaintiff's favour, and ordered the defendant to give up possession of land and to remove the mosque within 15 days from the date of the suit. The defendant took no steps to comply with this order, and on the expiration of the 15 days assembled about 2,000 of the local Muslims to resist an apprehended removal of the mosque.[36]

The mob, armed with sticks, assaulted and chased away some policemen of the local *Thana*, who endeavoured to explain that the Muslims had assembled under a misapprehension. The rioters then took possession of the main road which passes the mosque, and stopped all traffic, assaulting passengers. A Superintendant of Police and a Muslim Inspector with 25 men next endeavoured to pacify the rioters, but they were driven off and badly beaten. The Commissioner and the Deputy Commissioner of Police with European Police, foot and mounted, followed shortly but rioters had taken up position behind some wire-fencing and could not be dislodged. Twice the Police were beaten off. Gradually Police reinforcements arrived and the force, being armed with sticks, hastily collected, dispersed the mob about four hours after its assembling. Ninty-Seven rioters were arrested on the spot, and of these 26 were at once taken to hospital for treatment; 15 others were arrested shortly afterwards.[37]

Hindu-Muslim disturbances also broke out in the Nellore District, Madras in February 1913. The ultimate cause was friction between the parties over the building of a mosque in

---

[36]Home Public A. Proceeding Nos. 348-49 from Govt. of Bombay, No. 4801, dt. 9th July 1894 forwarding a statement of Hindu Muslim riots between 1889-93; pp. 21-22.

[37]Ibid, pp. 22-3.

a main thoroughfare despite the protests of the Hindus and the proximate cause was a Hindu religious procession passing the mosque during a religious recitation. An affray resulted and the Hindus who were attacking the mosque were fired on by the police under the order of the *Taluk* Magistrate and two were killed.[38]

In August 1913 the famous Kanpur disturbances broke out. The cause was Muslim's resentment over the demolition of a lavatory attached to a mosque in connection with municipal improvements.[39] It is well known that a new road, after much discussion, was to be opened through the city of Kanpur. The first alignment chosen in 1908 was altered in 1909 because it involved dismantling of several mosques and temples. Among the mosques was one in the quarter known as Machhli Bazar. The new alignment passed through a portion of the courtyard on the east of the mosque proper. At the north-east corner of the courtyard was a place, measuring 9 feet by 28 feet, used for purposes of ablution. It contained a small *istinja khana* (bathroom) and a massonry drain. The floor was raised 6 inches above the level of the courtyard, and the place was a later addition to the main building. In November 1911 the *mutawallis* of the mosque wrote to the Chairman of the Board stating that the materials of a house adjoining the mosque on the eastern side had been sold by auction. They pointed out that the western wall of the house was used by the mosque, the rafters of which rested on it. They feared that when the house was demolished this wall might be pulled down and the mosque thereby partly dismantled. A Sub-Committee of the municipal board, which constituted the improvement trust, noted on the 3 February 1913 that they understood the parties would come to an agreement under which the wall would remain. The Deputy Collector in charge of land aquisition had noted that the wall should not be pulled down and that a portion would probably be available when the bathroom was taken. The proceedings of the Sub-Committee were confirmed by the municipal board on the 6 February 1912. In September 1911 the question of

---

[38]Home Police B Proceeding Nos. 58-66 dated December 1913.
[39]Home Police A Proceeding Nos. 100-18 dated October, 1913.

demolishing a temple, which fell in the direct route, was brought to the notice of Government, and Sir Leslie Porter considered that no change should be made.[40] The question was again pressed a year later, and in November 1912 Sir James Meston visited the spot, and decided that the temple could remain if the road was splayed on both sides. On the same day a Muslim member of the Board asked whether the new orders about the temple would affect mosques. The chairman explained to His Honour that all that was intended was the removal of the bathing place from one mosque; and the questioner was accordingly informed that the splaying of the road would not affect mosques. After His Honour's visit some agitation took place in Kanpur, where the Muslims appear to have thought that the Hindus had gained while Muslims had obtained nothing. *Fatwas* were obtained to the effect that no part of a mosque could be alienated. The place was inspected by the chairman of the Municipal Board and a member, who were both allowed to enter the washing-place wearing shoes, and subsequently by the Collector who also entered it.[41] In February 1913 a Sub-Committee of the trust inspected the locality and decided that a plot to the north of the mosque should be given as compensation for the place to be removed. The decision of the committee was confirmed by the Board at a meeting on 18 March 1913, though a protest, which was ruled out of order, was made by one member raising the question whether any portion of the building should be acquired. A deputation waited on the District Magistrate, who heard them and advised them not to press the agitation, which he considered fictitious.[42] A requisition was then sent to the chairman of the Board asking for further discussion of the matter, and a resolution was passed and forwarded to Government asking that no portion of the mosque be acquired in deference to the feelings of the Muslim community. On 6 May 1913 orders were passed by Government to the effect that the mosque would not be interfered with but that the washing-place was not considered part of the sacred building. It was pointed

---

[40] Home Political A Proceeding No. 118 dated October, 1913.
[41] Ibid.
[42] Ibid.

out that similar alterations had taken place in connection with improvements at that place. The Municipal Board considered this letter at a meeting held on 20 May, and after some discussion a resolution was carried, by the casting vote of the chairman, to the effect that the decision of Government should be accepted as final. Further proceedings in regard to demolition were delayed by the local authorities in order to get the ground cleared and the new building erected before the washing-place was demolished. A petition had already been received by Government through a barrister of Lucknow in April asking that acquisition proceedings should be stopped. The Lieutenant Governor was also approached by Maulana Muhammad Ali, editor of *Comrade*, and by the Raja of Mahmudabad.[43] In view of the spread of agitation outside Kanpur the district magistrate was directed to get the washing-place removed as quickly as possible, and on 1 July 1913 it was demolished. In view of the well-known turbulent character of the mill hands, a force of armed police was present. No opposition was offered as the exact time of removal had not been known to the public. The spot was visited, as soon as the news spread, by a large number of Muslims. No disturbance was caused, and the Muslims held a meeting the same evening at which it was decided to send a telegram to His Excellency the Viceroy and to do nothing further till an answer was received.[44] Later in the month a second meeting was held, which also *saw* no violence. Meanwhile, a vigorous agitation was rising in the press and through the agency of the Muslim League and its branches. The agitation was largely engineered by the *Comrade* of Delhi, the *Muslim Gazette* of Lucknow and the *al-Hilal* of Calcutta.[45] But a number of well-known Muslims outside these provinces visited Kanpur and other persons took action by despatching letters calling on Muslims to hold meetings. The affairs of the mosque had till recently been managed by two *mutawallis*, but during the progress of the agitation the number had been enlarged to eleven. While hitherto the *mutawallis* had invari-

[43] Ibid.

[44] Ibid.

[45] Ibid.

ably been representatives of the *bisatis* or pedlars who were the chief worshippers at the mosque, the new managers included representatives from various parts of the city. On 1 August 1913 a notice was circulated summoning another mass meeting at an *Idgah* outside the city on 3 August. The date had obviously been chosen as it was a Sunday on which mill hands would be available to swell the throng.[46] The assemblage is estimated to have been from ten to fifteen thousands of persons. Many of the people marched barefooted and bareheaded and some of them were carrying black flags. A number of speeches were made, most of which, though rhetorical, were comparatively unobjectionable. Finally one Maulvi Abdul Qadir known as Azad Subhani, the chief local agitator and the sender of the telegram to the Viceroy, got up and made a violent speech, for which he was prosecuted under section 124A, Indian Penal Code. On arrival at the mosque some members of the crowd raised a cry that the washing-place should be restored, and a number of men began to pile up bricks. The city *Kotwal* with a few civil police men attempted to persuade the people to desist, but he was met by shouts of abuse and showers of brickbats. Police were summoned from another station, but they also were overpowered. Information was then sent to the Magistrate, who with the Superintendent of Police brought up a force of armed and mounted police. Attempts to quiet the mob were unavailing; the lives of the government servants were in imminent danger; and the District Magistrate finally ordered the police to fire. A number of lives were lost and a large number of the rioters were arrested.[47]

Coincidence of Hindu and Muslim Festivals

In 1910 serious disturbances blazed up in Peshawar over the coincidence of a Hindu festival of rejoicing the *Holi* with a Muslim occasion of mourning *viz.* the *Bara Wafat.* Briefly the facts are that in spite of arrangements agreed on by local influential Hindus and Muslims under the auspices of

---

[46]Ibid.

[47]18 persons were killed, 27 severely wounded, and several had minor injuries. See Home Police A Proceeding Nos. 100-18 dated October 1913.

the Deputy Commissioner, Peshawar, rioting broke out on the
night of 21 March 1910, owing partly to an infringement by
the Hindus of the terms of the agreement and partly to
Muslim intolerance of the Hindu rejoicings, and was renewed
in a serious form on the 22nd and 23rd when wholesale looting
of Hindu shops went on and violent fighting took place which
resulted in the death of three Muslims and nine Hindus and the
wounding of seven Muslims and thirty three Hindus. Four
hundred and fiftyone shops were broken into, many of which were
looted and much property was plundered.[48] The civil police was
unable to restore order and Indian troops had to be called in,
these having to be replaced later by British troops owing to
tension between the Hindu and Muslim elements in the Indian
troops.[49]

Obstruction in each other's places of Worship and in Festivals

Serious Hindu-Muslim disturbances broke out in Aligarh
in 1890 owing to obstruction at places of worship. It was
reported that a pot of filth was thrown at night into a mosque;
then beef was hung into two Hindu wells; subsequently a
young pig was thrown into a mosque and finally two Muslims
attempted to cut off the nose of Lala Badri Prasad, a lawyer,
the leader of the Hindu party. This assault was committed in the
compound of the Jndge's Court.[50] The criminals were arrested
and sentenced to seven year's rigorous imprisonment. Police
was also stationed at the expense of the people.[51]

Some disturbances occurred due to hindrance caused
by the Muslims in the performance of Hindu festivals and *vice
versa*. In Madras on the Hindu festival day, *Vijaya Dasami* a
small band of Muslims removed a small *pandal* (pavilion) put
up in a garden when an idol (*Viramakali Amman*) was being

---

[48]No less than 120 cartsful were recovered and the Hindus estimated losses
at five lakhs of rupees.
[49]Home Police B Proceeding No. 78 dated November 1910. See also Home
Police B Proceeding No. 46 dated August 1970.
[50]Home Public A Proceeding No. 352 from the Govt. of N.W.P. and Oudh,
No. 241 dt. 1st March, 1894.
[51]Ibid, No. 353.

taken by the Hindus in a procession. Seeing that the *Pandal* had been pulled down, the idol was taken back to the temple; but on the way the Muslims pelted it and the processionists with cow-dung. Seven Muslims were charged and sentenced to pay fine upto Rs. 100 each.[52] Again, a party of about fifty nine Muslims objected to a Hindu procession with a car (a four-wheeled platform arrangement newly made) passing a mosque They would allow the deity being carried on the shoulders of men, but not in the car. Inspite of all attempts by the Deputy Magistrate and the Police to conciliate the Muslims, many rushed out of the mosque, dragged the car close to the mosque, broke the wooden images and ran away. Eleven Muslims were ultimately convicted and sentenced to six weeks rigorous imprisonment and a fine of Rs. 50/- each.[53]

About this time in Madras, during the *Muharram* festival some Hindus disguised themselves as *Nabobs* at which the *Labbais*, a class of Muslims, felt themselves insulted, and a quarrel arose in consequence, which eventually ended in a fight. Ring leaders on both sides were arrested and charged before the Vellore *Taluk* Magistrate[54], who discharged them. In Bombay too disturbances occurred because some Hindus attempted to carry on a *Tabut* (i.e. *Tazia* or model of the tomb of Hasan and Husain) in front of one belonging to a Muslim. The disturbance was stopped by the Police; fifteen of the rioters were sentenced by the Magistrate to a fine of Rs. 25 each. A punitive post was also established in the village for one year.[55]

Next in December 1913 Hindu-Muslim disturbances took place in Agra in the United Provinces over the *Muharram*. The Muslim's opposed the taking out of *barats* by the Hindus during the *Muharram* according to recognised custom, and the Hindus

---

[52]Home Public A Proceeding No. 345 dated September, 1894 from the Government of Madras, No. 1149 dated 12th May 1894.

[53]Ibid, Nos. 346-7.

[54]Ibid.

[55]Home Public A Proceeding Nos. 348-49 dated September 1894 from the Govt. of Bombay, No. 4801 dated 9th July 1894.

retaliated. Sporadic fighting took place but more serious
disturbances were prevented by the strenous action on the part
of the district officials, aided by a British regiment and some
mounted men of the Royal Field Artillery and large reinforcements of police. Three Hindus were killed and 36 were injured,
as well as 17 Muslims.[56]

The Struggle for Government Posts

One of the main causes of religious disturbances was
the apprehension amongst Muslims that Islam and the
followers of that faith were generally suffering at the hands of
the Hindus. The impression that they were being gradually
edged out of the positions they had hitherto held in the country
was a predisposing cause of the disturbances.[57]   Dr. S.K.
Datta, an Indian Christian Member of the Legislative Assembly expressed this state of affairs in a somewhat different way.
The quarrel between the two communities, according to him,
was one of posts and positions and this had embittered the
situation. It implied that the Muslims became the victims of
the economic situation of the country and suffered from a feeling that the things of the world were not divided equally and
with any sense of justice.[58]

In 1926, Hadji A.K. Ghuznavi correctly depicted this situation in the following words: "Here in Bengal, we who but
yesterday were the conquerors and governors, are today
nothing better than doubly halots. [*sic*] We, who were once
not only the political but the intellectual power in India,
are today almost all mere tillers of the soil. We have been
gradually ousted from nearly every important walk of life.
Government employ—which was once the only source of
preferment and wealth, which enabled its holder to give
suitable education to his children who, in their turn, were
enabled to acquire wealth and position–is almost becoming

---

[56]Report on the disturbances in Agra between Hindus and Muhammadans on
the occasion of Muharram festival.
Home Police B Proceeding Nos 46-7 dt. February 1914.
[57]Home Public Proceeding No. 348 dated September, 1844.
[58]See Home Political F.No.27/IV/1926.

a monopoly of the members of the other community.[59] The following figures clearly illustrate this point. In the Executive branch of the Provincial Service there were 75 percent Hindus but 25 percent Muslims; in the Judicial branch 56 percent Hindus and 4 percent Muslims; in the Excise Department 69 percent Hindus and 31 percent Muslims; in the Education Department 80 percent Hindus and 20 percent Muslims; in the Veterinary Department 77 percent Hindus and 23 percent Muslims; in the Agricultural Department 95 percent Hindus and 5 percent Muslims; in the Medical Department $97\frac{1}{2}$ percent Hindus and $2\frac{1}{2}$ percent Muslims; in the Public Works Department, out of a total of 41 Indian appointments there was only one Muslim; in the Forest, Marine and Irrigation Departments, leaving out the non-Indian appointments, there were 100 percent Hindus and no Muslims. In the Calcutta Police there was 85 percent Hindus and 15 percent Muslims.[60] These figures tell their own tale and need no further comment.

The cup of Muslims degradation was almost full to overflowing, but whose fault was it? It was mainly the fault of the Muslims themselves,[61] more than anything else, if their condition was miserable.

> *The fault, dear Brutus, is not in our star.*
> *But in ourselves that we are underlings.*

> — *Shakespeare*

It was a great disgrace to allow educational backwardness to stain the fair name of Islam. The Muslims were once a great people — great in commerce, in science, in literature. It was given to them first to carry the torch of culture and learning into the dark corners of the western world, when it was full of ignorance and grovelling under superstition. They had estab-

---

[59]Past and present condition of Muslims-Presidential Address by Hajji A.K. Ghuznavi. Home Political F.No. 179/26 and 179/1/1926.

[60]Ibid.

[61]Home Political B Proceeding No. 198 of 1924.

lished the famous universities of Baghdad, Cairo, Muscat, Damascus, Nihapur, Cordova, Granada and Salamanca which were the wonders of the then known world. They also had among them great philosophers, brilliant mathematicians and eminent educationists of the calibre of el-Ghazi Ali, Rhazes, Abulcasis, Avicenna, Averroe's and Ibn-i-Janzi, whose names have become household words. But the Muslims, under the British administration were considered to be backward in all branches of human knowledge because they had neglected education which counts for the success and prosperity of a nation in the world.[62] But thanks to the heroic endeavours of Sir Sayed Ahmad Khan, they woke up from their slumber and took to western education the neglect of which had proved so harmful to their community. Though they did not make as rapid progress as was expected of them, there was now in the twentieth century, a distinct sign of general awakening among them and an increasing tendency to assert their legitimate rights in the administration of the country.[63] This progress of education, this awakened communal consciousness caused some uneasiness amongst the Hindus. For long they had enjoyed the exclusive monopoly of all votes and posts, and human nature being what it is, they found it difficult to part with the long held rights. So there was nothing to be wondered at that they hastened to mobilise the forces at their command to stifle the voice of the Muslim community. The Muslims too were now determined to fight for equal rights and equal opportunities for all people irrespective of caste or creed.[64]

Separate Representation

When in 1906 the Muslims, after long hesitation, decided to throw themselves more fully into politics and presented a memorial to His Excellency the Viceroy, Lord Minto, he gave a sympathetic reply, the gist of which is that in any scheme

---

[62]Ibid.

[63]Home Political B Proceeding No. 198 of 1924.

[64]*The Muslim Outlook*, Lahore dated 16.2.1924. See also Home Political B Proceedings No. 198 of 1924,

for associating the people of India more fully with the work of Government, he would undertake, to see that Muslim interests did non suffer.[65] The Council reforms of 1909 and subsequent enactments which introduced separate representation and separate electorates undoubtedly embittered relations[66] between the Hindus and Muslims. The illfeeling extended into the middle classes of society owing to the claim for separate representation of Muslims in local bodies. Thus political tension between the two communities now mounted up. Religious disturbances henceforth resulted more because of political than religious causes.[67]

The Hindus argeed that communal representation brought division in the country but the Muslims contended that it was not so; on the contrary it brought conciliation between the two communities, and if this communal representation were taken away it would be a fresh cause of religious disturbances which neither the Government nor the leaders of the two communities would be able to stop. A Muslim member of the Legislative Assembly rightly observed in this context :

> "If communal representation were taken away, where is the guarantee that the minority communities will be represented in the House? Try to do away with it and you will see rivers of blood flowing in the country.[68]"

Proximity of Census

The proximity of census also opened up new questions of dispute and the election controversy became prominent. It had never probably died out, because the Hindus were annoyed at the concessions given to Muslims and the Muslims were anxious to extend the scope of those concessions. This resulted in the appearance of the Hindu-Urdu controversy; the U.P. Muslim League petitioning for Urdu or at least Hindustani to be laid down as the common language in the census

---

[65]Home Political A Proceeding No. 118 dt. October 1913.

[66]Home Political F.No. 27/IV of 1926.

[67]Home Political F.No. 24/12 of 1933. See also Home Political F.No. 44/IX/27 of 1927.

[68]Home Political F.No. 27/IV of 1926,

schedules.   There also started an agitation in October 1911 for
the classification of depressed communities separately and not
as part of Hindu community.   The activity of the Muslims
was paralleted by an energetic propaganda carried on by the
Nagari Pracharini Sabha. It excited the Hindus to demand rights
of a semi-political nature such as the official use of Hindi. The
headquarters of the society were at Benares.[69]   It is thus clear
that the approach of the census was also made a reason for the
revival of language controversy.[70]

Swadeshi and Boycott Agitation

In April and May 1907, a series of dangerous disturbances
occurred in the Mymensingh District in Eastern Bengal.   In a
large number of places there was wholesale rioting and looting
by Muslims, bazars and shops were burned, images in Hindu
temples were broken and some murders were committed;
infact for a short time in certain areas the Muslims absolutely
terrorised and maltreated the Hindus.   Order was restored
only with considerable difficulty by the personal exertions of
the Commissioner, the Collector and District Suprintendent of
Police, aided by additional executive and police officers.
Gurkha military police were also drafted in and the local police
had to be greatly strengthened.   The reasons for the disturbances were partly the growing irritation of the Muslims with
the *Swadeshi* agitation and the boycott of European goods,
engineered by Hindus; agrarian and social grievances cherished
by the Muslims against the Hindus, who predominated as land
lords and money lenders.[71]   The local Government charac-
terished the state of events in Mymensingh at this time as
"perilously near to general explosion".[72]

Extra-Territorial Sympathies

Before passing on to other questions it is necessary to say

---

[69]Home Political Proceeding Nos. 100-17 dated October 1913.
[70]Home Political Proceeding No. 118 dated October 1913.
[71]Memo. from the Hon'ble Mr. H. Le Mesuries, C.I.E., I.C.S.,   Offg.
    Chief Secy. to Govt. of Eastern Bengal and Assam ʾdated 3rd June 1907.
    Home Political A Proceeding Nos. 6-16 dated July 1907.
[72]Home Pol. A Proceeding Nos. 57-63 dated December, 1907.

a few more words regarding "extra-territorial sympathies"[72A] of the Muslims, because on this account the Hindus always distrusted them. But the Muslims countered this criticism which becomes clear from the quotation below:

"They (Hindus) have woefully misunderstood the true spirit of Islam and constantly accuse us of want of partriotism. Muslims are indissolubly linked in the bond of a grand religious fraternity which has no equal in the world, and which is one of the standing miracles of the world—Prophet Muhammad (on whom be peace)—and for the Muslims, Islam comes above everything. But it is an error to suppose that Islam renders the Muslim, alien to patriotism." No, the Indian Muslims love India as passionately as anybody else...and strongly denounce the charge of unpatriotism levelled against them." If a foreign country, be it Muslim or non-Muslim invades India, Muslims would unflinchingly defend India and repel the attacks. If a Muslim country is in distress, our sympathies would go with it. So it is unbecoming of the Hindus to regard us with suspicion, and if they are desirous of seeing a united, free and enlightened India, they must treat the Muslims not as foreigners having no interest in the country but as people belonging to the same country they inhabit and having political ideals and aspirations similar to those of theirs. When they have developed such a conciliatory and sober attitude, side by side a sense of justice to part with our legitimate rights which have passed into their hands,[72B] inter-communal amity would be rapid and easy."

Missionary or Proselytising Movements

The period of extreme hostility between the Hindu and Muslim communities may be said to date from the inception of the *Shuddhi* (purification) movement directed by the *Arya Samaj* against the *Malkana Rajputs* (a sub-caste of Rajputs converted to Islam during the reign of Aurangzeb) of Agra and the neighbouring districts in 1923. This reclamation movement gave to the Hindus a definite objective and, directed

---

[72A] Home Political B Proceeding No. 198 of 1924.
[72B] Ibid.

as it was to a mass movement, called forth strenuous opposition from the Muslims who gradually realised the political significance of a nominally religious movement. The *Shuddhi* movement is of much older origin than 1923, but its application to mass rather than individual conversion gave it special prominence at this time. It is closely allied to the *Arya Samaj* movement.[73]

The *Arya Samaj* is a protestant and reforming movement within the Hindu church and originated in 1869, though the *Samaj* did not come into existence till 1885. The *Arya* religion is monotheistic and professes to be a reversion to the religion held by the early Aryans in the time of divine revelation, and as such claims to be older than Brahminism. The objective of the *Samaj* is the reform of the Hindu faith as practised under debased Brahminism with its opposition to advance in accord with world civilisation and to individual thought and freedom. An earlier reforming movement is the *Brahmo Samaj* but Dayanand (the founder of the *Arya Samaj*) was opposed to *Brahmo Samaj* on the ground that it was too cosmopolitian and tolerant and lacked the essence of patriotism in that it preferred foreign influence to that of ancient Aryan faiths. Thus from its inception the *Arya Samaj* had an element of political thought and this element, showed itself in a marked degree from time to time. Dayanand's objects, in addition to the reform of priesthood, included the accommodation of the masses in national religion freed of rigid ritual but incorporating certain platitudes to which the more educated Hindus could subscribe without misgiving. It was thus a religion acceptable alike to the enlightened Hindus, who desired greater freedom and to the outcaste who was crushed under rigid Brahminism. This latitude quickly proved popular and *Arya Samajism* developed rapidly and established a firm position throughout India.[74]

The proselytising work of the *Samaj* was effected largely

---

[73]Criminal Investigation Department. Note on the State of Hindu-Muslim feeling in U.P. Home Political F.No. 206 of 1926.

[74]Ibid, para. 2.

by a branch of the *Arya Pratinidhi* (representative) *Sabha*, known
as the *Shuddhi Sabha*, which early secured the conversion of a
number of non-Muslims, some Muslims, and a few Christians.
The permission to include Muslims and Christians was an
innovation, but as it allowed the return to the fold of Hinduism
of any who had espoused Christianity or Islam, it was a
considerable concession, and this, infact conciliated the more
orthodox but politically-minded Hindus who were now prepared to concede much to obtain a united Hinduism as a
political national force. The *Shuddhi Sabha* was started by
Pandit Bhoj Dutt Sharma of Amritsar, who in the years 1907
to 1909 was a pronounced militant worker of an inflammable
nature; he was prosecuted for obscene abuse of Islam and
warned on more than one occasion for inflammatory
speeches; the fact that the *Arya Pratinidhi Sabha* collected subscriptions for his defence indicated that the *Arya Samaj*
countenanced these attacks on other religions an also supported, or at least did not resist the political atmosphere
brought into the *samaj* activities by such persons. During this
period the *Arya Samaj* was controlled largely by men of advanced political thought, such as Lajpat Rai, Ajit Singh, Mul
Chand, Surendra Nath Banerji, etc., and the charges of sedition proved against several of the leaders demonstrated clearly
the use to which this reforming movement was in a large
measure being put.[75] The action of Government in prosecuting some of these leaders for sedition provoked a
storm of protest against what was called an attack on religion
but Government was emphatic in its reply that so long as the
Samaj confined its attention to social and religious reform it
had nothing to fear from Government. There were, at
that time, reasons to believe that the *Shuddhi Sabha* was
organized in reality to further the aims of these politicians and
to work for a national *Swaraj*. This phase gradually
passed and the *Arya Samaj* again became a social and
religious reform movement on the lines laid down by its
founder.[76]

---

[75]Ibid, para 3.
[76]Ibid.

The sympathisers with the *Shuddhi* movement were not content to leave the work unorganised or in the hands of a few people, and in 1909 a conference was held at Agra at which the *Bharat Shuddhi Sabha (or All-India Shuddhi Sabha)* was put on a definite footing; office bearers were elected and rules framed; Pandit Bhoj Dutt was made general secretary, but a strong committee was formed to control the work. The rules provided for provincial *Shuddhi Sabhas* to be established under the control of the central *Sabha*, and for a return to caste of any of the "twice-born" who had left the fold of the Vedic religion as well as the reclamation of outcastes in the ordinary sense; inter-dining was permitted amongst the members of the "twice-born" castes, including those reclaimed, and provision was made for a spread of education and the Vedic religion amongst the reclaimed outcastes.[77]

Meetings were held in various districts to organize local *sabhas* and the reclamation work was started. The *Malkanas* were early attracted by the scheme, as were a number of non-Muslims at Shahjahanpur; this called forth counter-measures from the Muslims of that place, who at once invited outside *Maulvis* to lecture on Islam; similar activity occured in other districts and the *Anjuman Islam* of Delhi took up the question of counter-activity.[78] In 1910 the office of the *Bharat Shuddhi Sabha* was transferred from Agra to Delhi. In 1911 the definite connexion between the *Arya Samaj* and the *Shuddhi Sabha* was denied, but it was admitted by the followers of the former that the latter was of much service to it, though certain doubted whether the work of *Shuddhi* was strictly in accord with the principles of propagating the Vedic faith. The movement spread to other provinces (and even to Zanzibar), and at the end of 1911 a conference was arranged at Amritsar. In 1913 the activity was directed largely to the *Doms* of the Kumaun division whose conversion to Christianity was at that time threatened. Isolated conversions were reported from various districts, but the movement seemed to have waned and little is heard of it from 1914 onwards, though Jaimini Das Mehta

---

[77]Ibid, para 4.

[78]Ibid, para 5.

and Shanti Sarup continued in their efforts as late as 1918.[79] Its sudden revival in 1923 is discussed later.

Another factor within the Hindu fold making for a communal awakening is the *Hindu Sabha Movement*. This started in the Punjab about 1910, and the stir caused by the *Shuddhi* movement probably was responsible for its origin. The movement gained strength in 1911, spreading into the United Provinces and forming branches in many centres. It then languished until 1914, when a branch was opened at Benares. In the following year, at the *Kumbh Mela* at Hardwar, a conference was held at the formation of the *All-India Hindu Sabha* (with its conference designated as the *Mahasabha*). Narayan Swami was prominent at the conference, as also was "Mahatma" Munshi Ram (known as Swami Shradhanand); many pnblic men were present at this meeting, and it is interesting to note that Mahatma Gandhi was there and took part in the proceedings. The outstanding cry at the conference was the weakness of the Hindu community through internal dissensions and vehement appeals were addressed to all Hindus to bind up the community for protection against Muslims and Christians; but it is noteworthy that nothing was said of any conversion propaganda. In October, 1915 the office moved from Dehra Dun to Delhi (but was again retransferred in 1916), and in the same month a (United Provinces) provincial *Hindu Sabha* was formed at a meeting held at Allahabad, with Madan Mohan Malaviya presiding; at the end of the year he also presided at the *Mahasabha* meeting at Bombay, and the theme of his address was an exhortation to all Hindus to strive to bring back the ancient glories and greatness of Hinduism.[80]

From this time onwards regular meetings were held and the energies of the *Sabha* directed to protests against any supposed favouritism extended to Muslims—chiefly in the matter of representation on legislative and local bodies. Purely Hindu matters, such as cow-protection, etc., naturally received atten-

---

[79]Ibid, para 5.

[80]Ibid, para 6.

tion; but the prominent current running through the various proceedings was the political advance of the Hindu body politic.[81] This position continued till 1923 (July) when a *Mahasabha* was held in Benares with Madan Mohan Malaviya presiding and impressing his will on the meeting, though not without opposition from the orthodox. The change in the policy may be shown by summarising some of the decisions. Briefly, these were (a) unity of races essential to *swaraj* (b) the formation of a *Samaj Sewak Dal* to encourage physical culture amongst Hindus, (c) advancement of *sangathan* (unity) necessary for the progress of the community and the spread of Hindi essential to the former, (d) *swadeshi* cloth, with the corresponding boycott of foreign cloth, (e) a recognition of *Shuddhi* extending to an agreement that all reclaimed, whatever caste, should be retaken into their former caste, and an appeal to all Hindus to extend a hearty welcome to Hindus returning from abroad and to all the depressed classes; this latter clause was urged as a means of preventing the thinning of the Hindu community. The clause relating to national unity was put in as a stop to Muslim apprehension; whilst that relating to *Swadeshi* was to capture the Congress politicians. The marked effort on the part of the President to force the question of the admission of untouchables produced strong opposition from the orthodox, and his action in regard to certain *Chamars* necessitated an apology from him to the *pandits* of Benares.[82]

A subsequent meeting (*Mahasabha*) was held in the *Kumbha Mela* at Allahabad in January, 1924, when the formation of active branch *sabhas* was urged for religious propaganda and social *sangathan;* the *Mahasabha* affirmed its previous decisions regarding the depressed classes, but modified this by declaring that such were not entitled, under the *Sanathan Dharma*, the *Shastras* and from public propriety, to the sacred thread, the learning of the Vedas and inter-dining. It further affirmed that non-Hindus may be admitted into Hinduism, but not into existing castes. A definition of Hindus was decided on, to include *Sanathan Dharmists, Arya Samajists, Jains, Sikhs,*

---

[81] Ibid, para 7.

[82] Ibid.

Buddhists and *Brahmos*. Rules for the *Hindu Sewak Dal* were drawn up to include a *Hindu Kumar Dal* in which young boys could be included; the vow to be taken on enlistment included unqualified obedience to the *Sabha* and a declaration of readiness to protect their religion.[83]

The change in the tenets of the *Sabha* can be attributed to the great interest displayed in the *Shuddhi* work of 1923 and the Hindu *Sabha* definitely sided with the *Arya Samaj* in its efforts to extend the Hindu community; Muslim apprehension was in no sense allayed by the platitudes expressed at these two meetings, and that community openly expressed its interpretation of the movement as a direct attack on the political and social life of the smaller Muslim race. Madan Mohan Malaviya was insistent at this time on the widening of the Hindu fold, and his efforts to capture the Sikhs were marked throughout the *Kumbh Mela*; members of the *S.G.P. Committee* were actually invited to attend a private meeting of the Hindu *Sabha* at Benares. His political aims were recognised by Hindus as well as by Muslims and the *Sadhu Sabha* at the *Kumbh Mela* objected to the introduction of politics into a religious festival. The campaign regarding untouchables was carried on during the *mela* with marked ostentation.[84]

Early in 1923 Swami Sharadhanand inaugurated his movement of the reclamation of the Malkanas, Gujar and Bania converts to Islam on the ground that united Hinduism was more conducive to national settlement in India, in relation to Islam than a disunited body having no central force. Within a very short time of its beginning the Muslim community became suspicious that Madan Mohan Malaviya was the real author and that Shradhanand[85] had been used as

---

[83]Ibid, para 8.

[84] Ibid, para 9.

[85]Swami Shardhanand, or Munshi Ram, as his real name is, lived in Punjab; in former days he was much connected with journalism and at one time was on the staff of the Swarajya of Allahabad; connected with the Arya Samaj, he was in close touch with Lala Lajpat Rai and Ajit Singh and was one of the leaders of the movement at the time when its control was entirely in the hands of Ajit Singh, and, in 1907, was convicted under Section 124A, Indian Penal Code.

a tool by him. The enthusiasm with which this movement was received suggests something in the nature of pre-conceived organisation, though conditions in India were such as to arouse lively interest in any religious revival movement. The fictitious *entente* between Hindus and Muslims during the days of non-cooperation had broken; the improvement in the economic situation and the disillusionment in the ideals of Mahatma Gandhi early in 1922 had broken the mass enthusiasm for the non-cooperation cause, and Hindu apathy towards the Muslim anxiety as to the fate of Turkey and the Caliphate rapidly became so marked that Muslims easily recognised that they had been used simply as a means to an end and that the unity cry so insistent up to this time was a political device pure and simple.[86] With the introduction of the Reforms and the consequent advance in democratic government, the Hindu aspiration to a Hindu swaraj became manifest in more ways than one, and the eyes of Muslims were opened to the possibility of a *swaraj* which meant Hindu domination. The cleavage between the two parties on political grounds was marked and definite. He who was responsible for raising the *shuddhi* cry at this time undoubtedly was a student of internal conditions, able to select the most opportune moment from his point of view for the inauguration of a definite Hindu campaign. As in 1907-09, the *Malkanas* were selected as an objective in the thought they would be the most accessible and amenable. The campaign developed with remarkable speed and spread rapidly from Agra to Mathura and Aligarh and neighbouring districts; by May the *shuddhi* enthusiasts claimed no less than 18,000 converts in Agra and the neighbourhood.[87] These conversions and the general religious activity on the part of Hindus were not allowed to pass without arousing deep resentment amongst the Muslims of that neighbourhood; relations between the two communities became strained to a severe pitch, necessitating preventive action under the Procedure Code and police reinformation at certain villages, Achnera being the most prominent; the readi-

---

[86]Note by H. R. Rao, Asst. to Dy. Inspector General of Police Criminal Investigation Department on Communal friction in United Provinces, para 12. Home Political F. No. 206 of 1926.

[87]Ibid.

ness of Hindus to carry arms at *shuddhi* meetings was indicative of the militant character of their campaign, and it became necessary to forbid the carrying of fire arms at all such meetings. The campaign, run almost entirely by *Arya Samajists*, was enlarged rapidly in scope; elsewhere *Chamars* and other depressed classes were chosen as the objectives, and the efforts of the *Aryas* to open wells, hitherto closed to the untouchables, provoked severe tension in several places; as early as April police interference over an incident of this nature was necessitated at Roorkee and a small riot, of a comic origin, occured at Chandausi. The tension between the two communities spread rapidly throughout the province[88] and affected all matters, social and political including elections to local bodies. The political leaders struggled, with little effect, to counter the adverse effect of this campaign on Hindu-Muslim relations, but their cry--'*swaraj* impossible without unity' —carried little weight when there was apprehension as to the dominant partner in the *swaraj*. The enthusiasm of the *Aryas* to obtain full recognition of reclaimed untouchables was not allowed to pass unopposed by the orthodox, and they met with considerable difficulties in certain centres. The period covering the *Id* was one of apprehension, and though no major trouble occurred, minor incidents were not uncommon: at Meerut relations were very strained and the readiness of the Hindus to close their shops and assemble with *lathis* at the first sign of trouble was indicative of the determined character of the protagonists.[89] As examplifying the complete separation of Muslims from Hindu thought, their abstension from all Gandhi Day celebration is worthy of note. Swami Sharadhanand himself made a tour of the province in July which tended to increase enthusiasm and interest amongst Hindus in the *shuddhi* movement; he was not allowed to speak in the Moradabad district owing to the delicacy of the situation there. The tension continued growing till the *Muharram*, when elaborate arrangements had to be made in every district; many incidents resulted from the strained relations and serious riots at Saharanpur and Gonda and sporadic faction fights at Agra and a riot at Alapur in the

---

[88]Ibid.
[89]Ibid.

Budaun district were the outstanding major events.[90] Jaspur
in the Naini Tal district was seized with panic and there was
promiscuous firing there. In Bulandshahr serious difficulties
threatened in several towns and the finding of a dead pig in a
mosque did not help to allay excitement. In connexion with
Hindu processions following the *Muharram* period sporadic
rioting broke out at Shahjahanpur and scares and panics
necessitated demonstration by the police in other places. The
Hindu Mahasabha at Benares, with its changed creed backing
the *shuddhi* propaganda, the presence on its platform of certain
extreme *Swarajists* suggested the political objective underlying the
religious-social reform movement.[91] Allahabad, Moradabad,
Jhansi and Pilibhit showed marked alarm and apprehension
during this period and trouble threatened at Benares, where
it was rumoured that Muslims intended to cut the *peepal* tree at
the Gyanbafi mosque, which stands in an enclosure of Hindu
temples. The *Chehlum* and the *Dasehra* passed off without
serious incidents, though elaborate arrangements were necessary
at Meerut and Agra, whilst in certain other places the restriction imposed on the use of music led to the abandonment of
processions; sporadic assaults occurred in Shahjahanpur subsequent to the *Dasehra* and a few days later a riot took place at
Bisalpur in the Pilibhit district due to the Hindus disturbing
a *Milad Sherif*. With the conclusion of the festival period
conditions became calmer, though a slight recrudescence of
shuddhi activity in Agra at the end of the year necessitated
magisterial action.[92]

The following year opened with a continuance of friction
and a general interest in communal affairs. A recrudescence
of *shuddhi* in Agra led to an attempt by the *Aryas* to re-open
the campaign in defiance of section 144 orders in village
Sandhan; hundreds of Muslims assembled and trouble was
narrowly averted by the authorities. In Lucknow a wave of
Hindu feeling arose over the demolition of temples on land
acquired by the railway authorities. Meerut showed consi-

---

[90]Ibid.
[91]Ibid.
[92]Ibid.

derable tension in February when an *Arya Samaj* demonstration had to be forbidden at one small town; and a small riot occurred in another village over the clashing of the evening prayers with the sounding of the *Sankh*; the *shuddhi* campaign there was extending throughout the district. Agra witnessed assaults on *Chamar* wedding parties by conservative Hindus. In April a communal riot broke out at Kandhla in the Muzaffarnagar district, with casualties on both sides; and in Hapur in Meerut district a similar riot necessitated the use of fire arms by the police. In Shahjahanpur a long drawn-out fight between two villages, one Muslim and the other Hindu, resulted in several casualties—one of them fatal; spears were used freely.[93] The *Id-ul-Zuha* passed off with no major incident, but extra vigilance was required throughout the province to achieve this result; in Jaunpur a chance quarrel led to a number of isolated assaults. Following this period, tension was most marked in Saharanpur and Dehra Dun, whilst the Rohilkhand and Agra divisions continued as unsettled as ever. A movement in Hardwar to expel all Muslims from the sacred limits of this town was exemplary of the general hostility prevalent throughout the province, which by this time was extending to local governing bodies in a marked degree—all matters before many such boards being contested on purely communal lines.[94] By June a new form of panic-mongering was becoming prevalent, with scare of kidnapping for conversion purposes; it was claimed that these had originated from Delhi, and in Meerut the *Hindu Sabha* took up the question of action to counter what was alleged to be an organised campaign on the part of Muslims to secure women and children for forcible conversion; in Kanpur similar stories were put about, and in consequence some Muslims were forcibly ejected from a bathing festival. The *Id* (*Bakr*) again passed off without major mishaps, but anxiety, based on well-founded apprehension, every-where necessitated elaborate precautions; Jaspur in Naini Tal again produced trouble, and in Bulandshahr the Hindu population

---

[93]Chief Secretary to Govt- United Provinces to Secretary to the Govt. of India. Home Deptt. No. 6522 dated Allahabad, 2nd January. 1925, Home Palitical F.No. 2 of 1926.

of one village showed a very truculent opposition to the passage of a supposed sacrificial; cow (actually a buffalo) many
arrests had to be made; small disputes arose in Fatehpur district and in Benares, while in Agra there were complaints of
stone-throwing.[95]   The   acquittal of some of the Muslims
accused in the Saharanpur (Muharram) riot cases of 1923 was
hailed by that community as a triumph and led to a Muslim
procession through the Hindu-quarters.   The Delhi riots had
the effect of increasing nervousness and bitterness.   In Meerut
the tension and rivalry extended to the villages, and an eager-
ness on the part of Muslim villagers to build mosques called
forth strenuous opposition from Hindu land-holders.[96] This
state of bitterness continued till the *Muharram*, when two small
riots occurred in the Bareilly district and more important ones
at Sambhal in the Moradabad district and at Amethi in the
Lucknow district; in Pilibhit brick-throwing on the *tazias* produced a panic and a certain amount of gun-firing.   In other
places elaborate precautions prevented trouble, and in certain
places (such as Najibabad in Bijnor) these had to be in the
form of armed pickets at nights.   In general the *Muharram*
intensified feelings, which led to the carrying over of dissensions
to the ensuing Hindu festivals; in one village in Kheri the
Muslims whose procession in the *Muharram* had been disallowed as an innovation, attacked a Hindu procession with
fatal results, whilst in Lucknow the protracted bickering intensified by the Amethi riot led to severe trouble over *Ram Dal*
processions and culminated in an outburst of sporadic fighting
throughout the city on September 12; the casualties included
deaths.[97] A similar serious outbreak occurred in Shahjahanpur
at the time of the *Chehlum*, though minor troubles, with casualties, had occurred in the intervening period; here sporadic
assaults continued for a considerable time, and an outstanding
feature of this outbreak was the readiness shown by the
villagers to come into the city to assist their co-religionists.
Tilhar, in the same district, was the scene of considerable

---

[95]Ibid.

[96]Ibid.

[97]Ibid para 13.

difficulties and mass demonstrations showed the temper of the different communities.[98] The *Ram Lila* was not allowed to pass off without incident. In Allahabad feelings had been growing in intensity during the past two years and an outbreak of this sort was regarded as more or less inevitable, every festival having been seized upon as a pretext by the community concerned to make a display of strength. In the intervals between festivals enthusiasm for physical prowess was engendered by the establishment of *akharas* and competitions in physical exercises. The *Ram Lila* processions produced disputes over the question of music outside mosques, but these were arranged satisfactorily and the processions passed without major trouble; but no sooner had the last procession dispersed than sporadic assaults broke out on the initiative of the Muslims, but followed immediately by the Hindus in retaliation; control was secured by the employment of troops, but further outbreaks of a sporadic nature showed the depth of feeling throughout the city and the panicky discharge of a gun by a *Kalwar* (resulting in one death and two other casualties) led to a determined attack on a Hindu suburb by a considerable body of Muslims.[99] In Bijnor disorders were narrowly averted in a number of small towns, whilst minor difficulties occurred in Azamgarh and Fyzabad. The increased bitterness occasioned by these various outbreaks led, in a number of places, to distrust in officials of both the communities and efforts were made to discredit any one engaged on investigations into actual outbreaks. The *shuddhi* movement continued actively in Agra and Mathura but the opposition by the *Sanatan Dharmists* at the inclusion of *Chamars* in the *Ram Lila* celebrations led to a number of conversions from this caste to Islam.[100] The continuance of the *arti-namaz* dispute in Lucknow inflamed the minds of both communities in that district. The Unity Conference at Delhi, convened by leading politicians to discuss a *via media*, attracted little notice throughout the province and its deliberations and discussions had no appreciable effect on the general situation and the prevailing bitterness continued.

[98]Ibid.
[99]Ibid.
[100]Ibid.

A serious riot occurred in connexion with the *Muharram* at Saharanpur in August, 1923. At that time this city had a population of 67,000, slightly more than a half of whom were Muslims. Consequent on the *shuddhi* revival, the *Arya Samajists* became active in *Shuddhi* work in this district, particularly in regard to *Chamars*; their activity was directed largely to permitting *Chamars* to use wells hitherto closed to them, and many of these wells were in Muslim centres; the action of Aryas was deeply resented. Friction was apparent and talk of communal boycott was common; irritation continued to grow in consequence of the spread of the *Sangathan* movement; Hindu *akharas* for training youths in physical exercises were arranged and this was considered by Muslims to be directed against cow sacrifice, but actually the *Id* passed off quietly.[101]

In reply to this Hindu activity Muslim *akharas* were started[102] for the *Muharram* (these had been in abeyance during the past four years owing to Shia-Sunni disputes); keenness rapidly developed, as also rivalry between the different *akharas* as to which could procure the longest bamboo for its *jhanda*; the winning *akhara* (Lakhigate akhara) actually secured one 72 feet long. The routes of the *Muharram* procession led through the Ramanandi bazar, where an *arti-namaz* dispute had arisen prior to the *Muharram*. In this bazar there was a temple with a large *peepal* tree with branches overhanging the bazar, and these had received no attention during the past four years owing to *akharas* being in abeyance. Now there was fear about the outcome of the *jhandas* passing this tree, and attempts to arrange matters were not very successful. The local Hindus eventually arranged to post selected persons on the roofs to pull back the branches when the *Jhanda* passed. The *akhara* did not obey orders as to which side of the road to take the *thela* on which this particular (Lakhigate) *jhanda* was mounted, and this resulted in extreme difficulty in getting the *jhanda* passed; delay occurred and hostility grew, and it seems that the action of some Muslims in mounting

---

[101]Ibid.
[102]Ibid.

the roofs to secure the stay ropes of the *jhanda* was interpreted as an attack and brick-throwing started and rapidly developed in intensity. The police, separated from magisterial direction, were compelled to open fire which stopped the riot itself; but it seems that this outbreak was the signal for the looting of Hindu shops and houses throughout the city. Simultaneous looting broke out as soon as the brick-throwing started, at which time it was observed that mounted messengers hurriedly left the Ramnandi bazar. Control was not effected until military patrols and pickets were secured, but by that time much damage to property had been done. In consequence of the behaviour of the inhabitants, a force of punitive police was posted in the city.[103]

Hindu-Muslim friction began to show itself in May 1923, when the *Anjuman-Raza-i-Mustafa* of Bareilly was already collecting funds in the districts to combat the *shuddhi* movement. Nervousness regarding the *Id* was general and a visit of Swami Sharadhanand in July accentuated Muslim irritation. During the *Muharram* there was considerable tension and apprehension. In the ensuing *Dadh-Kando* processions the Hindus made a great show of numbers and weapons, and in connection with one procession some thousands of Muslims assembled to prevent its progress. Trouble was narrowly averted, but the procession passed through safely. Immediately afterwards, however isolated assaults broke out and the state of tension was increased considerably. During the *Ram Lila* cases of attack occurred and considerable apprehension was experienced throughout this period. The aggressive action of the *Aryas* during these months was irritating alike to both orthodox Hindus and Muslims.[104] The year 1924 showed a continuance of *Arya* activity in connexion with the *Shuddhi* and a counter measure from the Muslims establishing of a branch of the *Tabligh-ul-Islam*. Communal tension remained the predominant note throughout the district. This resulted in a village fight in May, with one death and other casualties, while a continuance of communal meetings led to increased bitterness as the

---

[103]Ibid.

[104]Ibid, para 15,

Muharram approached. In Tilhar the Muslims refused to celebrate *Muharram* owing to a dispute regarding the blowing of
Sankh, and that town continued in a state of considerable
tension for a long period; mass demonstrations by villages,
armed with *lathis* showed the spirit of the communities.[105]
Thoughout the district incidents were common and tension
severe; it spread to the Police Lines where it became necessary
to forbid *Janmashtami* celebrations. All celebrations during
Muharram and the *Ram Lila* required detailed and elaborate
arrangements and disallowance of any procession promptly
produced *hartals*. Minor riots occurred over different matters,
and that in village Dhimra resulted in one death and other
casualties. The major outbreak occurred in Shahjanpur itself
during the course of the *Chehlum* procession when a Muslim
alleged to have beaten by Hindus and believed to be dead was
carried to the head of the *Chehlum* procession and immediate
justice demanded from the magistrate (the man was not dead
but was removed to hospital); the procession was induced to
move on with great difficulty, but this incident and the irritation of the Muslims led to reprisals, and during the next three
days isolated members of either community were chased
on and beaten and a large number of cases of riot, dacoity,
murder and arson occurred. A particularly dangerous feature
of this outbreak was the arrival of considerable numbers of
villagers from outlying villages, armed with *lathis* and obviously ready for a fight. Quiet was not restored until British troops
had secured control of the city. These disturbances show that
the bitterness between the two communities[106] was not
lessening at all.

Communal friction, which had been growing in intensity in Lucknow and its district broke into open trouble on
9 *Muharram* at Amethi[107]. Amethi is a Muslim town, but a
temple had been built some three or four years ago with the
knowledge, it is believed, of the *taluqdar*, though in conflict with
the general principles of the town. Its erection had provoked

---

[105]Ibid.

[106]Ibid.

[107]Ibid, para 10.

no particular comment during the years of the entente; but since relations had been strained, attention focussed on this and orders had to be passed forbidding the sounding of the *Sankh* during the *Muharram*. On 9 *Muharram* the *Sankh* was sounded while a *majlis* was being held at the house of the *taluqdar*; the incensed Muslims then attacked the temple and desecrated it.[108] This riot led to an increase in the bitterness in Lucknow city. Trouble arose in the Sadar Bazar over the question of *Ram Dal* processions during which the Hindus showed considerable provocation; the processions eventually passed through successfully, but the feeling engendered did nothing to help the strained relations between the two communities arising over the question of the sounding of the *sankh* at *arti* in the Aminabad temple, which coincided with the *maghrib* prayers. The reciting of prayers in the Aminabad Park had been going on in a small way for some years, but during the ostentatious revival of religious enthusiasm the number taking part in these prayers had grown considerably and objection was raised by the Muslim community as a whole against the sounding of the *Sankh* during these prayers. Orders were passed fixing definite periods for the *maghrib* prayers and for the *arti* and its associated *Sankh-blowing*.[109] On September 12, during the *maghrib* prayers some Hindus went to the Aminabad temple and tried to ring the bell there; they were prevented by the *kotwal* and the Hindus as a body then decided on a protest meeting in the Park; where meetings had been prohibited. The *kotwal* was again successful in inducing them to go off and hold their meeting behind closed doors in the *dharmshala*. During the course of this meeting, presided over by Narayan Swami, it seems that a party of Hindus came out of the *dharmshala* and attacked a Muslim shopkeeper ransacking his shop. Fighting broke out in various parts and casualties occurred. During the night sporadic fighting took place, and by the next morning fighting between small parties was going on all over the city; there was no mass fighting, but the whole city was engaged in a series of small conflicts with resultant casualties. Control was not

---

[108]Ibid, para 16.
[109]Ibid.

obtained until troops had been called in and regular pickets posted. This ended actual open hostilities, but the *arti-nimaz* dispute continued unsettled and provided a constant irritant to the two communities. This cause of dispute was given a political touch and Swarajists and liberals made us of it to further their election campaigns for the Municipal Board.[110]

With the exception of the interest taken in this conversion propaganda by the *Anjuman Islamia* in 1909, Muslims do not appear to have regarded the *shuddhi* activities as dangerous to the Islamic body and little in the way of organised counteraction was devised; this apathy continued till the war period when Muslim thought was directed to a new channel—the fate of Turkey. The general unrest in all the countries which had taken part in, or had been affected by the war extended to Muslim peoples throughout the world, who were imbued with a renewed hopefulness of a Muslim revival; the defeat of Turkey aroused within them a vague feeling of anxiety as to a possible downfall of Islam, and this feeling was shared by the Muslims of India. This anxiety was seized upon by political leaders, both Hindu and Muslim, to rouse the Muslims against the British Government; the opportunity was favourable in their eyes to reapproachment with a view to expel British from India. That the reapproachment was artificial was recognised by all but the economic stress throughout the country, combined with the world-wide indiscipline based on the cry of self-determination, was sufficient to cement superficially the two communities.[111]

As prominent Muslim political leaders were removed from activity by imprisonment, the cry of unity, never favoured by the orthodox Muslims of the old school, weakened. Attention was devoted to the more internal matters of Islam; and a renewed hope of a great Islamic revival based on the Turkish victory over the Greeks. The subsequent attitude of the Turks on the question of the Caliphate left the Indian Muslims with

---

[110]Ibid.

[111]Criminal Investigation Department's note on Hindu-Muhammadan feeling in the U.P. para 10. Home Political F. No. 206 of 1926,

no focus of interest, and they were at a "loose end" with no
outstanding individual to direct their energies and attention
to any objective. The *shuddhi* revival of 1923 supplied this
want and the Muslim community as a whole welcomed
the chance of active opposition as a cohesive force to cement
their scattered ranks.[112]   It is noteworthy that Swami
Sharadhanand, before starting his propaganda, had dissociated
himself from the Congress movement, and this deterred the
politically-minded Muslim leaders from adopting counter-
activity. Congressmen and Khilafatists were at a disadvantage; should they advocate either the *sangathan* movement
or its opposition, then down would fall all pretence of any
national movement to *swaraj*; they were therefore condemned
to remain aloof, but the natural result was that they lost
much influence and politics swamped the religious fervour.[113]
The *Jamiat-ul-Ulema* seized the moment as favourable for
asserting its influence and the *Khilafat Committee* and its members espoused the cause of opposing the *shuddhi* and
sangathan. Under its patronage the *All-India Anjuman
Tabligh-ul-Islam* was formed to combine the various
schools of thought for joint work; this proved impractica-
ble. The *Deobandis* refused to associate with the *Qadyanis*,
and the *Anjuman Razi-i-Mustafa* of Bareilly refused to
work with the *Qadyanis*; each however worked independently, not without dissensions and not with such
success as would have resulted from joint control. Various
bodies arose with objects, similar to the *Tabligh-ul-Islam*,
under such names as *Anjuman Tahaffuz-i-Islam*, *Anjuman
Hafazat-i-Islam*, *Anjuman Hurriyat-i-Islam*, etc., Their objects
were indentical, though their following differed somewhat in
different places. The *Tanzim* movement started in the
Punjab, but did not spread to this province, though its objects
were identical with those of the various bodies mentioned
above.[114] Seeing the growth of influence of this religious movement, with the resultant importance of the *Jamiat*, the *Khilafatists*

---

[112]Ibid, para 11.

[113]Ibid.

[114]Ibid,

set out to re-organise their various committees and to include
in their objects some of the items of *Tabligh-i-Islam* programme;
but they secured no following and religious propaganda continued to hold the field with the underlying thought of communal
advancement as opposed to national independence. The
introduction of the *sangathan* movement produced the parallel
of the Ali Ghol (Ali's band—the *Tanzimist* counter to
the Mahabir Dals of the *Sangathan*) movement and the
corresponding idea of physical culture; *akharas* became common,
especially in Allahabad but after a brief spell of popularity this
movement died and the Muslim community relied on individual
effort rather than on a trained band.[115]

During the campaign of these past two years much abuse
had been poured out by protagonists of both the parties; this
had taken the form of abusive speeches, articles in the press,
and pamphlets issued by individuals. The worst form of
this abusive propaganda has been the pamphlets. The
'*Dai-Islam*', attributed to Khwaja Hussain Nizami of Delhi, was
the first of such to attract wide attention; in it methods for
obtaining converts to the ranks of Islam were expounded, e.g.
Muslim officials of all ranks were to exert their influence and
pressure; the secrets of Christian and Aryan preachers were to
be secured, so that their proselytizing could be attacked on
their own ground; Muslim pedlars were to spy on Hindu house-
holds, as would also *fakirs* and female beggars; prostitutes were
to be brought into service for propaganda, etc.[116] This book
originally was issued for private circulation, but a later edition
was issued to Muslims in Africa, and it was from there that its
copies came into the hands of the *Aryas*; wide publicity was
given to it by reproducing much of it, with severe criticism,
in a pamphlet entitled the "*Alarm Bell*" and the *Aryas* and
others then poured out a flood of literature to counter its effect,
each new pamphlet seeming to outdo its predecessor
in filthy abuse of the Prophet. The *Islam-i-tilli-lili-jhar*
with its lines "When prostitutes have been entrusted with the
work of religion, how can such a despicable religion live? . . . .

---

[115]Ibid.

[116]Ibid, para 17.

Friends, the *Koran* has been torn into pieces . . . . . The braggings of Islam in India have passed away[117], "caused great offence to Muslims. A series of such pamphlets in circulation in Bareilly and Rohilkhand were typical of the abusive nature of allegations and criticism; these were responsible for considerable antagonism between the two communities; they dealt at length with Muslim "atrocities" in Malabar, Multan and elsewhere and dilated on the forcible conversion to Islam in the days of Islamic domination; they spoke of the boasting of Muslims over their violation of Hindu women and discussed the life of the Prophet at length attributing to him gross sensuality and claiming that Muslims in general followed his example; they claimed that the Muslim religion secured its followers by promising them polygamy in heaven as an inducement. Amongst these pamphlets were the *"Yannon ka ghor atyachaar"*, the *"Munh Tor"*, the *"Jarput"*, the *"Lal Jhandi"*, *"Taranai Shuddhi"*, *"Malakhash Tor"*, *"Bichitra Jivan"* *"Islam ka bhanda phut gaya"*. The Muslims replied with the *"Kufr Tar"*, in which Hindu women were accused of bestiality.[118]

The enthusiasts of lesser position followed similar strains in speeches, and certain women speakers, such as Saraswati Devi and Satyavati Devi, enlarged at length on the danger to Hindu women-folk from the shameful methods of Muslims and appealed for the arming of women for their protection and support to the *sangathan* movement as a general communal defence against Muslim aggression. Leaders of higher position, political and religious, refrained from employing such abusive methods; the former were anxious to use the enthusiasm aroused by this revival for political aims and attributed the bitterness between the two communities to the fact that they had left the common objective, namely, the fight against Government; they claimed that the differences were not religious and that strife had been engineered by a third party for definite aims; they appealed for the co-ordination of the

---

[117]Ibid.

[118]Ibid.

sangathan and *tanzim* movements so as to bring pressure to bear
on Government; Hindu speakers of this type used the argument
of cow-slaughter for the use of Britishers to show that Hindus
should direct their hatred to the English more than to the
Muslims.[119]   The political aim of Hindu enthusiasts is disclosed
at times by admissions as to the real objectives. For instance,
Krishna Kant Malaviya in a speech at Dehra Dun in 1924,
appealed for a Hindu-Muslim pact to include separate representation on a numerical basis, thus clearly demonstrating
the real motive behind the *shuddhi* movement.[120]

Thus the Hindu-Muslim feeling throughout the United
Provinces was based on political considerations as much as on
religious issues. During the non-cooperation period, for reasons
now well known, the Hindus decided to sink their individuality
for the time being and to play up to the Muslims on the
Khilafat question; "unity" thus became a main plank in the
Congress-*Khilafat* platform and, due to the economic position
of the province at that time, these movements and the non-
cooperation movement (none of which can be isolated from
the other) secured a great hold over the people, who were
ready to listen to any proposal for a change from their
then straitened condition. The "unity" cry thus obtained an
artificial importance which for the time being was successful in concealing the latent hostility always present between
the two communities. With the improvement of the economic
situation and the removal of the *Khilafat* question as a grievance
and the consequent downfal of the non-cooperation movement,
this artificial barrier to the natural expression was removed
and the Hindu community, which had ever been desirous of a
Hindu *swaraj*, began, through its leaders to propagate the
importance, from a political point of view, of a united
Hinduism, containing persons of all classes combined to present
a strong front against all antagonism.[121]   At the same time the
invocation to religious sentiment had been the deciding factor
in arousing the interest of all classes and races. The rivalry

---

[119]Ibid.

[120]Ibid.

[121]Ibid, para 18.

of different religious communities had not been confined to
the main differences between Hindus and Muslims; amongst the
Hindus themselves there had existed, acute differences between
the orthodox and the non-orthodox; amongst the Muslims
the different sects of *Qadyanis*, *Wahaqis*, etc. remained busy
promulgating their own ideas, while this period had not also
been free from open trouble between *Shias* and *Sunnis*. Among
the different Muslim societies much difference of opinion in
methods and direction had also become apparent; the Bharatpur
mosque affair is an instance of this, over which opinions were
very divided as to whether *satyagraha* could be offered or not.
Amongst Hindus the example of the *akalis* had not been over-
looked, and there was a distinct, though perhaps ill-defined,
movement towards securing the control of temples and temple
property to a body representative of the whole Hindu community; the formation of the *Tirtish Maha Sabha* at Benares by
the *Pandas* to protect the temples against outside interference
and the interest taken in the Bharat temple dispute at Rishikesh
by the *Sanatan Dharmists* are instances of the awakening in such
matters.[122]

Policy of Government

The question of prevention of religious disturbances
always remained under anxious consideration[123] of the Government and for several years it was even discussed and debated
in the Legislative Assembly. The primary duty of the Government in this matter was not only to maintain law and order
but also to bring about peace and reconciliation between the
two communities.[124] They upheld the action which its officer's
took all along in times of communal strain. Invariably when
communal trouble started brewing, the officers on the spot
first tried to allay it through influential members of each community and endeavoured to arrive at a solution in a given
situation on the basis of an agreement between the two com-

---

[122]Ibid.
[123]Notes Home Political F. No. 27/IV of 1926, p. 10, Home Political F. No.
24/12 of 1933, pp. 6-7.
[124]Ibid.

munities. Failing that the local officers passed orders on the basis of established custom and when such custom could not be definitely ascertained, they passed such orders as in their opinion were necessary for the maintenance of law and order always taking care to see that unreasonable claims of any community were not granted. Adequate police forces were also kept in order to enforce compliance with the orders passed to prevent a breach of the peace and in a vast majority of such cases, communal troubles were averted.[125]

The Government always tried to convince its officers as well as the public that they regarded it as their duty to foster good and friendly relations between the various communities and spared no efforts to bring disorder under control without the least possible delay.[126] Permanent boards of conciliation[127] were thus formed but their results did not prove to be encouraging. The Government followed a policy of religious neutrality[128] in such disturbances and felt that the only remedy to avoid them lay in the hands of the leaders of the two communities.[129] Sir Deni's Bray, Foreign Secretary, stated in his speech on Sir Muhammad Yakub's resolution regarding the regulation of the performance of religious festivals :

"what Government cannot do is to cure the disease itself— a disease which is within; it can tackle the outward and visible signs of the inward and spiritual disgrace that is eating into the heart of India but the cure must not come from without but from within.[130]

On this point it would also be quite fitting to quote Lord Irwins speech. He had remarked:

"The Government could watch advise and act, but they could do little to change the combustible nature of the

---

[125]Home Political F.No. 179/26 of 1926, pp. 1-3.

[126]Home Political F.No. 24/12 of 1933, p. 14.

[127]Note by D.V. Hodge Dt. 11.5. 1926, Home Political F. No. 27/IV of 1926.

[128]Home Political F.No. 206 of 1926.

[129]Note by D.V. Hodge dt. 11.5. 1926, Home Political F. No. 27/IV of 1926.

[130]P. 7, Home Political F. No. 27/IV of 1926.

mass of material or eradicate its potentialities for generating destructive heat . . . . The more he pleaded over the problem the more clearly he felt that the first work to be done was by the leaders within their own ranks, and the future of their communities and country alike demanded it.[131]

. . . "Let them throw themselves into a nobler struggle— the fight for toleration. He saw before him ancient and highly organized societies with able and esteemed public men as their recognised leaders. He could not conceive that a really sincere and sustained appeal by them to the rank and file of their co-religionists, sustained by active propaganda of the new gospel of peace would go unheeded[132]. . . . Communal strifes are senseless. They disorganise business and involve loss of life and property[133], they render goodwill between two communities difficult if not impossible, not only during the outbreak, but for a long time afterwards".[134]

The Government found it difficult to make laws to prevent clashing between the rites and ceremonies of different religions because it involved the curtailing of the common law rights of one party or another. They therefore considered it to be the right course to leave the existing rights undisturbed.[135] But this policy invited severe criticism. It was argued that the settlement of points of difference without government help or arbitration was useless because there was no force, no power and no sanction behind such a settlement for its enforcement. But if these principles had been put on a Statute Book in the shape of laws[136] the state of communal feeling would have been different in India. The Government's policy to grant separate

---

[131]P. 17, Home Political F. No. 24/IV of 1933.

[132]Ibid, p. 18.

[133]For example, the Bombay note took a toll of 214 human lives and resulted in injuries to 2,554 persons.

[134]Home Political F. No. 24/12 of 1933, and p. 18.

[135]Home Political F. No. 27/IV/1926.

[136]Legislative Assembly Debates Vol. VIII, No. 6.

representation for Muslims in the enlarged Legislative Councils also widened the breach between the two communities because it practically recognised the principle of separateness and distrust[137] between Hindus and Muslims. Some newspapers even advocated separation of Hindus from Muslims in all public matters—in schools, colleges and railways.[138] This clearly showed that government favoured one section of the community at the expense of the other[139] because it suited their vicious purpose to carry on their favourite *policy of divide and rule.* Lord Olivier, an ex-Secretary of State, had correctly remarked that they wanted to foment 'communal riots' and 'communal feelings'[140] but never intended to solve this problem.

The recurrence of these disturbances was also owing to the *'policy of liberalisation'* that was followed by the government. Commenting upon it a member of the Legislative Assembly at that time had remarked:

"If we cast a glance at the map of Europe and Asia we find that with the advent of modern democracy and the replacement of old ideals of Government there has been a general world wide unrest caused by the awakening of the East and the realisation of their rights and responsibilities by the people. So far as communal tension in this country is concerned these tensions are religious in appearance but in reality political. . . . We have therefore to find a remedy for the political discontent of the country. . . . In India this issue came to the forefront on account of the historic causes which led to the evolution of Indian society. . . . Long before we understood politics we understood religion and long before we understood religion we understood communities. The communal tie has been the genesis of all society, eastern and western. In the early days of Rome and Greece and in the medieval period of English

---

[137]*Akhbari-i-Am* dated 8th August, 1911.
[138]Abhyudaya, Allahabad dt. 5th October, 1911.
[139]*Rahbar* dt. 7th July 1911.
[140]Chief Commissioner, Delhi to A.S. Hands, Esqr., Deputy Secy. to Home Department, Govt. of India, Home Political F. No. 4/12/37 of 1937.

history and Irish history communal feuds and communal assertions of rights were as common and as violently and virulently asserted as they could have been asserted during the apex of Indian tension in the metropolis of Bengal and elsewhere. . . . We understand communalism; we understand religion; but so far as politics is concerned, our education is of recent growth and it is on that ground that I have always been a supporter of the Reform Act of 1919. It has brought into the arena of practical politics the realisation of responsible government, and with it a duty cast upon the people of the country to understand the meaning of politics. Immediately after the enactment of the Reform Act an attempt was made to educate public opinion in this country in the art of government through the instrumentality of communalistic and religious teaching. The result has been that the country galvanised into a new life and we felt for the time being that this life showed a manifestation of a dominant vitality possessed by our people and that it had come to stay. But the immediate causes which made the alliance of religion and politics became more or less shadowy and people very soon forgot the new lessons they had learnt about politics but remembered the adhesion to religious precepts and customs. The result has been that the religious instinct, being stimulated by an arti-ficial means inculcated in the wake of the Reform Act of 1919, has left an aftermath in the revolts and exhibi-tions of lawlessness which the country is witnessing today."

Another member of the Legislative Assembly had correctly remarked that these disturbances broke out because the Government was losing the '*moral leadership*' of the country. This becomes clear from the following extract from his speech :- "thirty or forty years back the Government did have the moral leadership of the country, what they said men listened to

---

[141]Home Political F. 27/IV/26 of 1926.

[142]Speech by Shri Hari Singh Gour, Home Pol. F. No. 27/IV-26 of 1926, p. 19.

[143]Ibid.

because they said words that inspired and the people were willing to follow their leadership. But now that leadership had gone.[144] Why? The Government of India was tied too closely to another i.e. the cynical authority 8,000 miles away, too much subject to the dictation of people who did not realise what the situation was, and were more concerned with their own interest."[145] It was now impossible for the government to get free from this bondage and use its authority to become again the moral leaders of the country.

---

[144]Home Political F. No. 27/IV of 1926, p. 6.
[145]Ibid.

2

Muslim Education in India

It is well known when the British first assumed the sovereignty of the Eastern Provinces of the Mughal Emperor of Delhi, the Muslims, in spite of many vicissitudes of fortune, still enjoyed power and wealth. The treaty of August 12, 1765, by which Shah Alam, the last of the Mughals, entrusted the collection of revenue of Bengal, Bihar and Orissa to the East India Company, made no alteration in the political condition of the Muslims.[1] Until the time of Lord Cornwallis the Muslim law continued to be the law of the land and the judicial and executive appointments remained in the hands of the Muslims.[2]

The Muslim community received the first shock from the Permanent Settlement. It elevated the Hindu collectors, who till that time had held unimportant posts, to the position of landholders, gave them a proprietary right in the soil, and

---

[1]Correspondence on the subject of the Education of the Muhammadan Community in British India and their employment in the public service generally. *Selections from the Records of the Government of India*, Nos. 205-6, para 10.

[2]Memorandum by **James** O'Kinealy, *Education A Proceedings*, Nos. 2-8A, dated August 19, 1871.

allowed them to accumulate wealth which would have gone to the Muslims under their own rule. The resumption laws fell heavily on the Muslims and deprived many of the learned classes in Bihar and Bengal of decent living. The annexation of the Oudh and the Mutiny had a similar effect on the Muslims of Delhi and Lucknow. These persons were quite naturally unfriendly to the Britishers.[3]

The government's firm determination to carry out a system of English education proved unfavourable to the Muslims and a great boon to the Hindus. The latter, who had been for ages under the Muslim rule, had no dislike to learn the language of their new rulers. As they had learnt Persian and Urdu under the Muslims, so they were willing to learn English under the British. But this was not so with the Muslims. They objected to the study English because they said they feared English education would undermine their religion. This objection did not, however, contain the whole truth. In reality, it was based on a far more serious consideration. According to the Muslim law, as expounded by Sunnis of the *old* school, it was not lawful to learn English or the language of any other non-Muslim people except for the purpose of answering letters, or of combating the religious arguments of those people. Learning a foreign language for any other purpose was not allowed.[4]

Such an attitude towards learning the English language weakened the position of the Muslims, and gradually they began to lose all important offices. They now possessed little influence, and that too in their capacity as government servants. The abolition of the Muslim law offices on the introduction of the Penal Code deprived the Muslims of almost all the respectable appointments and greatly checked vernacular education.[5]

From the first establishment of the Mughal rule in India

---

[3]Ibid.

[4]Ibid.

[5]Ibid.

till 1837, Persian continued to be the official language. The conquest of India by the Mughals had been achieved by men belonging to different races and speaking a variety of tongues, but the Persian language was considered sufficient for administrative purposes not only by the Mughal masters but also by their successors who were in power till 1837.[6]

The contact of the Muslims with the Hindus gave birth to the composite language which is known as Urdu. It was spoken by the Muslims all over India, with the exception of the deltaic districts of Eastern Bengal. From the Punjab as far down as Bhagalpur in the Lieutenant Governorship of Bengal, Urdu, more or less pure, was not only the vernacular of the Muslims but also of the majority of the Hindus. In 1837 an order was promulgated that office work should in future be done either in English or in the provincial dialects. The language of the people of each province and the character in which it was originally intended to be written were fixed upon as the most convenient and practicable substitutes for the Persian. This plan succeeded in those provinces where the language was not Urdu or Hindustani. Hence the Tamil, the Telugu, the Marathi, the Gujarati and the Bengali languages superseded Persian without much difficulty in Madras, Bombay, Gujarat and Bengal. In Bihar, the North-Western Provinces and the Punjab, where the language of the people had for several centuries been Urdu, this attempt not only caused great discontent both among the Hindus and the Muslims, but ended in absolute failure. The British Government wished to introduce the Hindi-Kaithi, written in the stiff archaic Nagri character, as the official language of these parts. But the change proposed was based upon a misapprehension and the attempt consequently failed signally. Urdu written in the Persian character was substituted for Persian in Bihar, the North-Western Provinces and the Punjab. The substitution of the vernacular dialects and the vernacular character for

---

[6]Correspondence on the subject of the Education of the Muhammadan Community in British India and their employment in the public service generally. *Selections from the Records of the Government of India,* Nos. 205-6, para 11.

Persian in other provinces resulted in throwing out of employment a considerable body of Muslim subordinate officers who were totally dependent for their subsistence upon the pay of the Government.[7]

The actual impoverishment of the Muslim middle class dates from this epoch. English educated Hindu youths, trained for the most part in missionary institutions, from which the Muslims naturally stood aloof, now poured into every Government office and completely shut out the Muslims. A few unimportant offices remained in the hands of the Muslims, but day by day their number decreased.[8] This led Dr. Hunter to observe that "there is now scarcely hope for any post above the rank of porter, messenger, filler of ink-pots, and mender of pens." The Muslims, who in the time of Lord Cornwallis were holding 75 per cent government jobs, no longer occupied the front rank among the Indian communities.[9]

While this radical change was introduced in the administrative policy of the country by making it necessary on all aspirants for office under Government to know the language of the rulers, no order was passed to make English education compulsory. On the contrary, till 1864 the Muslims were fed with the hope that their own classics were the *sine qua non* for Government employment, or for entering the legal profession. The orders of the Government permitting candidates for the offices of *munsif* and pleader to take their examinations either in English or Urdu remained in force till 1864. A year or two later, however, a sudden change was introduced. It changed the previous orders and declared that in future examinations for higher grade posts of pleaders and *munsifs* would be conducted only in English. This measure placed the Muslims under a complete disadvantage.[10]. For them the British system of education was a failure[11] because they were unable to participate in

---

[7]Ibid.

[8]Ibid.

[9]Ibid., para 10.

[10]Ibid., para 12.

[11]Note by His Excellency the Viceroy dated June 26, 1871. Education A Proceedings, Nos. 2-8A dated August 19, 1871.

the material advantages which the government education had conferred on the Hindus. The statistics available for the years 1860-61 to 1866[12] and 1871[13] proves the lamentable deficiency in the education of the Muslims who were not very long ago the most powerful rulers of India.

The special obstacles which hindered the education and social progress of the Muslims were very often discussed by the Government of India. In 1871 the Government issued a Resolution on the state of Muslim education and made it clear that the main drawback in their advancement was owing to their inability or unwillingness to take advantage of the Government system of education. Noting with regret that so large and important a class as the Muslims should stand aloof from the new educational system, and thus lose the advantages, both material and social, which the other people of India enjoyed,[14] the Earl of Mayo took steps to remove their disabilities. He decided to give systematic encouragement and recognition to the classical and vernacular languages of the Muslims in Government schools and colleges, appoint qualified Muslim teachers in English schools, assist the Muslims by financial grants to enable them to open schools of their own, and encourage the creation of a vernacular literature for the Muslims. The whole subject was commended to the attention of the Local Governments and of the three universities of India.[15]

---

[12]In 1860-61 there was only one Muslim to ten Hindus, in 1866 this proportion increased. There was now one Muslim to five Hindus.

[13]From the statistics collected by Mr Howell we see that in British India only 106,986 Muslims—out of a population estimated at more than 30,000,000—attended Government and aided schools, while the Hindus who attended these schools numbered 500,000. In Bengal the proportion of Hindu students to Muslims was 100,000 to 14,000, in Bombay, 114,000 to 10,000; in Madras, 45,000 to 1,900; in Central Provinces, 22,000 to 1,000; in the Berars, 7,500 to 1,400, while in the North Western Provinces and the Punjab, where Muslim education had greater encouragement, the proportions were 144,000 Hindus to 42,000 Muslims and 44,000 Hindus to 30.000 Muslims respectively.

[14]Extract from the Proceedings of the Government of India in the Home Department (Education),—under date Simla, August 7, 1871. Education A Proceedings, No. 7, dated August 19, 1871.

[15]Review of Education in India, 1886, para 259. Calcutta, 1888.

The reports which were received from the local governments showed that wherever the ordinary vernacular of a
province was Hindustani or Urdu, written in the Persian
character, or, again, where the Muslims used a form of the
provincial or district dialect, there the Muslims occupied
proper positions in the primary and secondary schools founded
or aided by the Government. But where, on the other hand,
they spoke a language different from that of the majority of
the population, or expressed in a different character, the special
arrangements necessary to meet these circumstances had not
always been carried out, with the inevitable result that the
claims of the Muslim community were disregarded. The
obstacles which kept the Muslim students apart from the ordinary school system naturally grew stronger as the higher standards of education were reached. With a strictly limited grant
for educational purposes, it was not possible to maintain a
double educational agency. Consequently, it was in high
schools, the colleges and the universities that the absence or
backwardness of Muslims was most conspicuous. The reports
all agreed that the existing system of education had not attracted them to the higher ranges of the educational course, or
induced them to persevere up to the point at which studies
impress real culture and fit young men for successes in the
services and the open professions.[16]

The reports of the local governments were reviewed at
length by the Education Commission in 1883. It laid much
greater stress on the educational than on the social or historical
difficulties that contributed to the backwardness of the Muslims
and debated the causes which kept them aloof from receiving
higher education. While some members of the Commission were
of the opinion that the absence of instruction in the tenets of
their faith, and still more the injurious effects of the English
education in creating a disbelief in religion, were the main
obstacles, others—a small minority—thought that religion had
little to do with this question.Some contended that the system of
education prevailing in government schools and colleges corrup-

---

[16]Ibid., pp. 311-12,

ted the morals and manners of the students. The small proportion of Muslim teachers in government institutions; the unwillingness of government educational offices to accept the advice and cooperation of the Muslims; numerous minor faults in the departmental system; the comparatively small progress in real learning made by the students in government schools; the practice among the well-to-do Muslims of educating their children at home; the indolence and imprudence too common among them; their hereditary love of the profession of arms; the absence of the friendly contact between Muslims and the Englishmen; the unwillingness felt by the upper class to associate with the lower; the general poverty among the Muslims, the coldness of government towards them; the use in government schools of books whose tone was hostile of scornful towards Islam—these and a variety of other causes were put forward at different times by members of the Muslim community to account for the scant appreciation which English education had received at their hands. But the Commission concluded that while all these factors must have combined in driving the Muslims away from English education, "a candid Muhammadan would probably admit that the most powerful factors are to be found in pride of race, a memory of by-gone superiority, religious fears, and a not unnatural attachment to the learning of Islam."[17]

Apart from social and historical difficulties, there were educational difficulties also in promoting education of the Muslims. First, whereas the object of the young Hindu was to obtain an education which would fit him for an official or a professional career, a young Muslim was not allowed to turn his thoughts to secular instruction until he had passed some years in going through a course of sacred learning because for him "the teaching of mosque must precede the lessons of the school."[18] The Muslim boy, therefore, entered school later than the Hindu. Secondly, he very often left school at an

---

[17] Johnston, J., Abstract and Analysis of the Report of the Indian Education Commission, pp. 86-7, London, 1884.

[18] Sharp, H., Progress of Education in India, 1907-12, para 601, Calcutta, 1913,

early age. The Muslim parents were usually poorer than the Hindu parents in a corresponding social position. A Muslim boy could not therefore receive thorough education. Thirdly, the Muslim parents often chose for their sons while at school an education which would secure for them an honoured place among the learned of his own community, rather than one which would command a success in the modern professions or in official life. The years which a young Hindu spent in learning English and Mathematics in a public school, the young Muslim devoted in a *madrasah* in learning Arabic, Islamic jurisprudence and theology. These were the three principal causes which retarded the prosperity of the Muslims.[19]

It now remains to examine the Commission's recommendations about the Muslims. The Commission treated the Muslim claims not merely with justice but with generosity to give them special assistance in view of their backward condition. The proposals of the Commission covered the whole field of education and, indeed, went beyond it into the domain of public life and employment. The following were its recommendations:

i. Indigenous schools for Muslims should be liberally encouraged to add purely secular subjects to their curriculum.[20]

ii. In public primary schools for Muslims, special standards should be prescribed.[21]

iii. Higher English education for Muslims both in schools and in colleges should be encouraged.[22]

iv. A graduated chain of scholarships leading from the

[19]Nathan, R., Progress of Education in India, 1897-98 to 1901-02, paras 1, 112. Calcutta, 1904.

[20]Report of the Indian Education Commission, 1882-83, Recommendation No. IX, 2. Calcutta, 1883-84.

[21]Ibid, IX, 6.

[22]Ibid, IX, 7.

primary school through all intermediate stages up to
the B.A. degree, and also a system of free scholarships in schools under public management should be
established for the exclusive benefit of the Muslims.[23]

   v.   The benefits of Muslim educational endowments
should be reserved for Muslims and applied to the
promotion of English education among them.[24]

  vi.   Special provision should be made to increase the
number of Muslim teachers and Muslim inspecting
officers.[25]

 vii.   Employment should be offered to the Muslims in
public offices by the local governments.[26]

The recommendations of the Commission did not escape
criticism. There were three main objections. First, it was not
in the interest of the Muslims that they should be offered
special facilities for learning Hindustani and Persian, instead
of the vernacular of the country in which they were to be
employed. (This objection, so far as it related to Persian, seemed
to spring from a misapprehension. Persian was not to super-
cede the vernacular but to take the place of Sanskrit which
was taught as a second language to Hindu boys in high
schools). Secondly, it was still less in the interest of the
Muslims to establish special schools for their benefit. The
spirit of exclusiveness or 'separatism' had been the worst foe of
the Muslims, and it was a duty incumbent on the government
to repress and discourage rather than to foster it. Muslim boys
could not begin too early to learn the lessons of tolerance and
emulation in association with those amid whom their lives
were to be spent. Lastly, it was unfair to other sections of the
community to establish scholarships for the special benefit
of Muslims, while they were also allowed to compete on equal
terms for the government scholarships that were open to all.

---

[23]Ibid, IX, 8, 9.
[24]Ibid, IX, 10, 11.
[25]Ibid, IX, 12-14.
[26]Ibid, IX, 17.

There was danger that sympathy with the Muslims might
result in unfairness to other classes. The Education Commission
in their "leaning towards generosity seemed to have overstepped
the limits of justice."[27]

In commenting upon the Report of the Education Commission, the Government of India, while explaining its policy
said :

> It is only by frankly placing themselves in line with the
> Hindus, and taking full advantage of the Government
> system of high and especially of English education, that
> the Muhammadans can hope fairly to hold their own in
> respect of the better description of State appointments...
> The object of the Commission is to attract Muhamma-
> dan scholars by giving adequate prominence to those
> subjects to which their parents attach importance, and
> to hold out special inducements to a backward class;
> but...due regard is everywhere to be paid to local circums-
> tances, and care must be taken to avoid unnecessary
> widening of the line between Muhammadans and other
> classes of the community.[28]

This policy of the Government of India showed good
results. The number of Muslim students increased from
114,816 in 1871-72 to 261,887 in 1881-82.[29] The educational
progress in the four years following the Commission's report
showed that the number and percentage of students attending
the school went up considerably.[30] In primary schools, the
percentage of the Muslim students was higher than that of
the other communities in India.[31] But in the higher stages of
instruction, the proportion of Muslim students rapidly declined.
Still, judged by the position in 1881-82, a striking advance was

---

[27]Review of Education in India, 1886, para 259.
[28]Ibid.
[29]Johnston, op. cit., p. 87.
[30]1881-2 ; 447, 703 students : 17.8 per cent.
  1885-6 : 748, 663 students : 23.6 per cent,
[31]Muslims : 21.1 per cent.
  Other communities 19.1 per cent.

recorded. From 1881-82 to 1885-86, great progress was made in the education of all classes, but that of the Muslim community was exceptionally rapid. The number of Muslims in Arts colleges increased from 197 or 3.5 per cent of the total number of students, to 330 or 4.4 per cent. In colleges giving instruction in law, medicine and engineering, the number increased from 73 to 132, and the percentage from 4.3 to 5.1. In secondary schools, the proportion of Muslim students increased from 9.3 to 13.5 per cent.[32]

The Commission's proposals and the objections taken to them were discussed in the Resolution of the Government of India in July, 1888. This Resolution thus described the principles upon which the education of Muslims should be encouraged by the State:

As to the principles upon which the education of Muhammadans should be encouraged by the State, His Excellency in Council need say little here, for they appear to be understood by all Administrations, and with general consent accepted by the people,—by none more openly than by the leading Muhammadans of India. The State has only to apply its education apparatus and aid, so as they may best adjust themselves to existing languages and habits of thought among all classes of the people without diverging from its set mark and final purpose— the better diffusion and advancement of real knowledge in India. His Excellency in Council is anxious that the attainment of this object shall in no class of the population be hindered by differences of language or of custom; and with this view the Government of India is very willing that the entire body of Muhammadan (as of Hindu) classic literature shall be admitted and take rank among the higher subjects of secular study; and that the languages shall form an important part of the examinations for university degrees. In short, His Excellency in Council is prepared to listen favourably to any well-

---

[32]Croft, Sir A., Review of Education in India in 1886, para, 261. Calcutta, 1888.

considered proposal for modifying or extending in these directions the existing educational system. One measure to which the Resolution of 1871 particularly adverted was the development of a vernacular literature for Muhammadans. His Excellency in Council would be slow to believe that such a literature still needed creation. To this suggestion Local Governments attach differing degrees of importance or practicability; and, on the whole, His Excellency in Council sees reason to believe that we must be cautious in attempting to proceed in this direction much beyond the point we have reached already. It is most desirable to frame a series of high class textbooks, to encourage the printing and publication of valuable Muhammadan works, and to offer prizes either for good translations of foreign works or for original studies. But in regard to the patronage of what may properly be called literature, the exercise of it must necessarily be restricted by the pressing demands of general education upon our finance, and by the difficulty of making a fair selection, or of distributing any money available with due discrimination and indubitable advantage.[33]

The Resolution concluded as follows :

His Excellency in Council has now reviewed rapidly the general measures which have been taken, or are being taken, for the encouragement of education among Muhammadans. The papers before him, received from all parts or British India, show that the Earl of Mayo's Resolution has succeeded in its main purpose of drawing the attention of all Administrations to needs and obligations which before had perhaps not everywhere been adequately realized. These needs and obligations may now be entrusted with confidence to the case of Local Governments. The Supreme Government has satisfied itself that

---

[33]Summary of the Principal Measures of the Viceroyalty of the Marquess of Dufferin and Ava in the Home Department, December 1884—December 1888, vol. I, pp. 49-50. Calcutta, 1888.

the principles upon which Muhammadan education should be supported or subsidized are clearly understood; while the conditions and rate of progress in this as in all branches of public instruction, the range of its operations, and all other practical details depend chiefly in each province upon local circumstances, administrative skill and financial resources.[34]

The Report of the Commission and the Resolution of the Government of India which was issued in 1885 gave a considerable impetus to Muslim education.[35] Under the patronage of men like Sir Salar Jang and other illustrious princes and nobles, and of such English gentlemen as Lord Stanley, Earl Lytton, Sir William Muir and Sir John Strachey, great pressure was put on the Muslims to receive education. But much of the good done was through the efforts of the Muslims themselves, of whom Maulvi Sayyid Ahmad Khan, whole life was devoted to the cause of liberal education, was the most distinguished leader. Many of the drawbacks which existed in 1870 had now been removed.[36]

From 1886 to 1897, i.e., in a period of 12 years, the total number of Muslim students rose from 754,036 to 966,632, but generally speaking the Muslim education did not advance beyond the primary stage.[37] A comparison of Muslim students, male and female, with general population during the period 1897-1902 showed that on the whole the comparison was unfavourable to the Muslim eommunity. Only 60 *per mille* of Muslim males were literate against 102 *per mille* on the general population.[38] This backwardness of Muslim education was due in a great measure to the traditions and character of the people, and the special efforts made by the government could

---

[34]Ibid, p. 50.

[35]Nathan, R., Progress of Education in India, 1897-98 to 1901-02, para 1, 158. Calcutta, 1904.

[36]Ibid, paras 1, 116.

[37]Cotton, J.S., Progress of Education in India, 1892-93 to 1896-97, p. 335. London, 1898.

[38]Nathan, op. cit., para 1, p. 119.

only have been successful if the Muslim parents had showed willingness to impart secular education to their children. The influential classes in several provinces showed appreciation of this situation and an earnest desire to improve it.[39]

Speaking as President of the Muhammadan Educational Conference in December 1909, Nawab Imad al-Mulk Sayyid Husain Bilgrami said:

> We usually take it for granted that everyone is alive to the benefits of education, that at any rate every literate parent is convinced of the duty he owes to his children of giving them a sound education, but in practice the majority of literate Muhammadans are accustomed to feel satisfied that they have discharged their duty in an effective manner when they have put their children under a village pedagogue at the door, or sent them to the nearest school. They think they have made an end of the matter, their consciences are satisfied and they give themselves no further concern about it. The result is that in the majority of cases the children grow up in ignorance and are perhaps led into evil ways, for which the parents are primarily responsible. They are responsible because they have not taken the trouble to find out what sort of education is wanted for their children and how it is to be obtained.[40]

Observations similar in tenor were made by His Highness the Agha Khan who was President of the Muhammadan Educational Conference which was held at Delhi at the time of the Coronation Darbar. The following quotation is of special interest:

> And now gentlemen, let us direct our attention to a question with which your conference is intimately concerned, namely, how have the Indian Muslims taken advantage of the chances which Providence has placed

---

[39]Ibid, para 1, p. 157.
[40]Ibid, para 1, p. 113.

in their way? We must all acknowledge with shame and regret that so far we have failed. Throughout the whole length and breadth of India, how many national schools are there in existence which educate Muslim boys and girls in their faith and at the same time in modern secular state? Is there even one to every hundred that our nation needs and which we should have established had we been like any other healthy people? There are, indeed, a certain number of old-fashioned *maktabs* and *madrasahs* which continue to give parrot-like teaching of the Quran, but even in these places no attempt is made either to improve the morals of the boys or to bring before them the eternal truths of the faith. As a rule, prayers are but rarely repeated, and when said, not one per cent of the boys understand what they say and why.[41]

From now onwards there was a remarkable awakening in the Muslim community to the advantages of modern education. The steady efforts made by the government to ameliorate their lot as well as the attitude of the leaders of their community towards education was more and more favourable.[42] During the nine years, *i. e.*, from 1904 to 1913, the number of Muslim students increased by approximately 50% and stood at nearly a million and a half.[43] In primary education, the number of Muslims had gone up a little as compared to children of all races and creeds in India,[44] but as regards higher education they still lagged behind and had much lee-way to make up before they could reach the educational level of the Hindus.[45] Various measures were, therefore, taken between 1913 and 1922 to encourage Muslim education. Chief among these were the appointment of special Muslim inspectors, the employment of Muslim teachers,[46] establishment of new Muslim schools in

[41]Ibid.

[42]Sharp, H., Progress of Education in India, 1907-12, para 601. Calcutta, 1913.

[43]Indian Educational Policy—Being a Resolution issued by the Governor-General-in-Council on the 21st February, 1913, p. 42, Calcutta, 1913.

[44]Ibid, p. 57.

[45]Sharp, H., Ibid, para, 601.

[46]Richey, J.A., Progress of Education in India, 1917-22, pp. 203-5, Calcutta, 1923.

suitable localities[47] and the reservation of scholarships for Muslim children.[48]   Similar steps were taken for the development of Muslim education in Bihar, Orissa, Madras, Bombay, Bengal, U.P., Sind and the Frontier.[49]

But the progress made by Muslims in the field of technical education was not yet satisfactory.   In 1913, the President of the All India Muslim Education conference commented upon this state of affairs in the following words:

> Thirty years ago the cry of the Indian Muslims used to be the cry of despondency, that in the matter of English education we have allowed ourselves to lag behind. Thirty or forty years hence I am afraid the burden of our cry would be that we have fallen behind all other communities in the peaceful avocations of manufacture, commerce and industry.[50]

In 1927-28, the percentage of literacy amongst the Muslims in the various provinces of India was as follows: Bombay, 9.6; Madras 7.8; Punjab 4.6; U.P. 3.2, and N.W. Frontier 2.0.   These figures show that the Muslims of Bombay stood first in the field of education.[51]   But even now they were worse than the advanced classes of the Hindu community because their percentage of literacy at this time was 16.1.[52] Mrs. R.S. Husain tells us that in India at that time all the doors to wealth, health and wisdom were denied to Muslims on the plea of inefficiency.   Some newspapers owned by Muslims admitted this fact.   The late lady Shams al-Huda often used to say that the Muslim public abused her husband because he gave certain high posts to Hindus ignoring Muslim claims, but

---

[47]Indian Education in 1913-14, p. 25, Calcutta, 1925.

[48]Ibid.

[49]Richey, J.A., Progress of Education in India, 1907-12, pp. 203-5, Calcutta, 1913.

[50]Indian Education in 1912-14, p. 25, Calcutta, 1915.

[51]Hidayatullah, Sir Gulam Husain, *Muslim Education, p.1; Progress of Education, Vol.* IV, No. 1, dated July, 1927.

[52]Ibid., p. 2.

they failed to see their own fault. The Muslim applicants were really unfit for the posts.[53]

It is an irony of fate that the Hindus, who were bound by their *Shastras* to treat women like slaves and cattle and to get their daughters married before they were hardly out of their girlhood, were as a matter of fact quite liberal in sending their children to modern schools. They were trying to get laws passed against childmarriage and raising the age of consent to sixteen years. They were also devising means to popularize widow-marriage heedless of their *pandits* who quoted *shastras* saying, "Not only should a woman refrain from marrying a second time but she should do penance by living only on fruits etc., after her husband's death." On the other hand, while Islam allowed every freedom to women so much so that a woman could not be given in marriage without her consent or free-will, thus indirectly prohibiting child-marriages, many people were giving away their daughters in marriage without their consent. Many a time a bride bitterly bewailed her fate on being compelled to marry a bridegroom whom she knew to be a drunkard or an old man of sixty, but the marriage celebrations proceeded despite her silent protest. Respectable families of Muslims took pride in preventing widow-marriages whether the widow was a girl of thirteen or a child of seven. In such a state of affairs, therefore, it was not surprising that in 1927-28 "not one out of two hundred girls even knew their alphabet." Much was, therefore, yet to be done to improve the standard of education amongst the Muslims.

Not much was however achieved till 1932 because the vast majority of Muslim boys[54] failed to reach higher classes.[55] The root cause for this unhappy state of affairs was loyalty to their traditional learning and religion.[56] Besides there were obstacles in their way in those provinces in which the

---

[53]Husain, Mrs. R.S., Education of Muslim Girls, p. 1; Progress of Education, Vol. IV, No. 4, dated January, 1928.

[54]Progress of Education in India, (1927-32), p. 241.

[55]Hartog Report, 1919, p. 199.

[56]Progress of Education in India, (1927-32), p. 242.

vernacular system of education was allowed to fall into decay. For the most part Muslims were agriculturist and lived in rural areas. A system of education by which only those who lived in towns could appear in the Matriculation Examination was therefore not suitable for them. But the greatest handicap to progress in higher ranges of education was mainly because children attended segregated schools in large numbers. As far back as 1919 the Hartog Committee had recorded the opinion that these institutions "undoubtedly brought Muslim pupils under instruction more extensively and more quickly than would have been the case and had the only facilities been those afforded by the undenominational and publicly managed schools. But these institutions have done but little to raise the general standard of education among Muslims to that of other communities. A continuance of these institutions on a large scale will be prejudicial to the interests of Muslims themselves and to the public interest."[57]

This situation had changed by 1937. The students realised the limitations of the segregated schools from the point of view of secular education and entered the general institutions in large numbers than before.[58] The Muslim community still regarded the absence of any provision for religious instruction in the ordinary schools as a deterrant factor. The politically conscious section of the Muslims felt that there was a danger of Muslim boys losing their individual outlook if they attended general schools which were manned very largely by non-Muslims and where the education given was more or less non-Islamic in character.[59] Efforts were therefore made, from now onwards, to provide special facilities for the encouragement of education among Muslims by reserving a certain percentage of places for them in Government institutions, by appointing special inspectors and by awarding free studentships[60] as had been recommended by the Hartog Committee in 1919.

---

[57]Hartog Report, 1919, p. 199.

[58]Progress of Education in India, (1927-32), p. 241.

[59]Progress of Education in India, (1932-37), pp. 247-8.

[60]Ibid, p. 248.

No wonder, as a result of these measures, the state of education improved a good deal by 1943.[61] The number of Muslims under instruction was now 3,414,460[62] whereas in 1921-22 it was only 1,966,442. The enrolment thus went up by over 14 lakhs. The percentage of Muslim students to the total number of all communities also increased from 23.5 in 1921-22 to 29.0 in 1943.[63] Unlike the year 1932, this increase in the number of students was shared by all stages of education —arts colleges, professional colleges, secondary and primary schools.[64] Proportionally there was increase in the number of girl students also. This progress was encouraging and was shared by all the provinces of India.

---

[61]*No. of students*
  1921-22 : 1,966,442
  1927-32 : 3,408,758
  1942-43 : 3,414,460

[62]The Indian Year Book, 1945-46, Vol. XXXII, p. 380.

[36]*Percentage of Muslim population to total population*
  1921-22 : 23.5
  1927-32 : 26.7
  1942-43 : 29.0

[64]Progress of Education in India (1932-37), pp. 245-6.

3

Mujahidin Movement

The word *Mujahidin* is an Arabic one. It is applied to a person 'who personally engages in Jehad'. 'Jehad', as defined in *Holy Quran*, is a Holy War against non-Muslim powers when Muslim places of worship are attacked or their religious interests are in danger. The word, as understood by *Mujahidin* who inhabited the Tribal Territory meant a crusade against non-Muslim powers such as the Sikhs and the British. To them "*Jehad*" did not necessarily or exclusively, mean "active engagement in a religious war".[1] They believed in the theory that, those persons who were unable to join in "active war" could fulfil their duty by assisting those so engaged with money or by others means. The "*Wahabis*" who lived in India gave full support to the *Mujahidin* because they were either engaged in or preparing for "*Jehad*". That is why they also contributed towards their maintenance in *Asmas*.[2] It is also significant to note that even though the headquarters of this movement were in Tribal Territory—a region difficult of

---

[1] Home Political Secret Consultation No. 101 of 1936, p. 3, para 1.

[2] *Samsas* in Pushtu means caves within the limits of the Mudakhal. In time Samsas was corrupted into Asmas—the headquarters of the *Mujahidin*.

access—recruits and funds were obtained[3] from places as far as Rajshahi in Bengal, Patna in Bihar and Amritsar in the Punjab.

Genesis of the Wahabi Sect

As practically all *Mujahidin* were *Wahabis* it is necessary, for a correct understanding of the movement, to briefly trace the origin of the *Wahabi* sect. This sect was created by Muhammad, son of Abdul Wahab, who was born at Najd (Arabia) in 1691.[4] The basic doctrine[5] of the *Wahabi* sect implied the oneness of God. The *Wahabis* believed that this holy doctrine could be violated by the paying of homage to Saints, *Walis*, *Pirs* etc. They accordingly called themselves "*Mowahidins*" (Unitarians). They had implicit faith in the *Holy Quran* and *Ahadees* (Sacred sayings of the Holy Prophet) and considered that the lessons taught by the *Ahadees* were flagrantly neglected by Muslims in general. The be-all and end-all of their faith was to promote the study of the *Ahadees*. They therefore earned the name of "*Ahl-Hadees*". They denounced the illumination of shrines, maintained that visits to them were irreligious and advocated that these should be razed to the ground. They believed in liberty of conscience and free-thinking. But they did not always follow the interpretation of religious books by old commentators and for this reason were known to some Muslims as "Ghair Muqallid"[6] (non-conformists).

Muhammad, son of Abdul Wahab, preached his faith

---

[3]Home Political Secret Consultation No. 101 of 1936, p. 3, para 1.

[4]Home Political Secret Consultation No. 101 of 1936, p. 3, para 2.

[5]The leading principles of this doctrine have thus been depicted by T.E. Ravenshaw : —

"1st   Reliance in one Supreme being.

2nd   Repudiation of all the forms, ceremonies and observances of Modern Muhammadan religion, retaining only such as are considered the pure doctrines of the Koran.

3rd   Expectation of an Imam (Guide or Prophet) who will lead all true believers to victory over infidels.

4th   The duty of Jehad or holy war for the faith against infidels generally.

5th   Blind and implicit obedience to their spiritual guides or Peers."

[6]Home Political Secret Consultation No 101 of 1936, p. 3, para 3.

vigorously but during his life time, failed to make any impression because the country was inhabited by orthodox Muhammadans. Like all religious reformers he was surrounded by enemies who did their utmost to discredit him. His opponents publicly declared that he and his followers were not true Muhammadans. The result was that in course of time this sect began to be known as *Wahabis*, after the name of the father of the founder[7] *viz* Abdul Wahab. After the death of Muhammad other, continued to preach the new faith and by 1936 there were a large number of *Wahabis* in Arabia. Ibn-i-Saud, the King of Najd, was a *Wahabi*. He was known for demolishing numerous tombs and domes but this action did not have any repercussions in India as Shias and Sunnis greatly out-numbered Wahabis. However, it is interesting to note in this connection that in Peshawar City Shias always cursed Ibn-i-Saud during their annual mourning for initiating any irreligious movement.[8]

Foundation of Wahabi Sect in India

The Wahabi sect was founded in India by Said Ahmad who was born at Rai Bareilly (U.P.) in 1786. He began life as a *sawar* under Ameer Khan Pindarry and accompanied him in many freebooting raids in Malwa.[9] Quitting that service about the time when Ameer Khan's followers were disbanded, he shifted to Delhi and became a disciple of Shah Abdul Aziz, a very celebrated devotee of that city. He preached a religious crusade or *jehad* only through his inspiration. His first disciples were two near relations of Abdul Aziz, one his nephew Moulvie Mahomed Ismael,[10] and the other his son-in-law, Moulvie Abdul Hye. Both of them paid great respect[11] to Said Ahmad.

---

[7]Ibid, para 4.

[8]Ibid, para 5.

[9]Home Judicial Proceeding Nos. 70-4 dated 27th September, 1865, p. 1501.

[10]Author of '*Suratul-Mustakim*'—a principal treatise on Wahabi sect—printed in Calcutta by an active member named Maulvi Mahomed Ali of Rampur about 1822.

[11]They rendered him the most menial services, running, it is said, with their shoes off by the side of his palanquin when he moved about, like common servants.

Accompanied by them Said Ahmad proceeded to Calcutta but took up a circuitous route first north to Saharanpur, and then west towards Rampur—the seat of a large and turbulent body of Pathans.[12] After leaving Delhi he assumed the character of a religious teacher. It was on this journey that he successfully preached and obtained ascendancy over the minds of Muhammadans particularly in Bengal, by spreading his reformed doctrines which supported Islam in its primitive simplicity and fervour, but rejected all idolatrous and superstitious innovations.[13]

Encouraged by this success he next reached the Lower Provinces. Here he obtained a large following and also enjoyed an extensive reputation.[14] He stayed for sometime at Patna, in the company of Moulvie Wilayat Ali and Shah Muhamed Hossein. Here he made many converts, but before leaving this place, he appointed his agents and delegated them authority to preach and proselytize in his name. Similar agents were then appointed in all large towns for collecting funds. These funds were raised by *takat*,[15] i.e. a tax, on the profits of trade and donations from well wishers to the faith. The chief agent appointed at Patna was Shah Mahomed Hossein. Besides him Moulvie Wilayat Ali, Moulvie Enayat Ali, Moulvie Murhum Ali, and Moulvie Furhat Hossein were also appointed as his *Khalifas* or Lieutenants.[16]

Proceeding from Patna, Said Ahmad went towards Calcutta, following the course of the Ganges, preaching and making converts and appointing agents at all the important towns which came on the route. In Calcutta and Baraset disciples flocked to him in such large numbers that he was unable to go through the process of enrolling them by separate laying on of hands. He had therefore to unroll his turban and

---

[12]Home Judicial Proceeding Nos. 70-4, 27th September, 1865, p. 1502.

[13]Ibid.

[14]Home Judicial Proceeding Nos. 70-4 dated 27th September, 1865, p. 1502, para 2.

[15]Ibid, para 3.

[16]Ibid, para 4.

all who could seize it became his *Murid's*.[17] In the early part
of 1822 he proceeded with his friends to Mecca from where
he returned in October of the following year. Then he stayed
for a fewdays at Bombay where his success in gaining followers
was as remarkable as it had been in Calcutta. In December
1823 he again started for Upper India and was joined at Bareilly
by Shah Mahomed Hossein with a number of followers.[18]

In 1824 Said Ahmad travelled through Kandhar and
Kabul, and reached among the Yusufzai tribes on the Peshawar
border. He made an alliance with the Barakzai Sardars and
proclaimed a *religious war* against the Sikhs.[19] The date of this
war is given in the following extract from "*Targhib-ul-Jehad*":

> "The tribe of Seikhs have long held sway in Lahore and
> other places, their oppressions have exceeded all limits,
> thousands of Muhammadans have they unjustly killed and
> on thousands they have heaped disgrace; the *Azan*, or
> summons to prayer, and the killing of cows they have
> entirely prohibited. When at length their insulting
> tyranny could not longer be borne, Huzrat Syed Ahmed
> (may his fortunes and blessings ever be permanent),
> having for his single object the protection of the faith,
> took with him a few Mussulmans and, going in the
> direction of Kabul and Peshawar, succeeded in rousing
> Muhammadans from their slumber of indifference and
> nerving their courage for action. Praise be to God, some
> thousands of believers became ready at his call to treat
> the path of God's service and on the 20th Jumadi-ul-Sani
> 1242 'Hijree (21st December 1826) the Jehad against the
> Kafir Seikhs begins."[20]

The events of this war were watched with much interest
by the Muhammadans. Many of the inhabitants of the
Western Provinces went in bodies to range themselves under

---

[17]Ibid, para 5.

[18]Ibid, para 6.

[19]Ibid, p. 1503, para 1.

[20]Ibid, para 2.

the standard of the *"Ameer-ul-Moomineen"*, or leader of the faithful, a title which he had now assumed. They gathered large contributions in jewels and money even from distant presidencies and from the Muhammadan Towns in the Deccan.[21] War with the Sikhs was kept up with great perseverence but Said Ahmad had only short-lived success. He was ultimately defeated[22] and fled to Surat.[23]

In 1828 Said Ahmad succeeded in extending the sphere of his influence over the area North of the Kabul river, and in 1829 he occupied the Peshawar valley. He took strong measures in enforcing Muhammedan law as interpreted by *Wahabis* and abolished many customary laws which were in conflict with the spirit of Islam. Populated as the valley was by bigotted Muhammadans, neither the *Wahabi* doctrines appealed to them, nor did they like the high-handed manner in which they were treated. Discontent spread rapidly and Pathans soon formed the opinion that no useful purpose would be served in replacing these Sikhs by a monster in the body of Said Ahmad. Accordingly a general massacre of Said Ahmad and his followers was secretly planned and on the appointed night every Hindustani in the area of Yusufzai was murdered. Providence, however, was kind to Said Ahmad, as he was at Panj Tar on the fateful night with a band of his devoted followers. He succeeded in crossing the Indus but was met by a Sikh force under Hari Singh, popularly known as "Hari Singh Nalwa", and was defeated near Phulra, on the right bank of Siran River, west of Mansehra. Said Ahmad's Tanauli followers numbering about 2,000, deserted him before the battle commenced by the "Hindustanis" put up a desperate flight and were annihilated. Said Ahmad however managed to escape. In 1830 he again tried to come to terms with the Sikhs in the Hazara district and paid for his folly with his life at the battle of Balakot.[24]

---

[21]Ibid, para 3.

[22]Ibid, para 4,

[23]There is some difference of opinion on the point. Some authorities say that Said Ahmad fied to Buner where he settled at Panj-Tar, the stronghold of Fateh Khan, a Khuddu Khel Chief. *See* Home Political Secret F. No. 101 of 1936, page 4, para 3.

[24]Home Political Secret F. No. 101 of 1936, p. 4, para 4.

In 1846 a few survivors of the Hindustani followers of
Said Ahmad gave out that Said Ahmad was not dead, and that
he would soon re-appear as the *Imam Mehdi* and lead them
again. On this pretext people of Northern Hazara joined
them in an attack on the forts of Shinkiari, Bhair, Kund,
Ghari Habibullah and Agror. The forts were captured and
the Sikh troops stationed therein were killed. Now all
Muhammadan chiefs of Hazara met at Haripur and chose
Said Akbar Shah of Satana; as their ruler. Nawab Khan
Tanauli and Ghulam Khan Tareen were appointed as ministers
to help him.[25]

Towards the close of 1846, a Sikh Army of ten regiments
moved from Srinagar to subjugate Upper Hazara. The army
was met by a combined Swati and Hindustani force at the
Dab Pass resulting in the Swatis surrendering to the Governor
of Kashmir. The Hindustanis retreated to Satana where they
decided to settle. Here they built a fort and subsequently got
into touch with Wahabi sympathisers in India who helped
them by obtaining funds and recruits.[26]

Having consolidated their position for the time being
in Satana, the Hindustanis or Hindustani fanatics, as they
came to be called, began fomenting trouble along the borders
of the Peshawar and Hazara Districts with the explicit object
of waging war against the Sikhs. But on the termination of
their rule they directed their hostilities against the British
Government. It was at this time that the Hindustani fanatics
assumed the name of "*Mujahidin*".[27]

In 1853 the Government of India blamed the Hassanzai
Tribe for the murder of two British officers of the Salt Department and sent a punitive column to Hassanzai limits. The
Hassanzai tribe, with the active assistance of the Hindustanis
attacked this column without any success. But enraged by
this attitude the Government allowed its column to demolish

---

[25]Ibid, pp. 4-5, last para,

[26]Ibid, p. 5, para 1.

[27]Ibid, para 2.

the fort of Hindustanis at Satana before returning to British territory.[28]

In 1857 the Hindustani Fanatics gave further trouble. But as soon as the Government informed the report of an attack on Lieut. Harne, Assistant Commissioner of Mardan, it decided to wipe out the colony at Satana and accordingly despatched a British column in May 1858. The Hindustani Fanatics offered stout resistance but were overwhelmed, and fifty of them were killed. The villages of Lower and Upper Satana were completely destroyed, and before the column returned a promise was exacted from the Ghadun and Utmanzai tribes not to allow Hindustanis to settle in their limits. The Hindustanis now moved to village Malka, in Amazai territory to the North of Hamban Hill, but here they remained inactive for about five years.[29]

In 1863 the Hindustani Fanatics resumed their turbulent attitude, and with the connivance of the Ghadun and Utmanzai tribes reoccupied Satana. Government therefore decided to punish the tribes and put an end to their activities across the border. A punitive expedition into the Chamla valley was accordingly sanctioned. The force marched through Yusufzai but was unavoidably held up near the Ambala Pass. The Hindustani Fanatics, taking advantage of the delay, incited the tribes to offer resistance, and succeeded in so exciting the tribesmen that eventually the force had to contend with 15 to 20 thousand of the enemy. The Akhund of Swat was also forced, against his better judgment, to join forces with the Hindustani Fanatics and tribesmen. Fierce fighting ensued but eventually the tribes submitted. A column was then despatched to destroy the forts of the Hindustani Fanatics in Satana and Malka, and it succeeded in doing so without much opposition. Following the termination of hostilities the Ghadur and Utmanzai tribes again promised not to permit the Hindustani Fanatics to re-settle in Satana and Malka, or anywhere in their country.[30]

---

[28]Ibid, para 3.
[29]Ibid, para 4.
[30]Ibid, para 5.

Disaffection of the Wahabis, 1876-86

Between 1876 and 1886 the Wahabi community became increasingly disaffected at being styled "*Wahabis*". Two quotations from the records of the Punjab Government exemplify this point. While forwarding a petition of 300 Wahabis to the Government of India the Secretary to the Punjab Government had once remarked as follows :—

"I am directed to observe that though the petitioners repudiate the name of Wahabi yet it is the one by which they are commonly known, and so far as it is used in this letter, is not intended as a term of reproach.[31]

"It is evident from the remarks we have made above that even those who believe the "Ahl-i-Hadis" to have been guilty of joining the Frontier plots cannot fairly brand the whole community with disloyalty. On the whole we trust that our long but necessary discussion of the subject will serve to convince the public and those officials who are ignorant of the real facts of the case that the so-called "Wahabis" are loyal subjects of the Queen. In conclusion we venture to express the hope that the above remarks will meet with the consideration they deserve at the hands of Government when considering the subject and that a circular letter will be issued prohibiting its officials from using this most offensive epithet in Government papers etc. with reference to a community which yields to none in loyalty and order than to be referred to by their old name "Ahl-i-Hadis".[32]

The Government of India on receipt of this petition in June 1886 proceeded to consider the matter very carefully. The following quotations show how the matter was dealt with. On

---

[31]Extract from letter from Secretary to Punjab Government, dated 29.10.1876 to 300 odd petitioners.

[32]Extract from an article in the "*Ishaat-us-Sunnah*" paper of Lahore, published in 1886, which article was enclosed with a letter to the Punjab Government in 1886 from the recognised leader of the Ahl-i-Hadis community.

the 26th June 1886 the Hon'ble the Home Member wrote as follows :—

"I am quite clear that the term "Wahabi" is inappropriate and offensive and should in official parlance be discontinued, but I am not all clear as to what should be substituted for it. C. J. Lyall might advise on this point."

"Wahabi" is no doubt the name given to the sect, which the petitioner represents, by their enemies, or rather by those who do not generally adopt their doctrines. This name is undoubtedly used by other Mussalmans in an approbrious manner, and Government officers have perhaps lent countenance to the idea that it necessarily connotes rebellion. I sympathise with their desire to rid themselves of its offensive associations. I send with this my copy of Hughes' "Dictionary on Islam". The author states on page 661 that "Ahl-i-Hadis" is the name of the Wahabis, by which the Wahabis of India and Arabia call themselves, and I believe he is correct, at all events, as regards the former. I am inclined to think that "Ahl-i-Hadis" is a sufficiently neutral and an objectionable designation to be, if the Wahabis desire it, generally adopted as their title. Strictly interpreted, it no doubt does imply that other Muslims are not as strict and single followers of the "tradition" as they. At all events, I can suggest no better name".[33]

The Home Department then referred the case privately to the great Muhammadan Syed Ahmad of Aligarh extracts from whose reply are as follows :—

"There is no doubt that in India the term "Wahabi" partly suggests the nation of disloyalty, and therefore on various political grounds I am decidedly of opinion that the word "Wahabi" should not be used in the official papers of Government. The use of the word "Ahl-i-Hadis", especially by the Government, is far from desirable because it has a special religious signification and is not

---

[33]Note by C.J. Lyall, dated 27-6-1886, *See* Home Judicial Proceeding Nos. 35-37, dated December, 1886.

a common word for any sect. It is likely that it will not
be accepted by the majority of Mahommedans. I do not
think it advisable that it should be used officially by the
Government".[34]

Syed Ahmad went on to suggest the name of *"Ghair
Muqallid"* (one who does not follow an *Imam*) for the persons
then called "Wahabis". But this suggestion, although approved by C.J. Lyall, was indignantly repudiated by the leader
of the community in several interviews with the Home Secretary. The former seemed to think the name was a suggestion
of the Evil One and abused Syed Ahmad roundly for having
put it forward. Finally the matter was discussed in Council,
and the decision arrived at was that the use of the term
"Wahabi" should be discontinued in official correspondence,
but that no decision should be arrived at as regards the substitute for it. The Home Secretary put the matter thus in his
private letter to the leader of the community, dated 29th
October 1886 : —

"Briefly, the Government will prescribe no appellation;
it will use no appellation hurtful to the feelings of any
class of Her Majesty's subjects; but, if an appellation be
accepted universally as properly applicable, the Government will consider favourably the wishes of Mahommedans for the general employment of such an approved term.

The official letter to the Punjab Government dated 3rd
December 1886 raed as follows :—

"In reply to your letter No. 1044, dated the 8th June
last, I am directed to say the Governor General in Council
is pleased to express his concurrence with the views of
Sir Charles Aitchison that the use of the term "Wahabi"
should be discontinued in official correspondence".[35]

---

[34]Extract from a letter from Sayad Ahmad of Aligarh to Sir Auckland
Colvin, Home Member, dated 16-7-1886. *See* Home Judicial Proceeding
Nos. 35-37, dated December, 1886, p. 4.

[35]From A.P. Mac Donnell, Secretary, Government of India to the Secretary
to the Government of the Punjab. *See* Home Judicial Proceeding Nos.
35-37, dated December, 1886, p. 7.

While issuing the above letter, the Home Department considered whether or not the decision should be communicated to any other Local Government, and the final decision was that the matter should be treated as a purely local matter and that the letter should issue to the Punjab Government alone. As regards the point that no title had been chosen by Government as a substitute for the discarded one of *"Wahabi"*, the Deputy Secretary, Home Department, on 23-10-1886 noted as follows :—

> "There seems nothing for it but to leave it to time to create a title, which shall be at the same time acceptable to the sect represented by Abu Said Muhammad Hossain and not displeasing to other followers of the Mahomedan faith.[36]

Developments since 1886

With Utmanzai and Gadun country closed to them since 1863, the Hindustani Fanatics sought and were provided with shelter in Chagarzai limits. The arrangement however was far from satisfactory as the tribes made them pay heavily for their food and the protection they enjoyed. Later, other complications arose. They incurred the displeasure of the Akhund of Swat who brought pressure to bear on the Chagarzai with the result that they were expelled from Chagarzai limits. Unable to obtain a permanent home elsewhere the Hindustani Fanatics took to roaming the hills on both banks of the river Indus north of the Black Mountains. Finally the Hazsanzai tribe took pity on them and gave them a tract of land near village Palosi, 20 miles from Darband on the right bank of the Indus. There they remained till 1888 when they joined in attacks on British Forces. At Kotkai a force of 200 Fanatics, made desperate attacks on Government troops but without any success.[37] The mud Fort at Palosi was destroyed and they were again compelled to retreat to Chagarzai limits where they lived for some years.[38] In 1893, the Hindustani

---

[36]Home Political (Deposit) Proceeding No. 12, dated September, 1917.
[37]Home Political Secret F. No. 101 of 1936, pp. 5-6, last para.
[38]In the second Black Mountain expedition of 1898 they again joined tribesmen against Government.

Fanatics moved to a site in Amazai limits near village Malka. This move was a deliberate breach of the agreement signed by the Amazai tribe on the 11 January 1864 after the Ambala Expedition.[39]

During the Malakand Expedition of 1897 and other minor operations in Upper Swat young hot-heads of the Colony joined the tribesmen against the British Government. Moulvie Abdullah then head of the colony was, however, opposed to making any settlement with Government. He maintained that an attack on British forces was only necessary when the British Government adopted an aggressive policy.[40]

In 1898, when British forces entered Buner, the Hindustani Fanatics, made preparations to resist. With the collapse of the Bunerwals, however, they were forced to fly accross the Brandu river back into Chagarzai country. They then settled in village Samasas, (Samasas in Pashtu means caves) within the limits of the Madakhel. In time Samasas was corrupted into Asmas—the headquarters of the *Mujahidin*.[41]

The Mujahidin

From 1898 to 1915 the Colony of Hindustani Fanatics of *Mujahidin*. as they were called from now onwards, gave very little trouble, but in the latter year they joined in the rising on the Sudhan Border engineered by the *Haji* of Turangzai.[42] The *Haji* of Turangzai remained, as he always had been, the stormy-patrol of the Peshawar District border. His real name was "Fazl-e-Wahid",[43] son of Faiz Ahmad Haji Khel Mohammad, Pirzada, of Turangzai. At the instance of Maulana Mahmud-ul-Hasan of Deoband he had fled to Tribal Territory in 1915 and raised the standard of *"jehad"* but he

---

[39]Home Political Secret F. No. 101 of 1936, p. 6, para 1.

[40]Ibid, para 2.

[41]Ibid, para 3.

[42]Home Political Secret F. No. 101 of 1936, p. 6, para 4.

[43]He was born in village Turangzai, Tahsil Charasadda. On reaching manhood he became a disciple of the late Mullah of Hudda and could on this account demand a considerable following in Tribal Territory.

failed to achieve any success. He then conspired with other disaffected Indians and the *Mujahidin* during the war to overthrow the Government of India.[44]

In 1914 Muhammadan feeling in India was deeply stirred when England declared war on Turkey. Leading disaffected Muslims such as the late Maulana Muhammad Ali of the *"Comrade"* and Maulana Zafar Ali Khan, Editor of the *"Zamindar"*, Lahore, took every opportunity to embitter Muslim feelings on this occasion. Leaflets which were distributed to pilgrims in Mecca found their way into India. In these leaflets England and her Allies were depicted as inveterate enemies of Islam. Small incidents like the pulling down of a wall of a mosque in Kanpur for public reasons and the subsequent firing on a Muhammadan crowd were highlighted to show the hostile attitude of Britishers. They were invariably accused of robbing Muhammadans and slandering the Holy Prophet.[45]

Such incidents had their repurcussions in Tribal Territory particularly amongst the *Mujahidin*. The *"Siraj-ul-Akhbar* of Kabul, which was read with absorbing interest by *Mujahidin* and leading Pan-Islamists in India adopted a very objectionable tone and described India as *"Dar-ul-Harab"* (Home of War). Following closely on this, news reached India that the Sultan of Turkey had declared *"Jehad"*. Turkish newspapers, which arrived in India during the month of November 1914, published five important *Fatwas* signed by the Sheikh-ul-Islam. *"Jehad"* was accordingly incumbent upon Muhammadans who, in Northern India looked towards the *Mujahidin* for inspiration and guidance.[46]

As time went on disaffected Muhammadans of the Punjab and the N.W.F.P. became convinced that their only hope lay in joining forces with Muhammadans of Tribal Territory. Consequently, a party of Indian students of the Medical and

---

[44]Home Political Secret F. No. 101 of 1936, p.6, para 5.

[45]Ibid, para 5.

[46]Ibid, pp. 6-7, last para.

Law Colleges of Lahore, left for Tribal Territory and were
welcomed by the *Mujahidin's*. This party included the notorious Moulvie Fazel Elahi, who, however, did not proceed further
than Haripur. The students were interviewed by the Amir
of Asmas and sent by the latter to Kabul. *En route* to Kabul
they stayed in village Tasha with Arbab Ghulam Navi Khan,
son of Arbab Ghulam Naqashband Khan of Tahkal Bala, who
was at that time a *Jagirdar* in Afghanistan.[47] But they
were arrested on suspicion in Kabul and on one
of them was found a letter from the Amir of Asmas
addressed to the late Sardar Nasrullah Khan, brother of the
late Amir Habibullah Khan. These students made a joint statement to the effect that they had fled from India as the British
Government wished to conscript them and send them to fight
against the Sultan of Turkey.[48] Following the flight of the
Lahore students to Asmas and Afghanistan Kala Singh, (*alias*
Gujar Singh, son of Man Singh of Akhara, P.S. Jagraon,
District Ludhiana) absconded to Asmas and was given shelter.
He had taken an active part in the Revolutionary Movement
in the Punjab in 1914-15 and had attempted to seduce Sikh
soldiers stationed at Mardan.[49]

Shortly after, Moulvie Abdul Rahim, (*alias* Moulvie
Bashir of the Chiniyawala Mosque, Lahore), who became the
Amir of the Chamarkand Colony, in 1926, joined the *Mujahidin*
and instigated the tribes to make inroads into British territory.
He and Kala Singh fought with *Mujahidin* against British forces
at Sudham in 1915.[50]

On the termination of hostilities in 1915 a section of
Mujahidin, consisting mainly of Punjabis founded a small
colony at Chamarkand in Mohmand Territory, near the Indo-
Afghan border because they wanted to be in closer contact
with Kabul and to engage in more violent anti-British activity

---

[47]Ibid, p. 7, para 1.

[48]Ibid, para 2.

[49]Ibid, para 3.

[50]Ibid, para 4.

than that approved by the majority of *Mujahidins* of Asmas. Moulvie Abdul Karim of Kanauj was appointed *Amir* by Moulvie Niamat Ullah who continued to be the *Amir* of the Asmas Colony. The Chamarkand Colony continued to exist in spite of a number of attempts to close it down.[51]

In 1916, a colony of *Mujahidin*, was established at Sarkash, a Kuki Khel village in Tirah, under the leadership of Maulvi Muhammad Hassan, of the Punjab. Kheri Beg and Ahmad Effendi, representatives of the Turkish Government at Kabul, were guests of the colony for some time. The colony did all it could to promote a rising of Afridis but was unsuccessful. The Afridis themselves in the same year externed the *Mujahidin* from their limits.[52] In August 1916, a conspiracy known as the *Silk Letter Case* also came to light. The conspirators aimed at overthrowing British rule by an attack on the North Western Frontier supplemented by a Muslim rising in India. In pursuance of this conspiracy Obedullah (a convert from Sikhism) passed through the N.W.F.P. early in August 1915 with three companions—Abdullah, Fatteh Muhammad and Mohd. Ali. Obedullah had been trained in the Muslim religious school at Deoband, in the Saharanpur District, U.P., and while there had infected the staff and students with his militant and anti-British ideas. Foremost amongst those he influenced was Maulana Mahmud-ul-Hassan who had left India for the Hedjaz in September 1915.[53]

Obedullah and his companions conferred with the *Mujahidin* at Asmas before proceeding to Kabul where they met the members of a Turco-German Mission with whom they were associated.[54] Obedullah and his fellow conspirators then devised a scheme for the *"Provisional Government"* of India after the overthrow of the British Raj with Mahindra Pratap—who was at that time in Japan—as President, Obedullah as Minister, and Barakatullah of Bhopal State—a member of the

[51]Ibid, para 5.

[52]Ibid, para 6.

[53]Ibid, para 7.

[54]Ibid, p. 8, para 1.

American *Ghadar* Party, who had also travelled to Kabul via Berlin—as Prime-Minister. He had also devised a scheme for the formation of an "Army of God" in which *Mujahidin*, including Moulvie Bashir and Fazal Illahi were to be given high ranks.[55]

Mujahidin of both colonies of Asmas and Chamarkand were, on the whole, quiescent from the end of the great war till 1920, when they took full advantage of the migration of large numbers of Indians to Afghanistan. This migration was known as the *Hijrat* movement and arose out of the *Khilafat* agitation. The presence of numerous disaffected Indians in Kabul and the anti-British activities of Soviet representatives in Afghanistan gave the *Mujahidin* the opportunity for which they had long waited. They immediately got into touch with extremists in Kabul, Bolshevik agents, and *Ghadrites*, and resumed their anti-British activities with renewed vigour but with little success.[56] A *Mujahidin* centre was opened at Makin, a Mahsud village in South Waziristan under the leadership of Moulvie Muhammad Hassan and Moulvie Bashir, well known Punjabi Fanatics. They encouraged the Mahsuds to continue their resistance and succeeded to some extent in prolonging the Waziristan operations. They could not, however, establish a permanent colony, and in 1921 after admitting their defeat returned to Chamarkand.[57]

Next Khan Bahadur, a member of the Chamarkand Colony, attempted to murder a Police constable at Ferozepore. Action following his arrest led to the recovery of eight bombs, two rifles, and a large quantity of ammunition from the house of one Abdul Rauf of Gujranwala. Investigations revealed that it was a deep rooted conspiracy against the British. Obedullah, a member of the Chamarkand Colony, turned approver, and disclosed that the bombs, arms and ammunition had been sent from Chamarkand by Fazal-e-Illahi through Mohammad Umar for the purpose of bombing

---

[55]Ibid, para 3.
[56]Ibid, para 3.
[57]Ibid, para 4.

British officers. Adequate sentences were awarded in this case and the appeals of the accused were dismissed by the Punjab High Court.[58] This case is popularly known as the Gujranwala Conspiracy case.

Shortly after the Gujranwala Conspiracy Case was settled five bombs were recovered from Ghulam Qadir at Turbella. These bombs were of the same make as those found at Gujranwala. Later, similar bombs were also thrown at a Military picket in Charsadda; at Deans Hotel, Peshawar; at the Peshawar City Church; at the Peshawar Market; and in Risalpur Cantonments. It was proved that the bombs were manufactured in Kabul and brought to India by members of the Chamarkand Colony.[59]

As a result of the disclosures of Obedullah in the Gujranwala Conspiracy Case, Mohammad Umar, Abdul Qadir, Siraj-ud-Din, Sadatullah, Abdul Sattar, Abdul Rahman, Saleh and Bilal of the Chamarkand Colony were arrested and tried in Peshawar for waging war against the King. In sentencing all the accused to imprisonment the Judicial Commissioner ruled that the very existence of the Chamarkand Colony depended upon a conspiracy to wage war against the King, and to overawe the Government of India, and that every member of the Colony was, by reason of his membership, a party to that conspiracy. This ruling was never reversed and was relied on for the arrest of all the members of the Chamarkand Colony.[60]

From 1922 to 1933 *Mujahidins* gave little or no trouble. In the latter year however they joined the Mohmand *lashkar* which opposed British forces. The same occurred in 1935, when, in addition to Chamarkand *Mujahidin*, about 20 members of the Asmas Colony reinforced the tribesmen. It is doubtful, however, whether the *Amir* of Asmas agreed to members of his colony identifying themselves with Chamarkand *Mujahidin* on this occasion.[61] In addition to these hostile acts

---

[58]Ibid, para 5.
[59]Ibid, para 6.
[60]Ibid, para 7.
[61]Ibid, pp. 8-9, last para.

Mujahidin gave asylum to Ajab Khan (the kidnapper of Miss Ellis of Kohat), to Chimnai (a notorious outlaw of Charsadda) and to Mahmud (the perpetrator of the Mardan Danish Mission outrage). Besides on various occasions they afforded help to members of the *Ghadar* Party and to Bolshevik Agents. Moulvie Bashir, the late *Amir* of Chamarkand, received a large allowance from the Afghan Government and was in close touch with the Russian Embassy in Kabul through Haji Abdul Razak. He received a regular subsidy from the Afghan Government but this allowance was stopped on his death in December 1934.[62] Thus, as a fighting force the *Mujahidin* did not pose a serious threat and were safely ignored. They remained however a source of constant annoyance as the colonies were hot-beds of intrigue, safe asylums for murderers, *Ghadrites*, terrorists and disaffected Indians, and centres from which emissaries were sent to incite the tribes whenever occasion demanded.[63]

Relations between Chamarkand and Asmas

The Chamarkand Colony was founded in 1916 and Abdul Karim of Kanauj was appointed its first *Amir* by Moulvie Niamatullah, then *Amir* of Asmas. The appointment made it evident that there was an understanding between the two Colonies, and that Chamarkand was, when first formed, a vassal colony of Asmas. Chamarkand *Mujahidin*, however, acted independently and took such extreme measures that Government was forced to take action to suppress them. At this time Moulvie Nimatullah the *Amir* of Asmas, made overtures to Government and entered into an agreement that he would not permit *Mujahidin* under his control to take any hostile action against them and do all in his power to wind up the colony at Chamarkand. The Government welcomed his attitude and granted him a small annual allowance for maintenance.[64]

When information about this agreement reached Chamar-

---

[62]Ibid, para 9, para 1.

[63]Ibid, para 2.

[64]Ibid, para 3,

kand it brought about a complete rupture between the two colonies. Plots were hatched for the murder of Niamatullah by Fazal Illahi, now *Amir* of the Chamarkand Colony.[65] After two years of careful planning Moulvie Niamatullah was murdered in 1921 by Muhammad Yusaf of Chamarkand. Following the murder, Chamarkand *Mujahidin* openly prayed for the soul of Muhammad Yusaf, who had been killed by the guard on duty, after he had murdered Niamatullah. The late *Amir* was openly condemned as having been untrue to his salt by making common cause with Government against *Mujahidin*, and emissaries sent to India were instructed to request supporters to cease contributing towards the upkeep of Asmas as the Colony had given up waging "*Jehad*" against the British Government. Sympathisers were told that Chamarkand *Mujahidin* would continue waging "*Jehad*" and were the only *Mujahidin* in Tribal Territory worthy of support. The messages carried by these emissaries, however, had little effect as recruits and funds continued to find their way both to Asmas and Chamarkand.[66]

In 1926 Moulvie Bashir of Chamarkand succeeded, after much intrigue, in deposing Fazal Illahi, the *Amir* of the Colony, on the ground that the latter was responsible for the murder of *Amir* Niamutullah of Asmas. By this act of deposition he enlisted the sympathies of Asmas *Mujahidin*, and it resulted in a resumption of traffic between the two colonies.[67] In 1932, however, Fazal Illahi gathered together the Punjabis at Chamarkand and formed a rival party with the object of deposing Bashir who had assumed the Amirship of the Colony. Bashir immediately summoned his adherents from Asmas and succeeded in counteracting the activities of Fazal Illahi. After that there was no concealment of movement between the two Colonies, and recruits and funds intended for Asmas found their way to Chamarkand. The fact that Chamarkand and Asmas were now in close alliance is proved beyond doubt by the fact that Shahzada Barkatullah of Asmas acted as publicity

---

[65]Ibid, para 4.

[66]Ibid, para 5.

[67]Ibid, para 6.

officer for both the Colonies.[68] One reason which probably
hastened the renewal of the alliance between the two Colonies
was that the income of Chamarkand, when independent, was
not sufficient for the needs of the Colony.[69]

The Policy of Government in the Past

The policy of Government since the conclusion of the
Gujranwala Conspiracy Case and the subsequent prosecution of
Chamarkand *Mujahidin* in Peshawar was to prosecute all members of the Chamarkad Colony whenever and wherever found
in British India, and to allow recruits and funds for
the Asmas Colony to pass through British India without
hindrance. This policy was agreed upon owing to the
conciliatory attitude of the Asmas Colony and the deep-rooted
hostility and aggressiveness of the Chamarkand *Mujahidin*.
Such a policy was followed to persuade the *Amir* of Asmas to
wind up the Chamarkand Colony. At one time Niamatullah
was even paid an annual allowance to bring this about. The
agreement, was however, terminated with the murder of
Niamatullah and thereafter no attempt was made to induce
the *Amir* of Asmas to liquidate Chamarkand. As a result
Chamarkand *Mujahidin* passed to and from tribal Terri tory
surreptitiously whereas Asmas *Mujahidin* made no attempt-to
conceal their movements.[70]

Collection of Funds

Having no sources of income in the N.W.F.P. *Mujahidin*
depended for funds and recruits on their co-religionists in
Punjab, Bengal and Bihar. The method of collecting funds
in Punjab differed from that in vogue in the other two provinces. In Punjab money was collected by secret begging or
by voluntary contributions from *Wahabi* sympathisers. *Madrasa
Selfia Ghaznvia Kucha Ganj Nazi* of Amritsar was a favourite
rendezvous of *Mujahidin*. Moulvie Muhammad Ismail Ghaznavi
managed this school and had trained thirteen students from

---

[68]Ibid, last para.

[69]Ibid, p. 10, para 1.

[70]Ibid, para 2.

Asmas. In addition to local contributions the school received financial aid from the Hedjaz Government primarily because Ibn-i-Saud was a *Wahabi*. The staff of the school consisted of two teachers one from Hazara and the other from Punjab. The school supplied funds to Asmas from its savings. Another school which assisted *Mujahidin* was known as *"Islamia Madrasa"* in village Lakhokai, District Ferozepur. This school was managed by Moulvie Muhammad Ali, an ex-*Mujahid* of Chamarkand. He was a keen supporter of the *Mujahidin* and very much wanted to return to Chamarkand if the *Amirhhip* of the Colony was offered to him. In Bengal and Bihar the method of collecting funds was more systematic than Punjab. *Wahabis* of these provinces were well organized, and had opened "centres" with subordinate branches in selected localities. Funds were collected as quietly as possible under the cloak of religion.[71]

The *Amir* of Asmas and his agents depended on a share of the money realized from the following sources:[72]

1. *Sale proceedes* of hides of cattle sacrificed during the *"Bakr Id"*.

2. *"Fitar"* — About $1\frac{3}{4}$ seers of grain or its value, per head, by every Mussalman during *"Id-ul-Fitr"*.

3. *"Zakat"* — Charity of 1/40th of the annual savings of each family (collected during the month of *Rajab*).

4. *"Muthi"* — A handful of rice, grain, or flour from each family during the two principal meals each day (collected weekly by the local leaders).

5. *"Kafara"* (Atonement)—fine for the commission of an act prohibited in Islam or for the omission of an act enjoined by Islam.

6. *"Ashra"*—1/10th of the produce of the field (collected during the harvesting season, but not very common).

---

[71]Ibid, last para.

[72]Ibid, pp. 10-11.

These recognized dues were collected locally and deposited with *Sardars* or leaders of subordinate branches who remitted them to their "centres". The collection was called *"Bait-ul-Mal."* (Public Charities, or funds dedicated to religious purposes). The proceeds were divided into five shares, 2/5th went to spiritual Moulvies, 1/5th was spent in charity, 1/5th was kept in reserve for the repairs of mosques and *Maktabs* (religious schools) and the remaining 1/5th was sent to the *Mujahidin*. The amount collected from these sources was reasonable owing to the presence of a large number of *Wahabis* in Bengal and Bihar.[73]

The Agents of the *Amir* of Asmas regularly used to visit *Wahabi* Centres with messages from the *Amir-ul-Mujahidin* and returned with funds to Asmas. These Agents were known in the localities they visited. Money was never handed over to unknown agents. The agents in turn were trusted to hand over what they were given, to the *Amir-ul-Mujahidin*.[74] It is interesting to know that money was collected from illiterate *Wahabis*. They contributed what they could either out of respect for their spiritual leaders or out of religious zeal.[75] In Bihar and Bengal there were eight[76] such centres for col-

---

[73] Ibid, p. 11, para 1.
[74] Ibid, para 2.
[75] Ibid, para 3.

[76]

Name of Centre	Name of Leader
(i) Duari, P.S. Pabba, District Rajshahi, Bengal.	Maulvi Akram Ali of Duari.
(ii) Sandbari, P.S. Gaptali, District, Bogra, Bengal.	Sirajur Rahman, son of Azizullah Sarcar of Sandbari.
(iii) Gulamunda, P.S. Jaldhaka, Rangpur District, Bengal.	Maulvi Mohd. Hussain, son of Abdul Hakim of Gulamunda.
(iv) Beraid, P.S. Rupganj, Dacca District, Bental.	Maulvi Wahid Ali of village Beraid.
(v) Jamtili, P.S. Phulbari, District Mymensing, Bengal.	Maulvi Ysaf Ali of Jamtili.
(vi) Sadiqpur Patna City, Bihar.	Maulvi Abdul Kabir of Sadiqpur, Patna.
(vii) Muzzafarpur, Bihar.	Maulvi Abdullah of Amba, P.S. Muzzafarpur District
(viii) Bilalpur, District Santhal, Parganas, Bihar.	Maulvi Aminul Haq, son of late Maulvi Mohib-ul-Haq.

lecting funds. In addition to funds received from the Punjab, Bihar and Bengal, *Mujahidin* were assisted by the Tribes living in the neighbourhood of Asmas with whom their relations were cordial. The assistance was generally in the shape of edibles which were received in such large quantities as to eliminate the necessity of local purchases. Further the *Amir* of Asmas owned six water-mills on the bank of the Brandu river from which he received a small income.[77] Up to the death of Moulvie Bashir in 1934 *Mujahidin* of Chamarkand continued to receive an allowance from the Kabul Government.[78]

Recruitment

Mujahidin were recruited through a number of residential schools[79] which existed in Bengal and Bihar. They imparted religious education and sent them to Asmas.[80] These were the only recruiting grounds for *Mujahidin*.[81] It is an open secret that Mohammad Sadiq Ali, Zahur-ud-Din, Mehrullah, Amanullah, Maner-ud-Din, Aseer-ud-Din and Mohy-ud-Din, were sent to Asmas from the Sandabari Madrasa, District Bogra, Bengal and that one Zamir-ud-Din, son of Nasir-ud-Din was sent there from the Dilalpur centre in Santhal parganas, Bihar.[82]

The method of recruitment of *Mujahidin* in Punjab differed from that in vogue in Bihar and Bengal. In Punjab

---

[77]Home Political Secret F. No. 101 of 1936, p. 11, para 4.

[78]Ibid, p. 11, last para.

[79]They were:-
   (i) Madrasa Islah-ul-Muslemin, Patna City, Bihar Province.
   (ii) Madrasa Dar-ul-Takmeel, Muzaffarpur, Bihar Province.
   (iii) Madrasa Iflah-ul-Muslemin, Duari, P.S. Pabba, Rajshahi District, Bengal.
   (iv) Madrasa Islamia Madhupur, Bihar Province.
   (v) Madrasa Sandabari, P.S. Gaptali, Bogra District, Bengal.
   (vi) Madrasa Gulmunda, P.S. Jaldhaka, Rangpur District, Bengal.
   (vii) Madrasa Beraid, P.S. Rupganj, Dacca District, Bengal.
   (viii) Madrasa Jamtilli, P.S. Bhulbari; District Mymensing, Bengal.
   (ix) Madrasa Shams-ul-Huda, Dilalpur, District Santhal Parganas, Bihar.

[80]Home Political Secret F.Ho. 101 of 1936, p. 12, para 1.

[81]Ibid, para 2.

[82]Ibid, para 3.

there were no regular recruiting centres. Agents of the *Amir* of Asmas usually proceeded there to preach the faith of *Mujahidin* and induced religious minded youths to join them. Through the preaching of one Moulvie Wali Muhammad, Abdullah, Nazar Muhammad, and Ahmed Ali joined the Chamarkand Colony in March 1936.[83]

Five schools[84] of course provided instruction in Theology to *Mujahidin* but these were not recruiting centres.[85]

Strength of the Colonies

The strength of the colonies was approximately as follows:[86]

Asmas	...	180
Chamarkand	...	50

The strength was kept low because the *Amir* wanted that everybody should live comfortably on the income he received.[87]

Arms, Ammunition and Transport

The Asmas and Chamarkand colonies kept the following arms and ammunitions:[88]

Asmas

Lee Enfield 303 rifles	...	70
5-shot rifles	...	40

---

[83]Ibid, para 4.

[84]They were :—
    (i) Madrasa Sulfia Ghaznavia Kucha Ganj Nabi, Amritsar City.
    (ii) Madrasa Masjid-i-Quddus, Kucha Dubgaran, Amritsar City.
    (iii) Madrasa Qazi Lakhoki, District Ferozepur.
    (iv) Madrasa Mian Sahib near Phatak Habash Khan, Delhi.
    (v) Madrasa Alia, Fattehpur Mosque, Delhi.

[35]Home Political Secret F.No. 101 of 1936, p. 12, para 6.

[86]Ibid, last para.

[87]Ibid, p. 13, para 1.

[88]Ibid, para 2.

Country-made rifles	...	200
Shotguns .12 bore	...	5
Revolvers and pistols	...	40
Machine guns or Lewis guns (looted in Waziristan campaign)	...	2
Ammunition in sealed boxes	...	6,000
Open cartridges	...	500
Bombs with wooden handles (country-made)	...	30
Bombs English (hand grenades)	...	50
Swords	...	200
Mules	...	30
Horses	...	20

Chamarkand

Machine guns	...	2
Lewis gun	...	1
Rifles, 303 bore	...	20
Rifles, French-made	...	5
Rifles, country-made	...	20
Shotguns, D.B. 12 bore	...	2
Webley revolvers	...	4
Pistols	...	3
Sealed ammunition	...	10 boxes
Open cartridges	...	1,000
Bombs wooden or hand grenades	...	80
Mules	...	5

The Dindar Movement

No account of the *Mujahidin* movement would be complete without a reference to the Dindar Movement (1935-36). Muhammad Sadiq Dindar[89] lived in Asafnagar in the Hyderabad State,[90] claimed to be the "*Imam Mehdi*", wanted to raise a large following and thereafter wage '*Jehad*' to convert disbelievers and to establish Muslim domination throughout India. He collected a small following in Hyderabad and Mysore States and in the Bombay Presidency, and succeeded in winning over several well-to-do persons. His doctrines, however, were not palatable to Muslims generally and therefore twice it was considered necessary to take action against him in order to avoid any breach of peace[91] in South India. But when Sadiq realised that he would not make much headway in Southern India he turned his attention to *Mujahidin*, and with his followers visited Asmas in 1935. He was cordially received there by the *Mujahidin*. Believing that Asmas would be a better base from which to propagate his faith he returned to South India to persuade his followers to concentrate in Tribal Territory.[92] But again in 1936 he returned to Asmas with about 20 followers and issued instructions to his disciples to sell their property and migrate to Tribal Territory, He promised to collect an army of a lakh, wage "*Jehad*" and capture the treasures of India. He succeeded in inducing about sixty of his followers to join him in Asmas, but before he could get any appreciable following he was arrested by the Nawab of Amb State and sent to the Deputy Commissioner, Hazara, so that he may take necessary action against him. Sadiq, and his followers, who subsequently surrendered, were deported from British territory.[93]

The *Mujahidin* held the view that Said Ahmad had not

---

[89]*Alias* "Chan Basweshwar."

[90]Home Political Secret F.No. 101 of 1936, p. 14, para 10.

[91]Ibid, para 11,

[92]Ibid, para 12,

[93]This was done under the Foreigners Act. The followers of Sadiq were subsequently sent under escort to their respective homes.

died and that he would reappear as the *Imam Mehdi* and lead *Mujahidin* again. Trading on this belief Sadiq claimed to be the re-incarnation of Said Ahmad and succeeded in duping some of the *Mujahidin*, including one of the leaders, as the following extracts from a letter sent by Shahzada' Barkatullah of Asmas to *Mujahidin* supporters in Bengal and Behar clearly show. It is definitely known that copies of this letter reached Moulvie Akram Ali of Rajshahi, Bengal, Moulvie Abdul Manan of Dalalpur, Sonthal Parganas, and Moulvie Abdul Khabir, of Sadiqpur, Patna :[94]

(a) "The condition of the Asmas Colony has not been satisfactory for the last ten years. The Almighty has, however, sent Hazrat Maulana Sadiq who has proved a pillar of strength. All members of the Association, including the Sardars of Mujahidin and the Amir-ul-Mujahidin have certified that Sadiq Dindar is the person whose arrival in the world has been long expected. The signs and marks on Dindar's body prove that he is the 'expected personality'. Mujahidin are prepared to accept his word and obey him implicitly[95].

(b) "Maulana Mohd. Sadiq has left a country of slaves and migrated to Yaghistan with a few followers with the object of waging "Jehad". During the last month he has been busy organising the tribes. We have given him shelter in Asmas. His sermons have created love for him in our hearts and he has awakened us. He has successfully explained to the Ulemas and tribesmen the importance of "Jehad" and has raised a lakh of recruits in the short period of one month. It is hoped that he will organise the whole of Yaghistan within a short time. After reorganizing the tribes, steps will be taken to serve down-country Muslims of India and render real service to mankind. Sadiq Dindar has prepared us for "Jehad" as was practiced by the 'companions of the Prophet'. We are deter-

---

[94]Home Political Secret F. No. 101 of 1936, p. 15, para 1,
[95]Ibid, para 1 (a).

mined to wage "Jehad" in the same way as the 'companions of the Prophet[96]".

(c) "We shall convert the whole of India to Islam. In this lies the solution of all the problems of India. We are prepared to sacrifice our lives in the cause. Every King can continue to rule in India provided he becomes a Muslim. Let Sovereigns enjoy their sovereignty. Our only condition is that they become Muslims. If they decline to embrace Islam they shall remain subject to our rule. If they refuse to be subject to our rule and also refuse to become Muslims we shall have to take to the sword. All Mussalmans who take part in the campaign shall be rewarded in this world and the next. Those Muslims who fail to do so will lead a life of degradation in both this world and the next. O Muslims of India it is your duty to leave the country of slaves in the cause of religion. You will be safe against all mischief and will gain strength and be the stronger for "Jehad". If you cannot leave the country of slaves, or are prohibited from doing so by Kafirs, help the Mujahidin liberaly. We have established our headquarters at Asmas in Yaghistan[97]".

Conclusion

It is thus not difficult to conclude that the Chamarkand Colony, for some considerable time, acted independently and was opposd to the moderate attitude of the Asmas Colony. In time, however, it was realised that Chamarkand could not do without the assistance of Asmas, and the first open sign of the renewal of the alliance between the two colonies came to light in 1932 when Moulvie Bashir summoned his adherents from Asmas to assist him in counteracting the activities of his rival, Fazal Ilahi. Thereafter there was no concealment of movement between the two colonies, and there can be no doubt whatever that Chamarkand was now, as originally, a

---

[96]Home Political Secret F. No. 101 of 1936, p. 15, para 1 (b).
[97]Ibid, para 1 (c).

vassal colony of Asmas, and that the *Amir* of Asmas had full control over Chamarkand[98].

The policy of intercepting and prosecuting Chamarkand *Mujahidin* thereby limiting their supplies in money and kind, an Afghan Government well disposed towards India, and the cutting off of supplies from Soviet sources, were obviously the fectors which led to renewal of the alliance between the two colonies. It is established that recruits for the Chamarkand Colony were now obtained direct from the Asmas. Although it was impossible to say whether recruits who passed through Peshawar and Hazara Districts, would ultimately settle in Asmas or Chamarkand yet it was quite apparent that, in order to avoid arrests they would choose their destination at Asmas[99].

During 1935-36 the Government of India made enquiries with the help of special staff placed on its duty by the Inspector General of Police into the connections of the *Mujahidin*, the manner in which they received recruits from down-country and the persons responsible for this recruitment and for the collection and forwarding of funds to Asmas from down-country.[100] The conclusions[101] drawn from these enquiries were as follows :

(a) The influence of the *Muahjidin* amongst the tribes was declining and was likely to become still smaller because the Afghan Government discouraged them;

(b) The connection of the *Mujahidin* with the *Wahabis* in Punjab, U.P., Bihar and Orissa and Bengal was largely based on old fashioned sentiments. The contributions made by the *Wahabis* were small and customary. They

---

[98]Ibid, p. 16, para 1.

[99]Ibid, para 2.

[100]Confidential Demi-Official Letter from A.J. Hopkinson, Esq. Chief-Secretary to the Government of North West Frontier Provinces, to Major W.R. Hay, C.I.E., Deputy Secretary to the Government of India, No. 78-P.C., dated the 5/6th January, 1937.

[101]Ibid, para 2.

were made on religious occasions only and had no
anti-British motive except in the cases of a few persons;
and

(c) The stopping of recruitment to Asmas and Chamarkand
and the seizure of money sent to Asmas from down-
country was not a practical proposition.

In 1936-37 on the basis of these enquiries, the Government
decided not to pay any further attention to the *Mujahidin* and
safely ignored them. Shortly afterwards this movement
collapsed.

4

Qadiani and Ahrar Movements

Mirza Ghulam Ahmad, the founder of the *Qadiani* sect was born at Qadian (the place from which the name of the movement has been derived) in the Gurdaspur District in 1837. He started his career as a *Muharir* in Sialkot in 1864 on a monthly pittance of Rs. 10 to 15. A few years later he sat for the *Mukhtarship* examination but failed.[1] He, however, came to public notice for the first time in 1883 when he claimed that he was inspired by God.[2] Eight years later he proclaimed himself to be the promised *Messiah*[3] of the

---

[1] Confidential Note on Qadiani Movement by Mr. S.N.A. Jafri, Deputy Director Public Information, Government of India. Home Political F. No. 150/1934.

[2] Note on the Ahmadiya Sect dated 1.11.1912, prepared by Mr. D. Patric on behalf of the Punjab Government. Home Political A Proceeding No. 46, dated November 1912.

[3] There is evidence to prove that Ghulam Ahmed had made the following declaration :

"These are not the vain words of a boaster and should be taken seriously. Believe it that save this Massiah no one can now intercede for you with God. Yes there is another intercessor too, the holy Prophet Muhammad, may peace and the blessing of God be upon him, but this Messiah, your

Muslim faith and won over a large number of people to his tenets. They were known as *Qadianis*.[4] Their strength increased considerably in course of time but headquarters remained at *Qadian* The census of 1890 revealed that they had 30,000 adherents but this number mounted to 18,695 in 1911.[5] In 1935 it was estimated that out of the total population of *Qadian* i.e. 9,000 at least 8,000 were *Qadianis* by religion.[6] As most of them lived in the Punjab it began to be called the 'chief home of the *Qadianis*'.

Mirza Ghulam Ahmad sympathised with all persons, Muslims or non-Muslims, and thought that the conquest of the world to Islam would be effected by peace and not by *jehad*. A *jehad* of pamphlets rather than the sword would according to him lead to the winning over all faiths[7]. He thus believed in the principle of universal brotherhood and unity of religious thought.[8] The cardinal principle followed by him was to respect the laws of the land. Thus during the anti-Rowlatt Act agitation, the non-cooperation movement and the Congress agitation he and his followers lent their whole-hearted support to the Government.[9]

Mirza Ghulam Ahmed died in 1908. His place was occupied by his talented lieutenant Nuruddin who was styled as *Khalifa*. The latter died in 1914 and his place was taken by Mirza Bashiruddin Mahmood, son of Mirza

---

intercessor for the present, is one with the Holy Prophet and his intercession is really that of the Great Prophet whose follower he is. Ye Christian Missionaries! Say no more that Christ is your God, for there is one among you who is greater than Christ Ye Shias! do not, take Hussain for your redeemer for I say to you truly there is one among you who is greater than Hussain. . .Moreover he has named this Messiah Ghulam Ahmed".
See Review of Religion, Vol. I, No. 6, dated June 1902, pp. 251-2.

[4]They are also known as *Mirzais* or *Ahmediyas*.

[5]But according to the return, which the Census Superintendent considered practically correct, their number in the Punjab was only 1,134.

[6]*The Muslim Times, Vol. I*, No. 15, London, December 19,1935.

[7]Home Political A Proceeding No. 46, dated November 1912.

[8]The Canton Truth, China, dated 12 October, 1935.

[9]Ibid.

Ghulam Ahmad, the founder of the sect. But after Nuruddin's death the *Qadiani* party was split into two groups — one called the *Qadiani* group who followed Mirza Bashiruddin Mahmood and the other one was the *Ahmediya* group who followed Mohammed Ali of Lahore. The former group regarded Ghulam Ahmad as a Prophet while the latter regarded him as only a *Mujahid* i.e. a religious reformer.[10] The *Qadianis* claimed to be staunch loyalists and supporters of the British government. The most popular amongst them were Chaudhari Zafar-ullah Khan, Minister of Viceroy's Executive Council and Munshi Mohammed Din, retired Deputy Commissioner of Punjab and member, Council of Jaipur and Council of State.[11] They always remained peaceful, law-abiding and constitutional but condemned hypocrisy, duplicity and all manner of violence. The prominent among the Lahore group were Dr. Mirza Yaqub Beg and Syed Muhammad Hassan, retired Assistant Chemical Engineer, Punjab. Khwaja Kamaluddin of this group was the head of the Woking Mosque for a long time.[12]

Both these groups had propaganda schools and centres in almost all the countries of the world notably in England, Germany, Africa, America, Malay Estates and East Indies with the exception of Afghanistan. Here, during the reign of Amanullah Khan they received a shock because one of their followers was stoned to death under the verdict of the *Ulama* who regarded him as a heretic. In England the head of the Working Mosque belonged to the *Ahmediya* group which regarded Mirza as a reformer while the head of the Southfield Mosque belonged the *Qadian* group which regarded Mirza as the *Messiah*.[13]

Mirza Ghulam Ahmad was the author of many works in Persian, Urdu and Arabic in which he combated the

---

[10]Home Political F. No. 150 of 1934.

[11]Ibid.

[12]Ibid.

[13]Note on Qadiani Movement by Mr. S.N.A. Jafri, Director, Public Information, Government of India. Home Political F. No. 150 of 1934.

doctrines of *jehad*. His first book entitled *Burahin-i-Ahmediya* (arguments of the Ahmadi in support of the Islamic faith), which was published in several instalments between 1880 and 1884 proved to be a success.[14] Critics however do not fail to point out that on the whole his writings were conflicting, created illfeeling and were assailed by Hindus, Muslims, Christians and Arya Samajists. Thus while he prophesised the speedy death of his enemies he also declared that Muslims must allow the members of all religions to live in peace. Likewise while he condemned the whole Christian religion as false and anti-Christ (*Dajjal*), yet he regarded Christ as a mighty prophet of God.[15]

Qadianis v/s Muslims

The *Qadianis* disagreed with Muslims on many grounds:

(1) The Qadianis held the view that Mohammed was not the last Prophet and that the chain of Prophets would continue for ever. They claimed that Mirza Ghulam Ahmad was one of them.

2. The *Qadianis* discarded *jehad*. They did not believe in active warfare, but only in propaganda through writing and debates.

3. The *Qadianis* believed that Christ was dead and that Mirza Ghulam Ahmad was his reincarnation and the promised *Messiah*.

4. The *Qadianis* regarded all those persons as infidels who did not regard Mirza Ghulam Ahmad as a Prophet.

5. The *Qadianis* regarded *Qadian* as their Mecca.[16]

---

[14]Ibid.

[15]Note on the Ahmediya Sect dated 1.11.1912 prepared by Mr. D. Petrie on behalf of the Punjab Government. Home Political A Proceding No. 46, dated November, 1912, p. 2.

[16]Note on Qadiani Movement by Mr. S.N.A. Jafri, Deputy Deputy Director, Public Information, Government of India, Home Public F. No. 150 of 1934.

The orthodox Muslims looked upon the *Qadianis* as heretics[17]. because Mirza Ghulam Ahmad claimed priesthood. They considered it heresy firstly because they did not want Mirza Ghulam Ahmad or any other man after the Prophet to regard himself equal, let alone superior, to Jesus, and secondly because Ghulam Mustafa and other *Qadianis* who had been publicly called upon to recant their statements made 3 years ago had not done so.[18] As such they kept aloof from such Muslim sects[19] and even refused to consider Mirza Ghulam Ahmad and his followers as Muslims.[20] They looked forward to the advent of a warrior *Mehdi* to put to sword all such 'infidels[21]".

During the first decade of the twentieth century the Muslims of Hong Kong refused to permit *Qadianis*[22] to make use of their mosque and the cemetry on the ground that they were not Muslims. This raised a big controversy and Mr. P.P.J. Woodehouse, Deputy Superintendent of Police, in a Minute dated 22 June 1912, pointed out to Mr. C. Clements, the Colonial Secretary, Hong Kong, that this step would create adverse reaction in India. He also remarked that "The ordinary Muhammadan belief is that at some future time an anti-Christ will arise, and dominate the whole world. The anti-Christ (who will represent all the Powers of Darkness) will appear in man's form and riding on an ass seventy yards long! After him will come the Mehdi, who assisted by Jesus Christ, will descend from Heaven and vanquish the anti-Christ. I am not clear as to what is supposed to happen

---

[17]Dictionary of Indian History (Calcutta University), p. 698.

[18]N.M. Bux, Hony. Secretary. the Board of Trustees of the Mosque and Guardian of the Muhammadan Cemetry to the Hon'ble Colonial Secretary Hong Kong, dated 15th June, 1912. Home Political A Proceeding No. 46, dated Nov. 1912.

[19]*The Review of Religion*, February 1902, p. 45.

[20]Home Political A Proceeding No. 46, dated Nov. 1912, p. 8.

[21]The Canton Truth, China, dated 12 October, 1935.

[22]Hon'ble Mr. C.A. Barron, C.I.E., Chief Secretary to the Govt. of Punjab to V. Dawson, Under Secretary to the Govt. of India, Home Department, No. 1738-S.B., dated 12 Sept. 1912,

after the anti-Christ is disposed of, as the Mahdi's role
is to convert the world to Islam by means of the sword.
What the *Ahmadiyas* believe is that the anti-Christ is simply
the Evil which exists in the world, and the *Mahdi* (Ghulam
Ahmad) and his successors will combat it by peaceful persuasion
and preaching. They do not believe in the reincarnation
of Jesus Christ, or that a *Mahdi* and anti-Christ will appear
on the earth in man's form. They also do not agree with
the principle of the *Jehad*. Moreover they deprecate
militant Islam, and profess benevolent toleration of other
religions".[23]

Mr. Clements, the Colonial Secretary, agreed with the
views expressed by Mr. Woodehouse and then sought a clarifi-
cation from the Government of India[24] on the following points:
(1) What was the position of the followers of Mirza Ghulam
Ahmed in India, (2) whether a similar situation to the one
which had arisen in Hong Kong ever arose in India, and if
so (3) what action was taken in the matter by the Government?[25] The Government of India replied that as regards (1)
"although, of course, the Mirza's speeches and writings had
led to much ill-feeling and some disturbances, and although
he and his followers were considered heretics by true Muhammadans, yet our records do not disclose a single instance in
which his followers have been denied the use of mosques or
Muhammadan burying grounds, or in any way molested,
except in one case at Cuttack, where some converts to *Qadiani*
faith wished to change the form of worship in the principal
mosque in the town — a course to which the rest of the
Muhammadan population naturally objected".[26]

---

[23]Minute by P. P. J. Woodehouse, dated 22nd June 1912. Home Political A
  Proceeding No. 46, dated November, 1912.
[24]Ibid.
[25]C. Clements, Colonial Secretary's Office, Hong Kong, to the Secretary to
  the Government of India, Home Department, Calcutta, No. 6634-1909,
  dated 26th June, 1912. Home Political A Proceeding Nos. 45-6, dated
  November, 1912.
[26]Hon'ble Mr. H. Wheeler, C.I.E., I.C.S., Secretary to the Government of
  India, Home Department, Simla, to the Hon'ble the Colonial Secretary,
  Hong Kong, No. 975, dated Simla the 6th November, 1912. Home
  Political A Proceeding Nos. 45-6, dated November, 1912.

As regards (2) and (3) the Government of India remarked, that "Though, no doubt, in the opinion of the orthodox they are heretics, the *Qadianis* have a prescriptive right by reason of their recital of the *Kalima*, to use Muhammadan mosques as individuals, if not as a sect. Orthodox-Muhammadans do not object to individual *Qadianis'* entering the mosque and reciting their prayers when public worship is not in progress; but they would resent their attending in numbers or attempting to worship collectively according to their peculiar rites. They are not permitted to have any voice either in the control of the buildings or in the management of lands or endowments connected therewith, but any attempt to deprive them of the use of Muhammadan graveyards would be regarded in India as indefensible. A situation similar to that which has arisen in Hong Kong does not appear to have ever engaged the attention of the authorities in India, except in one instance at Cuttack in Orissa. So long as *Qanianis* conduct themselves discreetly and inoffensively their exclusion from mosques and graveyards would not be countenanced......" This remark made by the Government of India settled the controversy regarding the position of *Qadianis* in Hong Kong and henceforth they were given the same treatment as was given to their brethern in India.[27]

Ahrar Movement

The *Ahrar* movement began with the establishment of *All India Majlis-i-Ahrar-i-Islam* at Amritsar in 1931 with Habib-ur-Rahman as its President and Daud Ghaznavi and Mazhar Ali Azlar as its Secretaries. Its aims and objects were (1) to work for the economic, educational and social uplift of the Muslims, (2) to awaken political consciousness and to infuse the spirit of Islam among Muslims and (3) to strive for the freedom of the country by peaceful methods[28]. It was started by pro-Congress Muslims with the main object of maintaining the position of the Muslims in the

---

[27]Ibid.

[28]A Note on Muslim political organisations. Home Political F. No. 150 of 1934, p. 27.

Congress itself and to secure seats in the Working Committee. They maintained the view that the Muslims would lose their entity if they absorbed themselves in the Congress and that on the termination of the Kashmir agitation against Hindu bureaucracy their attention would be directed to the future constitution of India and to the adoption of means to secure proper share in the Punjab and to fight against the British or the Hindus whosoever usurped their rights.[29] It should be remembered that this movement was essentially one of the urban middle and lower classes.[30] The loyal rural elements kept aloof from it.

Time showed that the *Ahrar* did not stick to any consistent policy. They did not welcome the Congress formula regarding the settlement of communal question and rejected it.[31] Thereafter they launched a people's movement in Kashmir and carried on an intense propaganda in the form of a press campaign, meetings, processions of the Kashmiri labourers and the celebration of a 'Kashmir Day' against the State.[32] But ultimately this agitation resulted in strengthening the influence of the British in Kashmir contrary to the intentions of the *Ahrar*. They frankly admitted that the change of Ministry in Kashmir had done no good for the Muslim cause because only the Hindu bureaucracy was replaced there by British bureaucracy which did not satisfy their demands.[33] The subsequent arresting of their prominent leaders coupled with chronic problems like lack of funds and volunteers decreased the enthusiasm for the Kashmir agitation.[34] The *Ahrar* complained that the British Government had stood between them and the Kashmir *Darbar* and prevented them from bringing this agitation against the *Darbar* to a successful

---

[29]Home Political F. No. 14 of 1914.

[30]Ibid.

[31]Home Political F. No. 150 of 1934.

[32]Ibid.

[33]Extract from a note recorded by an officer of the C.I.D. regarding his interviews with Ahrar leaders in District Jail, Delhi, on 21-22 February, 1932.

[34]Home Political F. No. 150 of 1934.

issue.[35]   They therefore constantly   grudged   against   the British.

The *Ahrar* left no opportunity to criticise the government for not making any announcement to grant a constitution to the people of India and looked upon them as nothing less than 'Satanic'[36] both from political and religious point of view. According to them India was a '*Darul Harb*' i.e. the house of war and it was the duty of the people to wage a Holy War against the British and other non-members of their religion. They argued that, under British rule, theoritically there was reign of law, justice and toleration but in actual practice it was all pure fraud and deception.[37]

The *Ahrar* now turned their attention towards the alleged government excesses in the North West Frontier Province but this agitation also proved to be short-lived.   Such an agitation in Kapurthala and Jind states did evoke considerable interest among the *Ahrar* who contemplated to stir the Muslim masses in the same way as was done in the case of Kashmir[38]   but it excited little sympathy in other provinces.

Civil Disobedience Movement

These developments convinced the *Ahrar* that they had failed (1) to get a constitution for India, (2) to secure any hold on Kashmir or (3) to stop repression in N.W.F.P. They now followed a programme to directly hit the Britishers because they were responsible for unprecedented oppression in India. Accordingly the *Majlis-i-Ahrar* directed all its subordinate bodies that out of five kinds of civil disobedience, they should on the basis of local exigencies, start any programme they liked. These five kinds of civil disobedience were (1) to   continue   to

---

[35]Ahrar Manifesto dated 29.2.1932. Home Political F. No. 14/14 of 1932, p. 2.

[36]*The Muslim Times, London, Vol. I, No. 8,* dated 12 September 1935, pp. 7-3.

[37]The *Mujahid* dated 12 November, 1935. *See also The Muslim Times,* London, Vol. I, No. 14, dated 5 December 1935, p. 1.

[38]Confidential letter from Punjab Civil Secretariat to Hon'ble H.W. Emerson, Secretary to the Government of India, No. 15267 (55) S.B., dated 4 March, 1932. Home Political F. No. 14/14 of 1932.

send *jathas* to Kashmir to defy the Kashmir Ordinance, (2) to violate the Railway Act and travel without ticket, (3) to violate postal act by sending unstamped letters, (4) to start peaceful picketing of foreign cloth shops, and (5) to start peaceful picketing of liquor shops.[39]   The chief centres of civil disobedience were Lahore, Amritsar, Sialkot, Gujranwala, Delhi, Wazirabad, Rawalpindi and Jullundur but the districts adjoining these centres helped them.   The *Anjumans* outside the Punjab complied with the first three instructions and also carried out a detailed programme.

These subordinate *Majlises* divided their volunteers into two groups.   The first group continued the struggle for entering Kashmir territory peacefully.   The second group, consisting of 25 volunteers, under a captain, as a matter of policy entered into a train without tickets so as to violate the Railway Act. If on account of any obstacle the group failed to enter a railway station then it purchased platform tickets or tickets for the next station but entrained and tore off their tickets after the train had started.   When tickets were demanded from them they clearly said that they were going to Kashmir without tickets to get arrested.[40]   At every place the volunteers occupied one compartment and stuck to their seats unless they were arrested but until that time they continued their demonstrations peacefully.   Where the number of volunteers was large more than one *Jatha* functioned at a time.   In case the Police or Railway officials succeeded in detaining the volnteers at any place they were directed to catch the next train peacefully.   All the subordinate *Majlises* regularly sent *jathas* for their respective centres in the largest number.[41]   In order to violate the Postal Act the Dictator of *Majlis-i-Ahrar-i-Hind* had directed the volunteers and members to post on Sundays to the Viceroy at Delhi unstamped letters containing the following subject matter "*That the Muslims are a living nation. They will neither be suppressed nor frightened by any repression, nor will they rest without getting their demands conceded*".[42]

[39]Ibid, p. 6.
[40]Ibid, pp. 8-9.
[41]Ibid, p. 9.
[42]Ibid, p. 10.

The Government crushed this movement with an iron-hand and arrested all the prominent *Ahrar* leaders. This brought about a change in the *Ahrar* policy towards the Congress. This also becomes clear from the discussions that took place between the C.I.D. officials of the government and the *Ahrar* leaders. Ataullah Shah Bukhari who was in Delhi jail for nearly three weeks, disclosed frankly enough in February 1932 that he had since converted totally to the Congress side. The company of Maulana Azad, Dr. M.A. Ansari, Faridul Huq Ansari—Bar-at-Law, Chaman Lal of Hindustan Times, Desh-bandhu Das, Devdas Gandhi and other men of their school of thought, in the prison, probably brought about this radical change in him. Subsequently he even authorised Mufti Kifai-tullah to convey his views to the then leader of the *Ahrar* party, Mr. Afzal Haq. When this was done it was disclosed by Afzal Haq to Ataullah Shah Bukhari that the British were no longer prepared to support the Muslims in any case and that "they kicked those who licked their feet".[43] This clearly demons-trated that the Government had ceased to have any respect for the *Ahrar*. They now patronised the Hindu community and the Raja in the Kashmir movement. Another *Ahrar* pri-soner Maulana Ahmad Said disclosed that the Muslims would not survive as long as the British remained in India and that the only goal of the Muslims should be to turn out the British because it would then be an easy task to crush the Hindus. But at the same time he did not rule out the opposition of three million Sikhs who were all armed.[44] The Government was somehow not the least impressed by their leaders and continued to keep them in jail-away with Congress leaders—because they not only preached sedition but were comparatively more unre-liable.[45] Nevertheless this was the first occasion when Muslims gave proof of their life and appealed for sacrifice to achieve their objects.

---

[43]Extract from a note recorded by an officer of the C.I.D. regarding his interview with Ahrar leaders Ataullah Shah Bukhari and Maulana Ahmed Said in District Jail, Delhi, on 21-22 February 1932.

[44]Ibid.

[45]Note by Non'ble N.W. Emerson, Secretary to the Government of India, dated 10.3.1932.

Three years later there was again a shift in *Ahrar* policies. They ceased to support the Hindus and appealed to Muslims for emancipation of their motherland. Addressing the *Ahrar* Conference on 1st May 1935 at Saharanpur, Ataullah Shah Bokhari said, "*There is no thought of making an alliance with the Hindus. When they die their dead bodies are cremated and carried away as particles of dust by a current of air. We Muslims are buried where we die and require three yards of land even after death. The country is ours ... India is our country*".[46] He also criticised Mahatma Gandhi's views on untouchability and remarked that "After twelve years of agitation Mahatma Gandhi came to the conclusion that the untouchables should be allowed to enter the temples and that there was no harm in dining with the sweepers. Our Islam can never tolerate slavery. Freedom is our faith and religion".[47]

The Shahidganj Mosque dispute created tension between the Sikhs and the Muslims for sometime in 1935 because the former injured the religious susceptibilities of the latter by demolishing an old mosque.[48] Riots broke out in Lahore and the government called out the military to control the situation. The *Ahrar* held aloof from this agitation[49] but received inspiration from *Mammons* and the Hindu capitalists.[50] The Government too supported the *Ahrar* and at first maintained the view that agitation over this issue would fizzle out. A paper supporting *Ahrar* stand was also started.[51] The *Ahrar* now came to be called 'nationalist', i.e. "*watan-prast, sarkar prast*"[52] by the Congress because they remained loyal to Government whenever it

---

[46]Speech by Moulvi Ataullah Shah Bukhari on 18 May 1935 at Saharanpur at Ahrar Conference. Home Political F. No. 36/5/935, p. 15.

[47]Ibid, p. 16.

[48]*The Muslim Times*, Vol. I. Ho. 14, dadted 5 December, 1935.

[49]India Office, White Hall, S. W. 1, Letter No. P and J 2417/35 dated 21 August 1935 to T. Sloan, C.I.E., Secretary to the Government of India, Home Department.

[50]*The Muslim Times*, London, Vol. I, No. 7, dated 29 August 1935.

[51]Intelligence Department Note dated 20.7.1935.

[52]*The Muslim Times*, London, Vol. I, No. 14, dated 5 December 1935, p. 4.

suited their convenience. Ultimately this affair was amicably settled in favour of the Muslim community.[53] The courage shown by the *Ahrar* at this time was appreciated by every sane Indian. By keeping themselves aloof from this agitation they not only rendered a great service to the province but also saved the lives of hundreds of Muslims who had decided to sacrifice their lives for the mosque.[54]

Criticism of Ahrar

The bulk of the Muslims felt insulted over this issue because the *Ahrar* forcibly ejected them from the public meeting with cooperation of the police. They accused them as the 'Reds of India'[55] and criticised Punjab Government for letting them down. They also accused the *Ahrar* leader Ataullah Shah as a traitor and an enemy of the Muslims and nicknamed him '*Ghaddar Shah*'. In retaliation they also turned out the *Ahrar* from the mosques with disgrace, attacked their office at Amritsar and tore down their redflag into pieces. Shouts were raised '*Ahrar Murdabad*', '*Down with the traitors*'.[56]

The Muslim press of India severely condemned the *Ahrar* for their selfishness, faithlessness and inconsistency. This becomes clear from the foregoing extracts: "O Muslims, can you think of anyone who is more selfish, faithless and treacherous than the *Ahrar*? These deceitful buffoons have appeared now in their true colours. If you will still have anything to do with them, you should be sure of your ruin and destruction. Let it be your duty for the future that the *Ahrar* should be flung out wherever they go". (The *Sarhud*, Peshawar[27])......"Some people are so constituted that they cannot be corrected even by experience. We have watched the political views of Ataullah Bukhari for a long time. He is an

---

[53]*Islamic Culture*, Hyderabad, Vol. XLIII. No. 1, p. 22.

[54]*The Muslim Times, London*, Vol. I. No. 7, dated 29 August, 1935, p. 7.

[55]India Office, White Hall, S.W.1 letter No. N and J 2147/35 dated 21 August 1935 to T. Sloan, C.I.E., Secretary to the Government of India, Home Department.

[56]*The Muslim Times, London*, Vol. I, No. 7, dated 29 August 1935.

[57]*The Muslim Times, London*, Vol. I. No. 8, dated 12 September 1935.

absolutely worthless fellow.   At one time he was such an
ardent supporter of the Congress that he ruined scores of
Muslims in connection with civil disobedience and caused
hundreds of them to be sent to gaol.   Then he disappeared
from the stage of the Congress at Bombay and kept unknown
for a long time ... During the recent disturbances at Lahore
he deserted the Muslims and is styled now the religious head of
the *Ahrar*.   We are glad to know the Muslims of Amritsar
flung him out of the mosque where he was making a speech.
This is the same man who caused Muslims to go to gaols in
obedience to the Congress and now has the cheek to speak
against civil disobedience.   We do not approve of such movements ... but ... these show what kind of man Ataullah Shah
Bukhari is".   (The *Inqilab*, Lahore[58])...... "The Ahrar
have been boasting that they are the leaders of the Muslims
and it appears that the ignorant masses were ready to dance to
their tune simply because of their propaganda.   Take the case
of Qadian.   The Ahrars collected a lot of subscription in its
name.   They issued posters and delivered speeches in which
they declared that "jathas" were being sent to the Qadian
where arrangements were made for free board and lodging as
a 'langar'.   This was the time when Section 144 was in force
at Qadian and an assembly of even five persons was unlawful...
We should see *why* the Ahrar have fallen so soon in the estima-
tion of the Muslims.   In view of the recent happenings it is
clear that the Muslims are disappointed in the Ahrar because
they have let them down when their services were needed
most.   At Amritsar the Ahrar could at one time gather thousands of people, but now nobody wishes to hear their
speeches."   (The *Rishi*[59])

A few years after the Shahidganj agitation the *Majlis-i-
Ahrar* was split up into two sections – one led by Maulana
Habib-ur-Rahman and M. Daud Ghaznavi decided to offer
civil disobedience from the Congress platform—the other led
by M. Mazhar Ali Azhar and Chaudhuri Afzal Huq supported
the view that Muslims should retain their separate entity and

---

[58]Ibid.
[59]Ibid.

manifested pro-Muslim League sympathies. The latter section was now more dominant[60] but it was not clear whether this section would fully support the Pakistan scheme. At the *All India Ahrar Conference* held at Delhi on 22 August 1941 Mazhar Ali Azhar did not at all seem to be enthusiastic about this scheme. He supported it only for want of a better scheme for "protecting the rights of the Muslims in the future constitution of India."[61] At the same time he also remarked that he was, still "prepared to lead the movement for country's freedom with the co-operation of Hindu brethren" but was not ready "to sacrifice the interests of Muslims of India at any cost."[62] Ataullah Shah Bukhari, on the other hand, remarked that the Muslim League had failed to give a proper lead to the Muslim community. But by the close of 1941 the majority of the *Ahrar* had definitely swung over to the Muslim side[63] because most of the pro-Congress members of their party continued to remain in jails and there was no good leader to guide them during this time.

The *Ahrar* have been criticised on various other grounds. In religion they were regarded as the dregs of the old *Mullah* school whose piety and devotion to religion demanded the blood of the innocent people who did not see eye to eye with them. In politics their unsightly acrobatics had corrupted the taste of ignorant masses. Their name signified that they stood for complete independence. The colour of their flag was red. They dressed in *Khaddar* and had served the Congress. Their vulgar behaviour in jails disgusted the British government.[64]

The *Ahrar* took pride in their notoriety, courted arrest and openly flouted the law. They roused the passions of the masses, and inflamed the people, and poured filthy and inde-

---

[60]A Note prepared by the Intelligence Bureau on the development in Ahrar politics. Home Political (I) F. No. 209 of 1941.

[61]Ibid.

[62]Ibid.

[63]Ibid.

[64]*The Muslim Times, London*, Vol. I, No. 8, dated 12 September, 1935.

cent abuse in an indiscriminate manner upon those who differed with them. They pelted their opponents with stones but felt
no compunction.   They took pleasure in ridicule; raised funds
but refused to render accounts.. They boasted of their influence
on the masses and propagated that conviction for a political
crime; a fine or a sentence for imprisonment was a passport to
get into their *Majlis*.   To be anti-government, to sing songs
and shout slogans of sedition and rebellion was the fashion of
their young-men.   To thwart government and purge India of
the British was the ambition of their children.[65]   They were
admired once but now they were "silenced, confused, ridiculed,
abused, and flung out of mosques and public places."   The
masses turned against them after the Shahidgunj agitation and
realized, that they had played "the part of wolves in sheeps
clothing".[66]   They were political gangsters untrue to their
community and country.   The majority of the Muslims thus
considered it suicidal to support them.

Qadianis v/s Ahrar

Unlike *Qadianis*, *Ahrar* used 'religion as a mere cloak' to
achieve their objectives and carried on a campaign of vilifica-
tion against them and tortured several of them to death.   They
also revived the doctrine of *Jehad* at Sialkot to expel the British
by force to secure freedom for India.[67]   Their movement in
its nakedness was thus far worse than the non-violent non-cooperation of Mahatma Gandhi. The *jehad* of *Ahrar* was violence
pure and simple.[68]   The *Qadianis* criticised them because this
doctrine of *jehad* was to be acted upon only in self-defence.
Taking of arms was allowed in Islam to repel the aggressive
attacks of the opponents.   The Holy Founder of *Qadiani*
movement condemned this doctrine in these words: "Bear
in mind", he says "that there is nothing so discreditable to
Islam as the doctrine of *Jehad* which is imputed to it.   A reli-

---

[65]Ibid.

[66]Ibid.

[67]Editorial entitled 'Jehad or Holy War' dated 5 December, 1935. *The Muslim
    Times*, London, Vol. I, No. 14, dated 5 December, 1935.

[68]Ibid.

gion whose teachings are excellent and to manifest whose truth Almighty God shows the signs, does not stand in need of the sword to propagate it."[69]

The *Ahrar* had traditional rivalry against the *Qadianis* because they did not believe in their ideology and remained law-abiding citizens. This is proved by an illustration. In 1934 the *Ahrar* decided to hold a conference at *Qadian* and sought permission from one Ishar Singh, a resident of *Qadian* to hold it on land in his possession. The *Qadianis* did not like it and prevented them to hold the conference by building a wall in the village round the site. Unable to find another site the *Qadianis* arranged for the conference on the grounds of D.A.V. High School premises in Rajada, a village one mile from *Qadian*. This conference was held on 21 October 1934. Sayyad Ataullah Bukhari, who presided at the conference for five hours attacked the *Qadiani* leaders and their religion and was subsequently prosecuted by the Britsh government.[70] The *Ahrar* organisation was then forbidden to hold its meetings at *Qadian* because they threatened breach of peace, strife and bloodshed.[71] The prestige of the *Qadianis* remained unchallengeable and unassailable.

---

[69] Ibid.

[70] Under Section 153-A, I.P.C.

[71] *The Muslim Times, London,* Vol. I, No. 16, p. 1.

5

Pan-Islamic Movement

Section I

The earliest information regarding attempts to stir up the Muslim feeling in India in favour of the Sultan dates from 1879, when news was received of the establishment in Constantinople of the 'Paik-i-Islam', an Urdu newspaper, of which the mission was to advocate a Islamic league hostile to British rule. This paper was soon suppressed at the instance of Her Britannic Majesty's Ambassador. In April 1880, the 'Wakt', a Turkish newspaper, announced a project for collecting Indian substcriptions for the purpose of a *Jehad*. It was said that a Turkish agent was on the point of being despatched to establish direct relations with Indian Muslims and Muslim chiefs, and that special agents were to be despatched from Constantinople to Kabul. The Grand *Sheriff* of Mecca was further alleged to be maintaining communications with the Muslims of India, through pilgrims and in combination with the Sultan and certain influential persons in Constantinople, in order to excite a seditious movement[1] among Indian Muslims. This report was corroborated from other directions.

---

[1]Foreign Secret E Proceeding No. 182, dated April 1898, para 2.

Before quitting Constantinople, Sir A. Layard called the serious attention of 'Her Majesty's Government to intrigues which, he said, were being carried on from Constantinople with Muslims in India. Of these intrigues Ghaza Osman Pasha was believed to be the chief instigator; they were directed by the anti-English party at the Palace and the Sultan was believed to be cognizant of them. The Sultan denied these rumours. In August 1880, however, Mr. Goschen informed Government that the Sultan had directed the chief *Ulama* to concert measures for an Islamic league[2] to oppose the Christian nations. Similar information reached the French Embassy.

Two Persian newspapers, the '*Akhtar*' of Contantinople and the '*Ghairat*' of London, as well as the *Wakt* advocated the cause of Islamic union, and the last named dwelt on the necessity for Indian Muslims supporting the *Khilafat*. Later in the same year information derived from apparently good authority, pointed to Bombay as the focus of intrigue between Constantinople and India carried on by Husain Effendi, the then Turkish Consul-General. The *Anjuman-i-Islam* was said to have been formed in Bombay to conduct an extensive correspondence with Calcutta, Delhi, Benares, Hyderabad, Jabalpur and other places. The Sultan was stated to have bestowed decorations on several prominent citizens of Bombay in order to enlist their services, and it was reported that the people of Peshawar, Lahore, Multan and other towns in the Punjab had been persuaded by the *Anjuman* to refuse to fight the Afghans. Finally, certain British Indian subjects were alleged to have formed a Committee at Constantinople to throw off the British yoke by preaching the spiritual influence of the *Khilafat* and championing the union of Islam.[3]

Efforts were made by the General Superintendent of *Thagi* and *Dakaiti* Department and the Commissioner of Police, Bombay, to ascertain the truth of these reports, but without success. There appeared to be some reason to believe that the

---

[2]Foreign Secret E Proceeding No. 18, dated December, 1899.

[3]Foreign Secret E Proceeding Nos. 157-87, dated April 1898.

reports were due to private malice on the part of the informant of the Embassy. Local Governments were warned, but nothing more was heard on the subject for seven years.[4]

In May 1888, a secret agent of the Goverment reported, after a visit to Constantinople, that the Sultan was not well disposed towards India, a feeling in which he was encouraged by some of the entourage who were in the pay of Russia. This agent gave detailed information regarding the persons at Constantinóple and in India engaged in propagating the doctrine of the Islamic League. Enquiries addressed to local Governments led to the collection of a good deal of information regarding the principal persons mentioned and the conclusion ultimately arrived at was thus summarised: "There is no reason to suppose that any active measures are being taken at the present time to organise any such League. During the abortive movement to this end in 1879-80, abundant information and warning were received from all sources and it is not likely that any serious effort can be made now without giving rise to rumours of some kind. The attention of the Indian Muhammedans at present is probably too much engaged in other directions to admit of a visionary scheme for the union of Islam meeting with much support from them".[5]

In May 1889, the Foreign Department received particulars regarding certain persons said to belong to the Pan-Islamic League at Constantinople. These persons, though very jealous of one another were stated to exercise a good deal of influence over the Sultan, leading him to believe that they were more valuable propagandists than was really the case.[6]

In 1892 a large number of Maulvis and Arabs were noticed travelling about the Central Provinces. It was, however, believed that these were merely tours for the *hajj*. In 1893 an attempt was made by one Abdulla Nadimto rouse the Sultan to circulate among pilgrims to Mecca an inflammatory indict-

---

[4]Ibid.

[5]Foreign Deposit (External) Proceeding No. 9, dated September 1901. *See* also Foreign Secret E Proceeding Nos. 157-87, dated April 1898, para 7,

[6]Ibid, para 8.

ment against the British treatment of Muslims generally. His Majesty was advised that this might lead to awkward and unforeseen consequences and dropped the matter. In April of the same year, the Secretary of State telegraphed that Abdul Hasn Mirza, known as *Shaikhu-r-Rais* a grandson of Shah Fateh Ali, Shah of Persia, was said to be at Bombay intriguing with Muslims and trying to raise trouble in Baluchistan and Egypt. The Bombay Government reported that Abdul Hasn was anxious to leave India.[7]

In 1895 an attempt was made to excite agitation among Muslims in connection with the restrictions imposed on the *hajj*. The principal leader in the movement was Maulvi Hidayal Rasul*, who in April held a meeting at Lucknow and raised a subscription of Rs. 300 for the purpose of memorialising Government. On the 14 July he addressed a meeting at Bombay, and in the course of his speech said that the Sultan was not in favour of the quarantine enforced at Kamran, but was obliged to impose it by the European powers, whose intention it was to create discord between him and the Muslims of India; that, as the Sultan was the spiritual leader of the Muslims and the *Khalifa* of the prophet, it was the bounden duty of every Muslim to obey and follow him; that there were 22 *krors* of Muslims in the world, all of whom were the army of the Sultan; that the English had intended to humiliate the Muslims in connection with the Armenian matter, which insult the Sultan bore with patience; and that, in the event of any breach between the Sultan and the English, the Muslims would sacrifice their lives. He expatiated on the glory of dying for the cause of Islam and said that the Muslims were connected with the English in temporal and with the Sultan in spiritual matters, but that the former could not take precedence of the latter. He further

---

[7]Foreign Secret Proceeding Nos. 27-50 dated October, 1906. *See* also Foreign Secret E Proceeding Nos. 157-87 dated April 1898, para 11.

*Maulvi Hidayat Rasul was sent to prison owing to his inability to furnish security for good behaviour which he had been called on to produce in consequence of scandalous language used by him regarding the Queen, at a meeting held at Kanpur to celebrate the Turkish victories.

stated that Maulvi Rafiu-d-din Ahmed, a barrister-at-law well-
known in England, and Rahmatulla (an ex-Mutineer) had
gone to Constantinople to interview the Sultan in regard to
this matter. The speakers now appeared to excite little
enthusiasm, no leading or influential Muslim was present
and among the 2000 who attended, only Rs. 80 were collected
and Rs. 200 promised.[8]

In 1895 the Armenian question excited a good
deal of interest among Indian Muslims, but this was
shown chiefly through articles in the newspapers, and there
was little, if any popular demonstration. A meeting of some
1,500 Muslims was said to have been held on the 24
February at the Fatehpuri *masjid* at Delhi. The meeting was
called and addressed by Hafiz Azizud-din, Pleader, and others,
but nothing of an objectionable character seems to have been
said.[9]

The *Shamsu-I-Akhbar* (Madras) on the 15 July published
an article saying that, notwithstanding the spread of Western
education, the sympathy and love of the Indian Muslims
towards the Muslim states, and especially the Turkish
Empire, the ruler of which is the Guardian of the Holy Places,
was as strong as ever. "If hostilities were to break out between the Sultan and the English, the loyalty of the Indian
Musulmans would be severely strained". A report received
in October from Hyderabad stated that much interest was
said to be felt there in the Armeinan question and that papers
were secretly going round requiring every true Muslim
to sign and declare his readiness to rise and join in a *Jehad*
on receipt of orders from Constantinople. Probably the state
of feeling in India was correctly described in the same month
by the District Superintendent of police, Karnal, who wrote:
"Some of the newspaper reading Muhammedans express regret
and sympathy that affairs are as reported in Turkey. A good
many of the educated class deplore the action that has neces-

---

[8]Foreign External proceeding Nos. 139-43 dated February, 1900. *See* also
Foreign Secret E Proceeding Nos. 157-87 dated April, 1898, para 12.

[9]Ibid.

sitated the British Government having to interfere in Armenian affairs, and hope that matters may be satisfactorily settled without recourse to force. The Sultan is looked on as the only Muhammedan power of weight and they fear his extinction. Any disaster to him will be looked upon as a calamity to the whole Muhammedan nation throughout the world."[10]

In August and September 1895, two Arabs, who called themselves Turks and were believed to be spies, came to Quetta from Kabul and eventually made their way to Karachi. It did not appear that they were engaged in propagandism. Again in the spring of 1896 definite information was received that a Pan-Islamist propagandist, Shaikh Kumalu-d-din, who was said to have been in India in 1894, was likely to visit this country again. He was ordered to be watched and all Special Branches were told to notice innovations by which the Sultan was alluded to as *Khalifa* in mosques during prayers in reading the *Khutba*. Kamalu-d-din's arrival was not reported by the Bombay Police.[11]

At this time was first heard of the '*Nadwatu-I-Ulama*' of Kanpur, a society which had met at Kanpur in 1894 and at Lucknow in 1895, and which proposed to meet at Bareilly in 1896, of which the purpose was *unification of Islam*. The object of the Society was apparently religious than a politica-union. It may be noted that the Secretary of the "Nadwatul l-Ulama" at Meerut informed the District Superintendent of Police in September 1897 that he had recalled his preachers and put them on half-pay for 6 months, as, in the excited state of India, he declined the responsibility of having to explain any possible acts of indiscretion on their part.[12]

About this time, Caron Mac Coll published an article in the '*Fortnightly Review*' on '*Some Fallacies about Islam*', which called forth the following reply from the *Muslim Chronicle* of

---

[10]Foreign Secret E Proceeding Nos. 157-87 dated April, 1898, para 13. *See* also Foreign Secret Proceeding Nos. 27-50 dated October, 1906.

[11]Ibid, para 15.

[12]Ibid, para 16. *See* also Foreign Deposit E Proceeding No. 9 dated Sept. 1901,

Calcutta. After rebuking the Caron's pedantry and refusal to recognise existing facts, the *Chronicle* went on to say: "At the risk of hurting the self-sufficiency and conceit of the Caron, we may take the liberty of telling him that amongst the *60 million* of *Muslims of India* with whom we are most conversant the regard and veneration for His Imperial Majesty the Sultan of Turkey, as the Chief Musulman Potentate of the world as the Guardian of the Holy Places, is a hard, stubborn fact, worth a hundred speculations and a thousand hackneyed third-hand historical references of the Caron. And not only that, on the occasion of the Id, from every mosque in India, Arabia, and Egypt, prayers are offered up for the Sultan of Turkey."[13]

On the 18 May, the '*Muhammedan*' of Madras reprinted a *fatwa* from Quilliam's organ, the '*Crescent*' (London) which said: "The *rendezvous of Islam* is under the shadow of the standard of the *Khalifat*. The *Kibla* of the true believer who desires happiness for himself and prosperity for Islam is the holy seat of the *Khalifat*".[14] Quilliam's proclamation was received in India without enthusiasm and was condemned by nearly all the papers that noticed it, except the '*Akhbar-i-Islam*' of Agra.

The '*Hablu-I-matin*' of Calcutta of the 27 April published a poem from Liverpool containing the words: "Awake, Musulmans, awake. How long will you remain asleep while the British Lion and the Russian Bear are rapidly making encroachments on Turkey, Persia and Afghanistan?"[15] Again, on the 9 July, the District Magistrate of Karachi reported that in some of the *Masjids* of Baluchistan the name of the Amir was being substituted in prayers for that of the Sultan.

In December 1895, the resident in Turkish Arabia reported that Sayyid Ahmad, son of Zainu-d-din and nephew of Sayyid Suliman, *Nakib* of Baghdad had left Baghdad for

---

[13]Ibid, para 17.

[14]Ibid, para 18.

[15]See also Foreign Secret E Proceeding Nos. 157-87 dated April, 1898, para 19.

India on the 9th instant. He was suspected to be the bearer of a message from the Sultan to the Amir inciting the later to stir up Muslim feeling in India in regard to the Armenian question. Enquiries showed that three persons,[16] who claimed to be related to the *Nakib*, had been travelling in India. They were:-

(1) *Sayyid Husain, Baghdadi,* who had visited Bombay, Hyderabad, Tonk, Bhopal and Delhi. He eventually reached Karachi from Lahore on 12 July and left two days later for Baghdad. He and his two sons, Sayyid Ali and Sayyid Sultan, appear to have visited India again in 1897, and to have been to Bombay, Bahawalpur, Hyderabad (Sind) and Karachi.

(2) *Sayyid Muhammad,* a nephew of the *nakib* who was subsequently identified with Ahmed, son of Zainad-din, and

(3) Abdu-s-Salam a younger brother of the *Nakb.*

Sayyid Muhammad *alias* Ahmed tried unsuccessfully to get permission to visit Kabul, stayed for a while with Sardar Muhammad Ayub Khan, and eventually went to Hyderabad. On the 18 September 1897 he was granted an interview by His Highness the Nizam and is said to have received 250 *ashrafis* (gold coins valued at Rs. 24 each). Abdu-s-Salam stayed with Ayub Khan, and at the end of 1896 went back to Baghdad. The main object of all these men except perhaps Sayyid Husain, seems to have been to raise money for themselves.[17]

Some communication apparently passed between the Amir and the *Nakib,* and it was reported from Peshawar that the former was preparing to send return presents to the latter. In October, Hashim Effendi and four other Turks, believed to be emissaries of the Sultan, reached Rampur, where the Nawab refused to see them. It was afterwards ascertained that this man, who knew Persian, Turki and Russian had been in India for sometime. He failed to obtain permission to

---

[16] Ibid, para 21.

[17] Ibid, para 21,

visit Kabul. A letter was found on him from the Nakib of Baghdad, in which he was commended to all pious Muslims.[18]

Two other supposed emissaries of the Sultan Ali Husain and Abdu-s-Samad—were also found travelling in the Panjab and numerous other Arabs and Turks were kept under watch from time to time, on the chance of their proving to be either emissaries of the Sultan or spies. In no case was it proved that they were engaged in propagandaism.[19]

In 1897 reports were freely circulated to the effect that a Turkish envoy was on his way to Kabul. Efforts were made to verify these reports, but without success. The Turkish Vice-Consul at Karachi, Husain Kiaum Beg Effendi, made a more or less begging tone in the Panjab and the Consul-General for Persia visited Hyderabad, where he was received with much honour.[20]

Sayyid Sahib, Khadim, of the tomb of Imam Husain at Karbala, also paid repeated visits to India since 1889. He returned to India again in 1897. In August he was reported to be at Hyderabad, and an informant stated that he had letters from the Sultan which he secretly showed to the people. There was no proof, however, that he was charged with any mission from the Sultan.[21]

In February 1897 a pseudonymous notice was distributed in Karnal and perhaps elsewhere, asking for subscriptions on behalf of the Sultan. It pointed out that Islam had fallen into decay for want of a leader: "The Muhammedans should be united with one rope and the Sultan should become their *Imam*. Their power would then be firmly established...The

---

[18]Ibid.

[19]Ibid, para 22.

[20]A rumour was also current that relations between Turkey and Persia had became very cordial. The *Khatib* of Medina is or was in India. He wanted also to go to Kabul, but the Amir refused to receive him.

[21]Foreign Secret E Proceeding Nos. 157-87 dated April 1898, para 25.

enemies of Islam will then know that millions of Muhammedans living in foreign countries not only consider the Sultan as
their leader and *Khalifa* but are ready to sacrifice their life and
property with true hearts for him and, when the time for sacrifi-
cing life shall arrive, no religious man will spare it...The Sultan's
influence will be firmly established over his enemies. The adver-
sity of the Muhammedans will be removed. As the Sultan is
the religious leader of the Muhammedans, it is a religious act
to assist him...Know well, ye orthodox Muhammedans, and
understand fully, *that our power is derived from the power of the
Sultan, our respect from his respect, and ruin from his ruin.*"

Information was first received in May 1897 of prayers
and thanksgiving being offered for the Sultan's victories.[22]
Subsequently reports were received of prayers and rejoicing in
Punjab, NWP and Oudh, Central Provinces, Bombay and
Sind, Madras, Bengal, Rajputana, Burma and Afghanistan.[23]

Muhammedan Revivalists' Proclamations of a religious
nature were also circulated to a considerable extent. These
had no direct political character, but were only calculated to
excite Muslim feelings. The worst desposed portion of the
Vernacular Press, both Hindu and Muslim, for sometime persistently put the action of England in regard to the
Eastern Question in the most unfavourable light, both as
regards bad faith and the power of England to enforce her
wishes. The Muslim Press exaggerated the significance
of the Turkish victories over Greece and represented the
Sultan as able to defeat any combination which might be
made against him. Naturally the Muslim Press in general
resented the language used about the Sultan in England by
certain politicians and newspapers.

In September 1897 the '*Subah*' of Constantinople published
an account of an interview said to have taken place between
the Maharaja of Kapurthala and the Sultan in the course of
which the Maharaja ascribed the frontier risings to British

---

[22]Ibid, para 26.

[23]Ibid, para 27.

disregard of Muslim feeling and stated that the Muslim were prepared to serve the *Khalifa*. The Maharaja wrote to the "*Levant Herald*" emphatically denying both the interview and the sentiments ascribed to him, but the press censor refused to allow the repudiation to be published. Tae Maharajah then wrote to the British Embassy, which pressed the Porte to compel the '*Subah*' to publish a denial of its report. The Porte promised to do this but failed to keep its words.[24]

It was reported from Constantinople in September 1897 that for some time past the Turkish press, notably the '*Malumat*' and the '*Subah*' had been reproducing from Indian and foreign newspapers articles on Indian affairs couched in a tone hostile to British Government in India. One of these articles in the '*Malumat*,' on the subject of the famine policy of Government of India, was violently worded, and was said to have been reproduced from the Indian '*Razghiar*'[25] (A very similar article appeared subsequently in a Russian newspaper and was taken from the Indian '*Ruzi-gar*'). The '*Malumat*' also had published a series of articles from its "*Petersburg correspondent*" whose name was "Jahangir and Jan", to the effect that the Maharajahs and the various races in India were becoming more and more hostile to British rule, and that the condition of the country was far worse than at the time of the Mutiny.[26]

The '*Muhammedan*' (Madras), in its issues of the 10 and 13 January 1898, published translations of two malignant articles which appeared in the *Cairene 'Alamu-l-Usmani*' and '*Al-Muaiyyad*'. These articles severely criticised and exaggerated the proceedings of Government in regard to the Calcutta riots, the Poona tragedy, the frontier disturbances, the plague

---

[24]Ibid, para 28.

[25]A very similar article appeared subsequently in a Russian newspaper and purported to have been taken from the Indian "Ruzigar". The columns of the "*Surma-i-Rozgar*', '*Jarida-i-Rozgar*' and '*Mantakhab-i- Rozgar*" were searched, but no such article was found in them, nor can the papers mentioned by the Constantinople and Russian newspapers be indentified with any paper published in India.

[26]C.S.B. Abstract, Vol. XI, para 1076.

measures, and the harsh treatment accorded to Muslims and the Muslim faith. The '*Alamu-l-Usmani*' called the Indian Government the "*fountain of disturbances*", a "*mine of mischief*", a "*quarry of violence and oppression*", a '*tyrannical and oppressive government*" and a "*wild and mean Government.*" It wrote: "Had we found at least one smallest virtue in the British, we would have, upon God, praised them so much as to cause an echo from earth to heaven, and we would have spoken very highly of them. Bnt what can we do—alas! Their greatest evils are manifest! These evils are such as cannot be enumerated even by the sharpest and most intelligent persons. Thereby it is understood that they have been created to harm the servants of God and ruin the country." It spoke of the Muslim as 'resting on a fiery bed', drinking the 'cups of disgrace and scorn', and of the Government as a "redcross" Government. It concluded: "O Lord, let the ways be easy for them (the Muslim) and simplify their troubles and difficulties. But the flags of their enemies be upset and the army and nation be dispersed and confused. Let the arms of the enemies become dull and strike at their faces. Let them be dispersed as the heavy winds disperse swarms of locusts." The article in the '*Al-Muaiyyid*' was less violent, though it dwelt on the oppression of the Indian Government, regretted that Indians were not allowed to carry arms, complained of heavy taxation and of the avaricious policy and great pride of Great Britain. The Editor of the '*Muhammedan*' was warned against letting such articles appear in his paper.[27]

Several reports were also received during the year 1898 and 1899 of persons from Turkey visiting India, but in no case was there any conclusive proof of these people being Pan-Islamic propagandists. The majority of them were probably merely religious mendicants, who had sought the charity of their co-religionists, either on their own behalf or for shrines or religious places in Baghdad and other towns of Turkey.

Accounts of a few of the more important of these visitors and suspected Pan-Islamists are given below :

---

[27]C.S.B. Abstract, Vol. XII, para 306 (v).

(1) *Sharif Nazr :* Intimation was received in August 1897 that Sharif Nazr[28], who had been given a letter of introduction by the British Embassy at Constantinople, was coming to India, and that he was a man whom it might be worthwhile to watch. He came to Bombay apparently in November or December 1897 and left for Hyderabad (Deccan), on the 18 December. At Hyderabad he stayed with Jamadar Kamal Khan and seemed to be trying to organise a sort of Turkophol Society, and to have won over several more or less prominent men and officials of the Nizam's Government, the most notable of the latter being Aziz Mirza, the Judicial and Home Secretary. Secret meetings were held in Kamal Khan's house, and the Pan-Islamic influence showed itself in the substitution of a new seal and monogram containing the *Tughra Uthmani* (Turkish Imperial Signature) on official letters and the establishment of a new shrine in the middle of the European bungalows. Both these innovations were the work of Aziz Mirza, but there was little doubt but that they were suggested by Sharif Nazr. Sharif Nazr came to Calcutta, on the 15 February 1898, asked and was refused an interview with the viceroy, and tried to obtain letters of introduction from the Foreign Secretary to the Political Officers at Bhopal and Rampur. He does not appear to have succeeded in ingratiating himself with the Calcutta Muslims, and he soon left for Burma. He arrived at Rangoon on the 20 March and left for Singapore on the 28 March, 1898.[29]

(2) *Ahmed Ratib Pasha* : In August 1897 Her Majesty's Embassy at Constantinople reported that Ahmed Ratib Pasha[30], Governor-General of the Hedjaz, was one of the persons engaged in writing to India in connection with the Pan-Islamic movement, and that Ahmed Faiz Beg, attached to the Turkish Consulate at Bombay, was one of his correspondents. It was ascertained in India that Ahmad Ratib, then Aide-de-Camp to the Sultan of Turkey, had come to Bombay in February 1892, had an interview with the Governor, Lord Harris, and received

---

[28]C.S.B. Abstract, Vol. XI, para 520.
[29]C.S.B. Abstract, Vol. XII, paras 60, 122, 288 & 329.
[30]C.S.B. Abstract, Vol. XI, para 1076.

letters of introduction to the various officials whom he was likely to meet in the course of his proposed tour through India. He left Bombay on 1 March 1892, visited Bhopal, Hyderabad, Agra, Delhi and other places and eventually went to Calcutta, whence he apparently returned to Turkey.

(3) *Shaikh Ibrahim*[31], son of Muhammad Ismail of Mecca visited Bundelkhand on the 4 October 1897, bearing sealed letters from the *Shaibi* (key-bearer) of the *Kaaba* building and the Shariff of Mecca, to the Nawab and the Superintendent of Baoni. He told the Superintendent that he had similar letters for all Muslim chiefs in India and presents for the principal ones, and that the Rulers of Hyderabad, Gwalior and Rampur had received him with all honour. He had a letter purporting to be from the Nawab of Rampur to the Shariff of Mecca. On discovering that the Superintendent was a Government official, Ibrahim became reticent and he left Baoni on the 6 October. The letters merely contained congratulations and appeared to have been written in India.

Muslim feeling was greatly stirred by the affairs of Turkey and Persia in 1911-13, by the repartition of Bengal in 1912, and by the fiasco over the Aligarh University, which cumulatively *created an anti-Christian feeling* and drove a wedge between Muslims and the British Government[32]. The *Kanpur Mosque* episode fanned Muslim resentment. Pan-Islamism became a force in Muslim politics, and Turkey used every endeavour to utilize the movement for her own ends. *The well known Anjuman-i-Khuddam-i-Ka'aba was utilised for this object.* The opposition of Turkey and Britain in the war severely strained Muslim loyalty, and there is reason to think that many of the more extreme among them became actively disloyal. Communication with Turkey was maintained through the Hedjaz till the Sherif's revolt closed this avenue, and several prominent Muslims who had foresworn their allegiance to Britain fell into British hands

---

[31]C.S.B. Abstract, Vol. XI, para 831.

[32]Note by W. Booth Gravely dt. 16.1.1918. *See* also Home Political (Deposit) F. No. 31, dated February, 1918,

after the revolt and were interned in various places. Frontier trouble instigated by enemies of the British Government had arisen on several occasions, and the Hindustani fanatics, a settlement fanatically hostile to the British Government, had been supported by both recruits and money from India. Finally, the revolutionaries in Kabul had not been idle and, apart from the part they played in stirring up frontier and other general trouble they engaged in a conspiracy to subvert the British Government[33] in India and join Turkey. The Silk Letters were one of the products of this conspiracy. But the alertness of the British Government, which had interned its leading adherents in India, did much to diminish its dangerous potentialities.

It is now necessary to throw some more light on *Nadwat-ul-Ulema* and *Anjuman-i-Khuddam-i-Kaaba*. Sections II and III which follow contain accounts of both these important Pan-Islamic societies.

Section II

NADWAT-UL-ULEMA

Little information is available about the *Nadwat-ul-Ulema*. The Government of India records mention about its working during the period 1894-99 but thereafter no information seems to be available. However, on the basis of the available data it would be worthwhile to examine its aims and objects; its scheme for the establishment of a University, and throw some light on the character and antecedents of the men who were connected with this movement.

According to the more important rules and regulations of the *Nadwat-ul-Ulema* only Muslims were eligible to become its members. The *Nadwat* had nothing to do with politics but when Government referred any political matters to it,

---

[33]Ibid.

the *Jalsa-i-Intizamia* or Managing Committee dealt with them.[1]

There were four classes of *Arakin* or members, and each member had to pay at least Rs. 2/—year as subscription, unless exempted from payment under the rules. The four classes[2] of members were as follows:

(1) Honorary Members possessing special qualifications, but exempted from the payment of subscriptions;

(2) Ruling Chiefs, the great *Ulama* or *Savants* and influential *Sheikhs* or leaders of any large section of the Muslim community inclined to promote the objects of the *Nadwat*, who were to be called patrons;

(3) The ordinary *Ulama* or *Sheikhs* nominated by the Managing Committee; and

(4) other members, i.e. those who paid the minimum rate of subscription.

The members were to follow strictly the *Shara* or the Muslim law, to promote concord and amity among themselves, and to further the objects of the *Nadwat*. The general meeting of the *Nadwat-ul-Ulema* was to be held once a year at any place fixed upon by the Managing Committee which would ordinarily meet once a quarter. The members of the first three classes would discuss any matter at the annual general session, but no member of the 4th class could speak without the permission of the President.[3]

The Managing Committee consisted of 35 members, elected from among the members of the *Nadwat*, of whom no less than two-third belonged to the 3rd class of members. The *Majlis-i-Mal* consisted of seven members and in no case of

---

[1] The *Zawabit-i-Nadwat-ul-Ulema* i.e. the rules of the Nadwat-ul-Ulema including a statement of its aims and objects. Printed at the Islamic Press, Kanpur, by Saiyid Muhammad Ahsan of Bihar, Manager of the *Tohfa-i-Muhammadia*, by order of the Managing Committee.

[2] Sub-enclosure, 5 (Enclosure No. 1) Foreign Proceeding No. 165 dated January, 1900.

[3] Ibid, p. 4.

less than four members, and had the full power to check the accounts of the income and expenditure of the *Nadwat*. A committee was to be formed under the name of *Majlis-i-Ishaat-ul-Ulama*, to collect funds for the establishment of a *Dar-ul-Ulama* (a college or a university) and to promote in other ways that scheme. The *Majlis-i-Ishaat-ul-Islam*, was a committee to collect funds and exercise control over preachers appointed to spread Islam. Branch offices could be established in connection with the *Nadwat-ul-Ulema* in different provinces with the sanction of the Managing Committee.[4]

The aims and objects of the *Nadwat-ul-Ulema* were described as follows by its founders :—

Firstly—As the *Ulama* or learned men among Muslims were scattered all over the country and did not correspond with one another, and each of them worked independently according to his own lights, they possessed little power and influence, and were therefore unable to control the religion and morals of the nation. New the *Nadwat* intended to concentrate the scattered strength of the *Ulama*, and to afford them an opportunity of meeting together once a year benefiting by an exchange of thoughts, settling disputed points and working in concert.

Secondly—Another chief object of the *Nadwat* was to promote concord among the different rival sects of the Muslim community which were constantly at loggerheads with each other. To merge these sects into one was, of course impossible, and no sane man would have ever thought of attempting such a thing. But the *Nadwat* impressed upon the importance of conducting their religious controversies with moderation and of refraining from harsh and abusive language; again, as Muslims, they ought to make common cause with one another, just as the King of Persia and the Sultan of Turkey had entered into an alliance against the *Kafirs* (unbelievers).

----

[4]Ibid, pp. 4-5.

[5]Ibid, p. 5.

Irreligion (atheism) being rampant in Europe, the Europeans struk at the root of religion and Islam with all their might and main, and it was therefore incumbent on the different sects of Muslims to unite and offer strong resistance to them in their evil endeavours.[6]

Thirdly—The course of Arabic studies had been changing from time to time during the last three hundred years, the last change having been made by Mulla Nizamuddin. The *Nadwat* would prepare a new course according to the requirements of the present times.[7]

Fourthly—The instruction given in Arabic and religion at the existing schools was of an ordinary kind. The *Nadwat* had resolved to establish a college, with a sufficient staff of able professors to give education. Promising students, after going through the college course, were to be induced by offers of scholarships to prosecute their further studies at the college for two years more, with a view to acquire a proficiency in any particular branch of knowledge. A large library was to be attached to the college.[8]

Fifthly—The *Nadwat* aimed at encouraging the spread of Islam in India and other countries in two ways, *viz.* by inducing Muslims who did not strictly observe their religious customs and duties to do so, and by makiug *conversions*. Muslim preachers were to be appointed for the purpose. Preachers intended for foreign countries were first to be taught the languages spoken there.[9]

Sixthly—Many persons wanted *fatwas* (judgments or decisions) from the *Ulama* in secular and religious matters, but they found it difficult to obtain such *fatwas*, either because they did not know any *Ulama* or the *Ulama* had not the time to answer all references made to them. The *Nadwat* intended to establish a *Dar-ul-Ifta* (a seat or court for giving *fatwas*), to readily give judgments in any matter referred to it.[10]

---

[6]Ibid, p. 5.
[7]Ibid, p. 6.
[8]Ibid, p. 6.
[9]Ibid.
[10]Ibid.

It is now necessary to examine Nadwat's scheme for a University *(Dar-ul-Ulum)*. The pamphlet "*Tajwiz-dar-ul-ulum-Nadwat-ul-Ulema*" which was printed at the Intizami Press, Kanpur, and appears to have been written by Muhammed Ali, *Nazim* or Secretary to the *Nadwat-ul-Ulema* contains the views expressed by the *Ulama* and other Muslim gentlemen in support of the proposal. It opens with a preface which reproduces two letters written by Maulana Haji Imad-Ullah. He was in entire sympathy with the movement set on foot by the *Ulama* of this country, regarded the *Nadwat-ul-Ulema* as a boon from Heaven and called upon the Indian Muslims to promote, by all means in their power, its aims and objects. The writer of the pamphlet called attention to these remarks as evidencing the interest which holy men like the Haji had commenced taking in the *Nadwat*, and after alluding to the "happy tidings" which have been revealed to certain holy men by the Prophet regarding the *Natwat*—an indication of the Prophet's own sympathy with the *Nadwat*—warns those persons who labouring under a misapprehension or owing to their imprudence are opposed to, or prejudiced against, this assembly (the *Nadwat*), against incurring the displeasure of the Prophet, which would bring down upon them the wrath of God, and damn both their present and future lives."

The writer stated that the *Nadwat* had taken steps to carry out two of its three principal objects, namely, the *Dar-ul-Ifta*, i.e. the seat or court for giving decisions and the *Mahakma-i-Ishaat-i-Islam* (the department for the spread of Islam) which was badly needed, have been opened. Questions already received from various places have been answered by the *Dar-ul-Ifta*. For the present a preacher has been appointed, who preaches in different quarters of the city (Kanpur) against the Christians and the Arya Samajists—opponents of Islam—and the measure is having good effect on the Muslims generally, and the followers of other religions particularly, who are becoming converts to Islam. Mention is also made of the Muslim orphanage which has been established at Kanpur, and is making progress.

---

[11]See scheme for a University *(Dar-ul-Ulm)* Sub-enclosure No. 6 (Enclosure No.1) Foreign Secret F-Proceeding No. 165, dated January 1900, p.7.

The main object of the *Nadwat* according to this writer was to encourage those branches of knowledge which were connected with religion and to improve the condition of the Muslims. With this object in view, three important schemes were sanctioned during the last two years, namely, the establishment of a *Dar-ul-Ifta*, the appointment of preachers and the establishment of a *Dar-ul-Ulum*.[12] These schemes, especially the third one, were a *sine quo non* for an improvement of the condition of the Muslims. The Muslims who desired to live according to the *shara* will at once recognise the necessity for the establishment of the *Ifta* Department, which will prove of immense advantage to the Muslim community, and will, it is hoped, grow into a department of *raza* (administration of justice) to which the Muslims may refer their civil suits for decision. The preachers appointed by the *Nadwat* will seek to ameliorate the condition of Muslims by inducing them to follow lawful trades and industries, and by enlightening ignorant Muslims on the subject of their religious duties — the Muslim peasantry in many places being Muslims only in name. But by far the most important was the university scheme. It was calculated to revive the drooping spirits of Muslims. A draft scheme was also laid by the writer of this pamphlet before the members of the Managing Committee which met on the 12th of *Muharram* 1313 *Hijra* (6 July 1895), and was then published in accordance with the decision of the said Committee and qualified Muslims, especially the *Ulama*, were invited to express their opinions regarding it......The proposal received the approval of the meeting, and was declared by Maulana Maulvi Muhammad Lutf Ullah, the President, to have been unanimously sanctioned[13].

It is now necessary to throw some light on the character and antecedents of such men as Hafiz Abid Husain, Maulvi Abdul Hai, Abbas Ali and Gul Muhammad Khan who were connected with the movement.

---

[12]Ibid.

[13]Ibid, p. 8.

(1) A *Hafiz Abid Husain*[14], Honorary Magistrate of Jaunpur. He was a *Vakil*, practising in the Judge's Court, and was also a member of the Municipal Board. He was a bigotted narrow-minded Sunni who took great interest in religious matters, and provided money for the purpils in one of the Jaunpur Masjids. He was not well disposed to Government, but was not connected with any political movement. He did not take a prominent part in the religious disturbances at Jaunpur and the report on the *Muharram* of 1885 didn't contain his name.

(2) *Abdul Hai*[15], was son of one Fakhr-ud-din of Rae Bareli, who owned a few *bigahs* in sub-proprietary tenure, and also practised as a *hakim*, was at one time employed in Bhopal, and later by the *talukdar* of Gaura on Rs. 25 per mensem. Abdul Hai, a youngman of 26 or 27, was educated in Lucknow, where he learnt Arabic and Persian, but he had no English education. He studied at Kanpur with some Maulvis when he became Joint Secretary to the *Nadwat*. He then went to Bareilly, and in July 1899, was at Lucknow, where he carned Rs. 30 per mensem, and had a house and office at Golaganj (value Rs. 10,000). A cousin of his Saiyid Khalil-ud-din, was an Honorary Magistrate in Rae Bareli, but a man of no importance.

(3) *Abbas Ali*[16], a Shia, was an Arabic teacher in the Aligarh College for over 24 years, and was drawing Rs. 100 per mensum. His home was at Jarcha, Police Station Sikandrabad, District Bulandshahr, and he was educated by Maulvi Tafazzal Husain Mujahid, who lived at Sambhal, District Moradabad. He obtained his *sanad* as Maulvi from Mufti Abbas of Lucknow. His relatives lived at Jarcha.

---

[14]Copy of notes on the character and antecedents of Hafiz Abid Husain, Honorary Magistrae of Jaunpur. *See also* Sub-eneloswre 1 (Enclosure No. 1) Foreign Secret. F. Proceeding No. 165, dated January, 1900.

[15]Copy of notes or the character and antecedents of Abdul Hai. *See also* Sub-enclosure 2 (Enclosure 1) Foreign Secret Proceeding No. 165 dated January, 1900, p. 4.

[16]Copy of notes about the character and antecedents of Abbas Ali. *See also* Sub-enclosure 3 (Enclosure 1) Foreign Secret Proceeding No. 165 dated January, 1900, pp. 4-5.

He himself resided in the city of Koil (Aligarh) with one Hakim Yakub. Before joining the college he held no appointment. He was about 50 and was the most highly reputed Shia in Aligarh and the neighbouring districts. He had a strong prejudice against all non-Muslims, especially Europeans, and washed his hands after every occasion on which he shook hands with one. He was visited by *Raises* of Aligarh, Bulandshahr, Lucknow and Muzzafarnagar. His father, Jafir Husain, was a Shia Mujahid and a well-known reader of the *Koran* and a popular teacher. Sir Saiyid Ahmad Khan selected him, as he did not wish the Shias to hold aloof from the college, and, therefore, engaged a man, likely to attract him. He never preached sedition.

(4) *Gul Muhammad Khan of Aligarh*[17]: This man was actually a resident of Ghazni. He succeeded Maulvi Lutf Ullah as Maulvi of the Jumr Masjid at Aligarh when Lutf Ullah left Aligarh to take up an appointment at Hyderabad. At that time a religious controversy existed between Maulvi Lutf Ullah and a leading Maulvi, named Ishmail, regarding the chanting of the "Amen", and it was following an attempt to poison Lutf Ullah that he left for Hyderabad. The majority of the Muslims at Aligarh were opposed to the recitation of the "Amen", and it was with general concurrence of the Muslim community that Maulvi Gul Muhammad Khan succeeded Lutf Ullah as being a man of character who was not likely to be influenced. He received a salary of Rs. 30 a month, which was contributed to locally.[18]

As regards the work done by *Nadwat-ul-Ulema* the proceedings of its fifth meeting held at Kanpur on 8th and 9th March, 1898, make it clear that upto 1897 it had done no practical good but yet much was done towards advancing its two

---

[17]Copy of notes or the character and antecedents of Gul Muhammad Khan. *See also* Sub-enclosure 4, (Enclosure 1) Foreign Secret F Proceeding No. 165, January, 1900.

[18]Extract from a letter No. D.O. 72, dated 13th March 1899, from the Inspector General of Police, N.W.P. and Oudh, to the Under-Secretary to Government, N.W.P. and Oudh.

principal objects, *viz.* the reform and improvement of education and the promotion of mutual concord among Muslims. The mere agitation of the *Nadwat* for the revival of Arabic learning has led the Anglicised Muslims, who condemn the study of Arabic as utter waste of time, to recognise its importance, and convinced orthodox Maulvis, who were opposed to any change in the prevailing system of Arabic education, of the necessity for reform. The efforts of the *Nadwat* had been still more succcessful in preventing disputes among the rival sects of the Muslims. The difference of opinion between the *Muqalhids* (Muslims who accept the interpretence of the Koran and the *Hadis* as made by the four schools) and the *Ghair-i-Muqallids* (Muslims who do not accept such interpretations) formally led to serious riots and there were also disputes regarding *Amen-bil-Jahar* (i.e. uttering the word *Amen* in prayers in a loud voice), and so forth.[19]

These riots and disputes which cost lakhs of rupees had become things of the past through the good offices of the *Nadwat*. Such riots were very common in the Eastern districts, but the reconciliation effected by the *Nadwat* between Maulana Shah Amanat Ullah of Ghazipur and Maulvi Abu Muhammed Ibrahim had put an end to them. The preceding *Nadwat* held at Meerut had amicably settled the dispute regarding a mosque which had long been the subject of a costly litigation between the *Hanafis* and the *Ghaur-i-Muqalhids* of that town. Again, as the *Nadwat*, had afforded the *Ulama* of the various sects an opportunity to meet together on friendly terms once a year, the feeling of love and amity had grown up between them, and the existence of concord among them was the best guarantee for the maintenance of peace among the masks who followed them.[20]

It is now necessary to examine how far efforts were made to carry out the resolutions passed by the preceding Meerut *Nadwat-ul-Ulama*, and how far other work was done during the year 1898:

---

[19]Proceedings of the 5th Annual Meeting of the *Nadwat-ul-Ulema*. Foreign Secret F Proceeding No. 165 dated January 1900, p. 8.
[20]Ibid, pp. 8-9.

(1) According to a resolution of the Meerut *Nadwat-ul-Ulema*, students who received a sound English education were to be given scholarships and instructed in Arabic and Muslim religion, so that the *Nadwat* might send them to foreign countries to preach Islam. But none of the then existing Muslim schools could arrange for their education.[21]

(2) According to another resolution some intelligent students were to be encouraged by offers of scholarships to go to Egypt to complete their education. A subscription was at once opened, and subscriptions promised were Rs. 35 a month, and Rs. 140 a year, and donations promised amounted to Rs. 1,204. But when a copy of the rules of the *Dar-ul-Ulum* in Egypt was obtained, it was found that candidates possessing a necessary knowledge of English and Arabic were not forthcoming.[22]

(3) According to the 3rd resolution, some preachers were to be engaged to instruct ignorant Muslims in their religious observances and duties. Provision was made for four preachers in the budget. But as the appointment of a preacher in Meerut led to a deep sensation, the scheme had to be suspended.[23]

(4) Funds were to be raised for the establishment of a *Dar-ul-Ulum* or University. Applications were received from several towns in the Panjab for the despatch of a deputation to raise funds, but it was not considered expedient to send a deputation to the Panjab owing to the frontier disturbances.[24]

(5) Good work was done by the *Dar-ul-Ifta* during the year 1897, though it consisted of only one *mufti*. 572 references were made to him and he was able to answer 565 of them.[25]

(6) The Muslim orphanage at Kanpur established by the *Nadwat* was in a satisfactory state and had 43 orphans.[26]

---

[21] Ibid, p. 9.
[22] Ibid.
[23] Ibid.
[24] Ibid.
[25] Ibid.
[26] Ibid.

(7) A branch association was established at Aurangabad in the Gaya District.[27]

(8) There was a steady increase in the number of members. This becomes clear from the following table.[28]

1st year	...	242 members
2nd ,,	...	443 ,,
3rd ,,	...	782 ,,
4th ,,	...	1,015 ,,

(9) Though no deputations were sent to other parts of the country to promote the objects and interests of the *Nadwat*, no pains were spared to do so by letters and pamphlets. 1,964 letters were received, and 2,515 letters and 1,268 copies of pamphlets issued.[29]

(10) The income, including the surplus of preceding year, amounted to Rs. 8,386-15-9 while the expenditure was Rs. 3,946-59 during 1897.[30]

Dar-ul-Ulum was to be established at Lucknow. On 10 March 1898 a deputation of the *Nadwat* made the selection of a site for the *Dar-ul-Ulum* building. The deputation approved of a plot of land offered by Munshi Ihtisham Ali, son of Munshi Imtiaz Ali, deceased, later Wazir of Bhopal. Then on 11 March, the Managing Committee appointed a committee to take necessary steps to carry out the University scheme. It consisted of: Maulvi Hafiz Abdul Majid, of Farangi Mahal; Maulvi Abdul Rauf Majid of Farangi Mahal; Munshi Athar Ali, Khan Bahadur, Vakil; Munshi Ihtisham Ali; Raja Tassadaq Rasul Khan, of Jahangirabad; Chaudhuri Nasrat Ali Khan, Kahan Bahadur, and others.[31]

---

[27]Ibid.

[28]Ibid.

[29]Ibid.

[30]Ibid.

[31]Ibid, pp. 9-10.

The enquiries made by the Government revealed that the *Nadwat* had political as well as religious aims[32] but it was confident that time had not yet come when the Pan-Islamic ideas preached by *Nadwat* could effect its policy adversely. This becomes clear from the following extract:—"Sir A. MacDonnel's view as to the impossibility of drawing the line between Muslim politics and religion seems to me to be correct—at any rate so far as the more orthodox and the more ignorant Musalmans are concerned.[33] ... I would invite attention to the passage in the proceedings of the Nadwat-ul-Ulama which shows that their scheme included the provision of scholarships to enable Musulman youths to study at Cairo. Al-Azhar is, I believe, a centre of bigoted and reactionary Muhammedanism, and Indian students who return from it are likely to come back thoroughly imbued with Pan-Islamic ideas. Fortunately upto the present time students with the qualifications requisite for admission have not been forthcoming".[34] The Government thereafter did not pay much attention to the activities of the *Nadwat*.

Section III

THE ANJUMAN-I-KHUDDAM-I-KAABA

The *Anjuman-i-Khuddam-i-Kaaba*, or Society of Servants of the *Kaaba* was established in May 1913 with the ostensible object of protecting Mecca and other holy places of Islam from

---

[32]Despatch to the Secretary of State for India correcting a mistake made in a previons despatch regarding the meeting of the "Nadwat-ul-Ulama" of Kanpur in March 1998. Aims and objects of the society. Pioceedings of meeting held by the Society, a at Kanpur in March 1898. Foreign Secret Proceeding No. 165 dated January 1900.

[33]Note by C.S. Bayley dated 9.7.1899 in the Foreign Department. *See also* Foreign Secret F Proceeding No. 165 dated January, 1900.

[34]Ibid. *See also* Page 3 of enclosure No. 3 Secret F Proceeding No. 123 dated June, 1889.

non-Muslim aggression.[1] The society owes its origin to the general feeling of uneasiness that became manifest among Muslims in India during the Turco-Italian and Balkan Wars. It appears that the scheme was first propounded in Lucknow by a barrister named Mushir Hussain[2] Kidwai and Maulvi Abdul Bari[3], of Faranghi Mahal, Lucknow in January 1913 and an outline of the Society was sent to Abdul Kalam Azad, editor of the *Al-Hilal*, Calcutta for publication in his newspaper but the latter took no notice of it for a time.[4] This seems to have been due to the fact that Abul Kalam Azad was himself occupied at the time in working out a scheme for a secret society, which never fully developed. The earliest public announcement regarding the society was made on 31 March 1913, when Shaukat Ali of Rampur, late of the Opium Department, United Provinces, and brother of Mohamed Ali, editor of *The Comrade*, suggested in a speech at Amritsar that all Muslims should combine in a society to be called the *Anjuman Khuddam-i-Kaaba* with the object of protecting the holy places of Islam from non-Muslim aggression.[5]

On 9 April, a letter written by Mushir Hussain appeared in the *Al-Hilal* asking the editor to publish his scheme and this was done subsequently in the issue of 23 April. On 6 May Shaukat Ali and Mohamed Ali came to Lucknow and, at a meeting held at the house of Maulvi Abdul Bari discussed and amended the details of Mushir Hussain's scheme.[6] This discussion seems to have turned

[1] Home Political A Proceeding Nos. 33-8 dated November 1914, pp. 3-16.

[2] He was a Kidwai Shaikh of Bara Banki District and belonged to a petty Taluqdari family.

[3] He came into prominence at the beginning of the Turkish war by virtue of a somewhat turculent attitude on Pan-Islamic questions. He soon busied himself in collecting subscriptions in attending meetings and in entertaining other agitators and took a leading part in stirring up excitement amongst the Muslims of Lucknow.

[4] Hon'ble Mr. R. Burn Chief Secretary to Government, United Provinces to the Secretary to the Government of India, Home Department, No. 1532 of 1913, dated Nainital, the 17th September, 1913. Home Political A Proceeding No. 118 dated October, 1913.

[5] Note by F. Isemonger, Assistant Director, Criminal Intelligence dated 20th February 1914. Home Political A Proceeding No. 46 dated May 1914.

[6] The Society comprised two sections—the members of general section, took

chiefly upon the subscription and the remittance of a part or whole of the sum so collected to the Sultan of Turkey as *Khadim-ul-Harmain*.[7] All present at the meeting took an oath on the Koran to abide by the amended rules, and a committee was appointed consisting of Maulana Abdul Bari as *Khadim-ul-Khuddam* (Servant of the Servants), Shaikh Mushir Hussain Kidwai and Shaukat Ali as Secretaries, Hakim Abdul Wali of Lucknow, Dr. Nazir-ul-Din Hassan, Barrister, Lucknow, and Mohamed Ali, Editor of the *Comrade*, as *Mautmidin Khadim-ul-Khuddam* ('Assistants of the Servants of the Servants). The provisional rules framed at this meeting laid down that its chief aim was to maintain the honour and safety of the *Kaaba* and to defend the holy places from non-Muslim aggression. In order to effect this the society decided to form an association of lovers of the *Kaaba* whose members were at all times to be ready to sacrifice their lives and property for its safety. Futher the society decided to undertake measures to spread Islam, to establish Muslim schools and orphanages, to improve the existing relations between Muslims and the *Bait-Ullah Sharif* and to render every facility for the voyage (*Haj*).[8]

The annual subscription was fixed at one rupee for rich and poor alike so that the equality of Islam may be held supreme. The money thus obtained was to be divided into three equal shares;

(a) one share being allotted to that independent Muslim State which may have the duty of looking after the *Kaaba*;

(b) one share to be given to different orphanages, schools and missionary societies; and

---

an oath to maintain the respect of tke Kaaba and to sacrifice life and property against non-Muslim aggressors, and the special section, known as Shaidi or devotees, expressed readiness at any time to carry out any orders of the Society without delay or objection. The Shaidis were maintained by the Society. *See also* Home Political A Proceedings No. 118 dated October 1913, pp. 187-88.

[7]Servant of the two Sacred places i.e. Mecca and Medina.

[8]Home Political A Proceeding No. 46 dated May 1914.

(c) the third share to be reserved so that it may be advantageously spent in time of need for defending the *Kaaba*.[9]

It was further laid down that this last portion was to be devoted in part to any commercial undertaking which advocated the good of the *Kaaba* and other holy shrines, as, for example, the purchase of vessels in which pilgrims may be conveyed easily, cheaply, and comfortably to the holy places of Islam.[10]

When the society was formed members were required on joining to take the following oath :—"I, son of......being in the presence of God, after repentance for my past sins, with *Kalima*[11] on my lips and with my face turned towards the *Kaaba*, solemnly affirm that I shall try with my whole heart to keep the respect on the *Kaaba* and shall sacrifice my life and property against non-Muslim aggressors. I shall fully carry out the orders of the *Anjuman-i-Khuddam-i-Kaaba* given to me."

There seems to have been some idea of utilising the services of some of the more earnest members for special work — though the nature of this work was not specified — for there was a special provision in the rules in which it was laid down that those associates who were ready to sacrifice their lives, property and honour at the direction of God and in the interests of *Kaaba* and would like to become volunteers (votaries), would have to take the following solemn affirmation:

"I, son of......with my face turned towards the *Kaaba*, being thereby in the presence of God, hereby solemnly affirm that I have given up my life for the service of God. I now must only serve the *Kaaba*, and keep up the respect of the *Kaaba*. The orders of the *Anjuman Khuddam-i-Kaaba* will be my most responsible duty which I shall always be ready to

---

[9]Hon'ble Mr. R. Burn, Chief Secretary to Government, United Provinces to the Secretary to the Government of India No. 1532 of 1913 dated Nainital, the 17th September 1913.
Home Political A Proceedings No. 118, dated October, 1913, para 9.
[10]Home Political A Proceedings No. 46 dated May 1914.
[11]The profession of faith.

carry out with my heart and soul, and without any objection or delay. I will, without delay or objection, start for any destination to which I may be ordered to go; no difficulty will keep me back. With this solemn promise I enter into the society of *Shaidaian-i-Kaaba* (votaries of the *Kaaba*) swearing for a second time by my God and my Prophet, the Qoran, my religion, and my honour to remain faithful to the above promise".[12]

These oaths, coupled as they were with an undertaking on the part of the *Anjuman* to be responsible for meeting the requirements of a votary and his family according to his social position sufficiently indicate that the promoters of the society contemplated action other than mere proselytism or educational work.[13] In fact the ideas of the founders were most extravagant.[14] It was said that they hoped to collect a crore of rupees in a year to be in a position to build ships and to maintain an army and navy for the protection of Mecca and other sacred places. It was also broadcast that the original intention was to send 5,000 men abroad for military training[15]. This proposal was however vetoed and the schemes of the society were greatly modified though the objects of the special order of votaries were not yet defined.

It will not be inappropriate perhaps to quote here some extracts from an article published by the *Comrade* in its issues of 31 May and 7 June 1913 regarding the society and its aims.

"We who are living today have witnessed perhaps one of the most decisive wars of any period in history. Forgetting the determination of the Powers to maintain the *status quo* in the Balkans," and also forgetting the agreement of England to Austria's proposal, with regard to the Note presented in

---

[12]Home Political A Proceeding No. 118 dated October 1913. *See also* Home Political A Proceeding No. 46 dated May 1914.

[13]Ibid *vide* Appendix, page 9 (Rule. 6)

[14]Home Political A Proceeding No. 118 dated October. 1913.

[15]Ibid *See also* Home Political A Proceeding No. 46 dated May 1914.

the Capitals of the Balkan Confederacy, "for the addition of words making it clear that the Powers were determined to secure respect for the integrity of the Ottoman Empire," Mr. Asquith announced even before the war was over that "things can never be again as they were", that "the victors are not to be robbed of the fruits which cost them so dear", and that "the map of Eastern Europe has to be recast". But if to Europe it means something strange and startling to have to recast the map of Eastern Europe, can it mean nothing to the Moslems of the world to entirely recast the map of the Moslem world?......Those who foretold a future for the Turks only in Asia have occasion to rejoice as the true prophets of evil. But even some of them, such as His Highness the Agha Khan, who could not but feel distressed at this result, cannot foretell with anything like the same certainty whether Turkey's control over her Asiatic empire would be allowed to remain adequate and effective. Her robe of power is indeed in rags and totters, and even these are being pulled at and torn by grasping hands on every side. Russia is openly casting greedy eyes over Armenia. France is fomenting disturbances in Syria and rousing the Arabs against the Turks, just as Russia is encouraging Armenians to entice the Kurds into acts of violence in order to make the excuse of intervention plausible. Trouble is also brewing in Baghdad and Basra, and one may be sure that every effort will be made to make the differences of Arabs and Turks in the Hedjaz and Yemen as dangerously acute as possible. The future of Turkey is, therefore, no less dark and gloomy than her recent past.[16]

"The Musalmans of the world who have seen enacted before thier very eyes the tragedy of Turkey in Europe, who have watched the strangling of Persia, who have witnessed the independent kingdoms of Africa being one by one practically lost to Islam, cannot now find the same comfort in their past achievements or present temporal power when they are reminded to think of the future of their sacred places. Islam is no longer a conquering power. It does not rule any more over a large part of Europe. In Africa, too, the days of its domination

---

[16]*Comrade* dated 31st May 1913.

are over...... With the realisation of all these depressing facts can the Moslems of the world seek solace in indolence and indifference to the fate of their holy places? Can they sit with folded hands, ruminating over the past or fretting against the stern and inexorable decrees of fate? No, Mr. Asquith is right; "things can never be as they were"; and if those Moslems who have hitherto formed part of the ruling races of mankind cannot safeguard the effective sovereignty of some Moslem States over the holy places of Islam, the hundreds of millions of Musalmans, who are numbered amongst the subject races, must now make up their minds to do so.

"When we in India received a London wire dated November 1st, saying that "the Bulgarians are now only twenty-five miles from the Capital," and that "they declare their resolve to make peace in Constantinople and nowhere else," we know what Indian Musalmans felt and what terrible apprehensions penetrated their bosoms and brains. It was then that for the first time they began to think uneasily of the safety of their holy places. But the war was still going on, and all hope was not lost......Besides it was apprehended that at such a time any reminders to the Musalmans of the situation of their holy places may possibly excite them to acts of desperation. It is certainly not by acts of desperation that the *Kaaba* of Islam could be safeguarded, and it was resolved that when the war was over, and there was no fear of any violence of thought and feeling, the Musalmans should be invited to deliberate over this question and arrive at a carefully determined conclusion concerning ways and means"......[17]

"Apart from the work of safeguarding the sanctity of the *Kaaba* and other sacred places of Islam from violation, and maintaining an independent and effecting Moslem Sovereignty over these lands, the Society of the servants of the *Kaaba* is destined to do much useful work in connection with the Moslem propaganda, the establishment of Moslem primary schools where Government assistance is not easily available, and saving the lives and faith of Moslem orphans, and it would be

---

[17]Ibid,

most appropriate for such a society to remove the existing difficulties of pilgrimage to the Hedjaz and other sacred places of Islam, which have already caused no little trouble to the Government.[18]

"As regards the main object of the Society, we wish to point out that in its essence it is a purely religious organisation, for the duty of pilgrimage is enforced by the law of Islam on every Moslem who is not exempted under that law. In order to free the performance of this duty from all dangers of interference, the prophet had to declare war on the Quresh of Mecca, and at last he forced his way into his birthplace as the head of a victorious army of pilgrims. Since then Mecca has acknowledged none but a Moslem ruler, and it has been the uninterrupted practice of the last thirteen centuries, based on the most clear injunctions in the Quran, that non-Moslems are not allowed to enter the Kaaba or its proceedings. It is, therefore, no new duty which some politically minded zealots have invented for themselves and their co-religionists that this society is to preach in India. As a matter of fact the society disclaims all connections with the politics of any community or country. The work of the society is such that every violence whether of feeling, thought or deed, is more likely to injure it than to assist it, and the huge network of local societies that is the essence of the movement cannot be created and maintained by appealing to the passions of the moment. Nor can such an organisation, emracing as it does every town and village of India and every Moslem living therein, remain secret in its aims and actions.[19]

"Its servants are expected before very long to number millions, and it is they who will form the rank and file of this society. But as work at the headquarters of provincial societies and the central society requires whole-time men who have dedicated their lives for a specified period thereof to this work, the society shall receive at provincial headquarters and at the head quarters of the central society about

---

[18]*Comrade* dated 7th June, 1913.
[19]Ibid.

twenty votaries for each, and it would also entertain the services of other votaries for the establishment of Moslem primary schools and orphanages and missionary work in somewhat inaccessible tracts. About four hundred votaries working at the headquarters of provincial societies and the central society would form the main spring of the mechanism.

"We have stated all this with a view to make it clear that nothing is farther from the minds of the organisers of this movement than to identify themselves with lovers of secret societies, and the only revolution that this organisation aims at creating is a revolution which would convert millions of illiterate, indifferent, indolent and unproductive Moslem units into a united and well regulated society of productive workers true to themselves and therefore false to none.[20]

"To the Mussalmans of India we have just one word to say. You know well enough that the protection of the holy places of Islam is a religious duty which is as much yours as that of the Turks, and you also know that it is a duty more sacred than any other. You know well enough that the Turk, who has for centuries stood as your sentinal at the gate of the Kaaba is weaker to-day than he ever has been since he planted the Crescent over St.Sophia, and you also know that he has to guard his own hearth, and that much, if not most of his vigilance is now needed nearer home. You know well enough that you do not feel the same security about your sacred places in 1913, than you did even in 1912, and you also know that if any sacrilege did occur before you could organise yourself, as it occurred at holy Meshed, you could do nothing but suffer in silence. It is true that God is himself the Protector of His House; but it is also true that he works through what he has created. When the people of the Elephant attacked Mecca, he did not have to crush them with his own hand. "He sent against them birds in flocks; claystones did they hurl down upon them, and he made them like stubble eaten down". And if the people of armoured cruisers and Dreadnoughts, of guns and magazine rifles, of shots and shrapnels and bombs

---

[20]Ibid.

hurled down from the clouds, attack the holy places of Islam,
may he not "cause their strategem to miscarry?" But should
the means employed be once more birds in flocks that could
only hurl claystones down upon the enemies of God, or men
in organised society, that could watch their weapons with
similar weapons and defeat their stratagems with their own.
Shall the honour of the deed go to the birds again, or shall it
this time go to you and to us?"[21]......(*Sic*)

Once launched, the promoters made earnest efforts to
popularise the movement by touring and holding meetings
and by advertising the society in the press. Maulvi Abdul
Bari accompanied by Shaukat Ali left Lucknow on 2
June and visited Bareilly, Badaun, Delhi, Ajmere, and
Deoband. All these places became important Islamic
centres—Deoband being the home of Islamic orthodoxy.
This visit to Ajmer was timed to coincide with the celebration
of the *Urs*, when large numbers of people from all over India
collect at Ajmer. At the same time Mushir Hussain visited
Kashmir in order to organise a branch of the society there. The
movement, however, did not succeed at first to the extent anticipated. The society was therefore regarded with suspicion, and in
particular the oath of membership caused so much distrust
that a number of newspapers published warnings, advising
their readers to have nothing to do with it. The society was
described as "an association for the purpose of preaching and
waging religious war (*Jehad*) and the honesty of the promoters
was questioned. A *Shia* paper warned the followers of its
particular sect not to be taken in by the political tricks of the
Sunnis, and remarked that the *Anjuman* was bound in course
of time to disturb the public tranquillity. A circular letter
addressed to leading Muslims in Bombay, containing
an appeal to join the society, and enclosing forms of membership was rejected by many of the recipients on the score that
the rules of the *Anjuman* were most objectionable and likely to
bring ruin to Indian Muslims.[22]

---

[21]Ibid.

[22]Home Political A Proceeding No. 46 dated May 1914.

On 9 July a letter from Shaukat Ali was published notifying changes in the societie's rules. The most important of these was the abolition of the oath of membership, and the substitution of a vow or promise in which the words *"all possible help"* replaced the words *"life and property"*.[23]

The occurrences at Kanpur and subsequent agitation diverted public attention from the *Kaaba* and its hypothetic dangers to actualities nearer home, and little was heard of the society until October, though one or two preachers were reported to be moving about lecturing on its behalf and endavouring to rally Muslims in the defence of their sacred places. On 26 and 27 October 1913 public meetings were held at Delhi with a view to explaining the objects of the society and pushing on the movement and from this time the society appears to have made steady head-way. It was then explained that owing to the unfortunate occurrences at Kanpur the society had kept itself in the background lest its motive should be misunderstood, but since a settlement had been arrived at, the promoters were desirous of advancing this religious movement.[24]

A statement regarding the working of the society up to 31 October 1913 was published soon after these meetings by Shaukat Ali. According to this statement the society began with twenty-three members, and by 31 October had enrolled 3,431 persons. As regards practical work two *Shaidais* (votaries) had been employed at first, namely Syed Ayub Ahmed of Shahjahanpur, and Syed Manzur Ali of Delhi, and their work had been supplemented by the services of six more votaries.[25] The names of these men were given as Hasan Ahmad Ranbari, Maulvi Habibu-ul-Hasan,[26] Maulvi Irshad Ali Khan, Maulvi Mehdi Hasan, Taj Mahomed, Mir Mahomed and Maulvi Ata Mahomed. They were said to be

---

[23]*Zamindar* dated 9th July, 1913, p. 12.

[24]Home Political A Proceeding No. 46 dated May 1914.

[25]Ibid.

[26]Formerly a sub-Inspector of Police.

employed chiefly an clerks and accountants, though occasionally they acted as preachers also.

Branches of the society were established at Hyderabad (Deccan), Lucknow, Sukkur, Khost (Baluchistan), Ajmere, Jamnagar, Amritsar, Naini Tal, Saharanpur, Benares, Sandela, Dhuan village, Kathiawar, Shabaznagar, Akbarpur, Makhdumpura, Gaya district, Narain Pinth (Deccan), and Bhainsa in Bareilly district.[27] The Aligarh branch was, however, the most popular.

The total receipts of the *Anjuman* upto 1 November 1913 were reported to be Rs. 3,974-2-3, of which Rs. 3,430-14-0 is shown as having been obtained by subscriptions and Rs. 139-7-0 by donations. Expenditure amounted approximately to Rs. 1,500 and half the receipts were deposited in the Bank of Bengal.[28]

The formation of this society in India attracted attention and enquiries regarding its rules and objects were said to have been received by Shaukat Ali from Egypt, Morocco, Turkey and other countries. The requisite information had been supplied on the understanding that membership of the society in India was confined to citizens of India, whether living in India or abroad, and consequently that if members of other nationalities desired enrolment in such an Islamic institution they must also then establish such societies in their own countries. This precaution was taken to counteract the criticism that in India an association had been formed, with branches in other countries, to promote Pan-Islamism. In spite of this avowed intention of taking no part in establishing branches in other countries Shaukat Ali had the rules of his society translated into Arabic (including a revised version of the oath of membership suitable to other countries) and printed in that language with the express intention of sending copies to Egypt

---

[27]Home Political A Proceeding No. 46 dated May 1914.

[28]The statement of accounts is not clear, and it will be seen from the above figure that the totals do not correspond.

and other countries where this language was spoken. Moreover
the society proposed to publish a paper in Arabic and it was
reported that the services of one Hafiz Wahabi[29] had also been
engaged to edit it. Hafiz Wahabi we know was chief editor of
Al Haq Yallu, a newspaper published in Constantinople. He
had come to India at the close of 1913 with the object of
studying the condition of Muslims in various parts of the
world.[30] His appointment as editor of the Arabic journal of
the *Anjuman Khuddam-i-Kaaba* was announced in the *Al Shaab*,
a newspaper published from Cairo.[31]

As regards the active preaching of the society little information is available. In the meetings held at Delhi during
October, the proceedings of which may be regarded as typical
as far as the bigger towns of India are concerned, speakers
described the ancient history of the *Kaaba* and depicted its
glory as the birth-place and home of the Prophet and the
accepted house of God. Those who loved God, it was urged, must
love the Prophet; and, those who loved the Prophet must love
the *Kaaba* and defend it from danger. While no definite statement was made that the holy places were in actual danger the
audience was left to infer this and that it was their duty to combine against an impending attack. The conclusions to be drawn
by the speeches were further emphasized by a printed letter,
which was distributed in these meetings, in which it was definitely stated that while the society sympathised with such objects
as the propagation of Islam and advancement of education, the

---

[29]Hafiz Wahabi was an Egyptian by birth, and was born at Boulac, Cairo. He
was educated at the Azhar University and subsequently studied at the College
of *Cadis*. He obtained a degree after five years and was working for a second
degree when he met Sheikh Abdul Aziz, Shawish. He formed a great
friendship with the latter and accompanied him to Constantinople where
he worked in collaboration with Abdul Aziz in editing the Hilal *Osmani*
and *Hak Yallu* Newspapers. It it said that he met Zafar Ali Khan, editor
of the *Zamindar*, at Constantinople during the Balkan War and received
introductions from him to India, which ultimately resulted in his appointment.

[30]Home Political A proceedings No. 46, dated May 1914.

[31]Ibid. *See appendix* E for translation.

promoters had no intention of adopting or limiting themselves to such objects nor of relinquishing the original aim of the society which was to maintain the respect and honour of the *Kaaba*.

The Government had received only one report regarding this society's work in villages. In this case a preacher who was touring in Lahore district was alleged to have openly stated that the infidels (Christians) were threatening to capture and demolish the holy places of Islam, and for this reason villagers should join the *Anjuman*.[32]

It is interesting to note that the society did not preach to men alone, but to women also. Under the rules Muslims of either sex were eligible for membership, and both in launching and pushing their scheme, the promoters did not neglect the idea to appeal to women. In Delhi the society organised a number of meetings for women but even then, on the whole[33] by September 1914 it had not made much progress. The Government agreed with the view expressed by its inner promoters that it wanted to have a direct influence on the politics of India. Moderate minded Muslims took fright at the blind oath which they had originally taken and became sceptical as to the motives of its originators. Money was not forthcoming in sufficient quantity but the society had now decided to carry on its work of establishing a secret and political organisation for the Muslims.[34]

The society throughout had remained anxious to get Government recognition[35] or some sort of official patronage but without success. The Government was convinced that

---

[32]Ibid.

[33]Ibid.

[34]Hon'ble Mr. R. Burn, Chief Secretary to Govt. United Provinces to the Secy. to the Govt. of India, Home Dept. Dept. dt. Nainital, the 17th September, 1913, Home Political A Proceedings No. 118 dt. October 1913.

[35]This may point to inherent weakness or to the desire to get the better of the Hindus.

it had 'dangerous capabilities[36], and refused to give it any recognition or advertisement[37]. Some Government officials however advocated that a society like this needed direction because its leading exponents were favourably disposed towards British rule. This view was very strongly asserted by Mr. S.A. Imam a Muslim civil servant in the following words: —

"*This society is based upon one of the deepest sentiments of Islam.* The protection of the Harmain Sharifain is regarded by the Faithful as a religious duty and has an abiding place in almost the very essentials of their creed. The appearance of Italian men-of-war in the Red Sea has brought home to the Muhammadans of India the probability of non-Moslem control of the sacred places of Arabia in the event of a collapse and disintegration of the Turkish Empire. It is not probable, therefore, that the Khuddam-i-Kaaba movement will die out, nor is it possible for us to check its growth without departing from our traditional policy of non-interference with the religious notions of Indians. At the same time it will be unwise to ignore the dangerous potentialities that are inseparable from a society that is based upon a militant spirit that must animate its Khuddams. An attitude of indifference does not commend itself to me. The movement is young and at its very inception. This is a stage at which it is possible to direct it. Maulvi Abdul Bari, to the best of my information is honest and well-disposed towards British rule. I have felt for some time that it is possible through him to introduce into the constitution of the society such safeguards as may protect the movement from degenerating into a secret society hostile to us. The personal equation counts for a great deal in such matters, and I, for one, do not feel hopeless of giving the right direction to the movement by securing the good offices of the Maulvi".[38]

---

[36]Home Political A Proceedings Nos. 33-8 dated November 1914.

[37]Home Political (Deposit) Proceeding No. 7 dated July 1913. *See also* Home Political Proceeding No. 19 (Deposit) dated May. 1914.

[38]Note dated 26.3.1914 Home Political A Proceeding No. 46 dt. April 1914

But the Government countered this criticism in the following words:

"The efforts of the various communities are being directed to start organisations under the cloak of religion, with ostensible objects which appear on the surface to be unexceptional and in which, owing to this vague religious cloak, active Government interference is not to be expected.

"Their great desire is to secure some kind of Government benediction in the hope of this being a protection against inquisitive police. It is only natural that they should do this.

"Sir Ali Imam recognizes potentialities of mischief in the movement, and dwells upon the importance of controlling it for good through its head Maulvi Abdul Bari. Now, it may be quite correct that Maulvi Abdul Bari's loyalty is assured, but that *does not mean that this movement of young men should not be regarded with great caution.* Munshi Ram's personal loyalty may be quite firm, but that does not connote that the whole of the Hardwar *Gurukul* is to be trusted. Dr. Rash Bihari Ghose was at the head of the so-called National University but the examination papers set by that body to the National High School at Amraoti were examination papers in sedition. Sooner or later Abdul Bari will either be led astray by the young men, or he will sever his connection with the movement. The idea that these enthusiasts will be able to supplement Turkey's warchest, take effective action for the protection of holy places in Arabia, and build and run a line of steamers for pilgrim traffic is too absurd for serious consideration. They must either collapse altogether, or keep themselves going by religious agitation on local events which will at once assume a political tinge; and they will speedily take to secret methods, secret preaching and so forth, and no amount of encouraging or guiding by Abdul Bari can effect the question".[39]

On 20 March, 1914 the Director, Criminal Intelligence corroborating the views of Government remarked:

---

[39]Note by Lord Hardinge dated 31.3.1914. Home Political A Proceeding No. 46 dt. April 1914.

"My own individual opinion is that the present leaders of the party, of which this society is intended to be a powerful weapon, aim at their own personal interests first and those of their own way of thinking in the matters of religion and politics next. I also think they are careless of the excitement and dangers into which the pursuit of their own ambition may lead the country or sections of the public. I therefore look upon the society as dangerous and I, personally, find it impossible to believe that the founders and organisers do not intend it to be dangerous. *It is aggressive and not pacific*, and other Indian communities as well as the British Government are likely to feel its aggressiveness in an unpleasant manner. From the point of view of the enthusiast of the society it is at least a weapon of justifiable retaliation. The society will no doubt pass through various states. Just at present the leaders are anxious to appear before Government in lamb's wool but in my opinion the disguise is ill-concealed. In any case the society is necessarily an object for study at the hands of the Provincial and Imperial Criminal Investigation Department and that this should be the case for a Moslem organisation in India is regretted by nobody more than by myself".[40]

The *Anjuman-i-Khuddam-i-Kaaba* remained lifeless from 1914 to 1917 but in 1918 Maulana Abdul Bari of Lucknow, President of the Society, published a leaflet which aimed at the resuscitation of the *Kaaba*.[41] The Government had intercepted this leaflet in the post and it was addressed to one Syed Muhammad Mahmud in Washington. It is reproduced below :—

> "*Translation of an Urdu leaflet*[42] (*printed at the Ashul Matafa, Lucknow) written by Maulana Abdul Bari of the Anjuman-i-Khuddam-i-Kaaba Society and addressed to Syed Muhammed Mahamud, University Station, Washington, U.S.A., Box 123.*"

---

[40]Note by Mr. C.R. Cleveland dated 20th March 1914. Home Political A Proceeding No. 46 dated April 1914.

[41]Note by C.R. Cleveland, dated 29/4/1918. Home Political (Deposit) Proceeding No. 12 dated February, 1918.

[42]Ibid , pp. 3-4.

Please have it distributed 786 (In the name of God,
among members.   to most Compassionate
  Sd/Abdul Bari   and Merciful)

My respected one, may His greatness be everlasting!
"Salutation to you. The rapidity with which time has
changed its side, and the swiftness with which it has
presented its events before us, has no other example of
its nature in the pages of history. Hence agitation in the
thought of men of views and wisdom, or uneasiness in
their movements are not surprising. Time must have
its effect on the people. We ourselves admit of our
uneasy conditions (of mind) and perturbed thoughts.
But we think that every deep thinker should have the
same state (of mind), because the results of causes and
exceptions are so very similar that no opinion can be
formed definitely. The establishment of the *Jamiate
Khuddam-i-Kaaba*, the suspension of its activities and now
the movement of resuming its work again are the effects
of all these changes.

"We had information from a reliable source that Russia
and the Kings of her views had intention to lay their
hands on the honour of the Musalmans and the prestige of
Islam, and that they wanted that independent government
be wiped out from the Islamic world, the Islamic Caliphate
be allowed to remain nominally and that the holy places be
placed under the influence of non-Muslims. After these infor-
mations, we thought that serving the two sacred places
(Mecca and Medina) and the protection of the holy places
were not the share of any particular nation. All the Musalmans were responsible for them, and hence we too should be
prepared for that. Accordingly, the *Jamiate Khuddam-i-Kaaba*
was started after due consultation, discussion and
deliberation.

"This movement was started after clear announcement
and we refrained from adopting any intriguing or secret
working. But, as we opposed some of their secret designs,
our organisation was dubbed as something very big. Before
the present war, I had discussions with some responsible

officials of the Government or this subject, and we were
forbidden to send money without permission of the Government. We agreed to do so or the condition that, if our
holy places remain in their present condition under the
control of the *Khalifatul Muslemin* (Caliph of the Muslims)
Amirul Mumerin (Commander of the faithful) His Majesty
the Sultan, may his kingdom be everlasting, then we shall
have no objection to enter into any treaty. Accordingly
it was promised to us and His Excellency the Governor
General made it clear in his reply to the Delhi deputation.
We became satisfied, acted fully according to the treaty,
and did not send any amount to the Government Islamia
from the *Jamiate Khuddami Kaaba*, and brought the office to
Lucknow and locked it up. We did not take any
notice of the internment of the *Motamid* of the
Jamiate, and gave up collecting subscription as it was
objectionable to send it, and it was difficult to keep it
deposited with us, and hence it was better that the Musalmans should keep their money with themselves. During this
period the *Jamiate* became a forgotten thing. But now and
then it continued to be mentioned in the history of the war
in connection with the report of the Commission through
European newspapers and we published writing's (in reply)
as suited the occasion. Now, owing to the change of events,
we have decided after (due) consultation (with one another)
that the management of the *Jamiate* be organised and it
should be reconstituted, and that a *Motamid* be
appointed to act for Shaikh Shaukat Ali and another
for Shaikh Mushir Hussain for the present, and that
all the braches be again made ready (for action) with
a view that, if it be necessary, to protect
the holy places, our organisation be fit for complete
action. For the present its work should be to give
attention to the internment of our Secretary, and the
other members of the *Jamiate* who are also interned, and
the *Jamiate* should sympathise with them in consideration
of the causes for which they are interned, and the subscriptions which are paid by the members of the *Jamiate*
should be taken and spent only with a view to help the
internees in general and the Secretary in particular.

I hope that anybody, whether he is a member of the Head *Jamiate* or any of its branches, would inform me by the *9th of Rabi-us-Sani 1336*, if he disagrees with the above decisions, otherwise it will be considered that he is in favour of it. It is also hoped that all the servants of the *Jamiate* would inform me with their views as soon as possible. The *Jamiate* will commence work after the 9th of *Rabi-us-Sani 1336 H.* It is also proposed that the office of the Head *Jamiate* should be opened temporarily at Lucknow.

The finish. Salutation.

Faqir Mohamed Qayamuddin Abdul Bari the Servant of the Servants of the *Jamiate asliah* (head) from Feringhi Mahal, Lucknow".

The Government of India strongly objected[43] to the reasons given by Abdul Bari for reviv ng the society's activities at this time. It also intercepted in the Aden post a letter from the Secretary of the Delhi Branch addressed to a Muslim soldier of the Indian Army calling upon him to collect subscription's for the current year, to send on any money he had already collected for the past year and to enrol new members. It was not certain that this effort on the part of the Delhi Secretary was the direct outcome of the decision to revive the society at Lucknow but the two matters were probably inter connected.[44] The interception of the Delhi letter, however, showed clearly that some Muslim soldiers of the Indian Army were members of the society and the Government therefore rightly decided to advise the military authorities to take suitable action against such soldiers who remained members of the society. This was done and the *Anjuman* there after completely collapsed. This is corroborated by the fact that Government's post-1918 records upto 1947 find no mention about it.

---

[43]C.R. Cleveland, Criminal Intelligence Office No. 022 dated Delhi the 29th January 1918 to Hon'ble Mr. S.P. O'Donnell I.C.S., Chief Secretary to the Government of the United Provinces, Allahabad.

[44]Ibid, para 3.

6

Lucknow Shia-Sunni Controversy

The Shias who are very numerous and influential in Lucknow held that the three *Khalifas* who immediately succeeded the Prophet and who were succeeded by Ali, were usurpers, that they were guilty of acts of tyranny and oppression against Ali and his wife Fatima, who was the daughter of the Prophet, and that the result of their policy was the terrible tragedy at Karbala when Hussain, a son of Ali and his family members where massacred.[1] This massacre is mourned at the period of *Muharram*.[2] The Sunnis on the other hand regard the first three *Khalifas* as rightful rulers, and hold them in profound respect and regard them as men of great honesty, virtue and courage.[3]

---

[1]Government of India Note dated 4.5.1939. Home Political F. No. 5/6/39 of 1939, para 1.

[2]In Northern India the Muharram is celebrated as a tragedy and in the Deccan as a Comedy. With the exception of the Wahabees all sects of Muslims revere tombs of saints and ancestors. The state of religious animosity between the Sunnis and the Shias and between the Sunnis, and the Traditionists or Non-Conformists of Muslim Church is well known. Muharram riots took place at Bombay, Lucknow and other places. The Mosque is often the scene of sectarian dissentions leading to litigation. *See also* Home Political B Proceeding No. 85 dated September 1912.

[3]Government of India Note dated 4,5,1939, Home Political F. No. 5/6/39 of 1939, para 1.

About the year 1906 disputes arose in Lucknow between the Sunnis and Shias about the celebration of *Muharram*, and the Sunnis began to recite verses in praise of the first four *Khalifas* whom they described as friends and comrades of each other and of the Prophet. These are the recitations which have now crystallised into what is known as the *Madhe Sahaba* or praise of the Companions. The Shias retaliated by employing the *Tabarra*, that is, curses on the first three *Khalifas* for their inhuman treatment of the descendants of the Prophet, and the praise of Firoz who had killed one of the three *Khalifas*.[4]

As a result of these demonstrations serious rioting took place between Sunnis and Shias in Lucknow in 1907 and 1908, and the Government appointed a committee under the chairmanship of Mr. Justice Piggott, a High Court Judge to investigate into the Shia-Sunni controversy. Next year, on the 7 January 1909, the Government issued a Resolution[5] on the basis of the evidence afforded by the report of the Piggott Committee. This resolution asserted the impossibility of restoring the *status quo ante* the separation of the *karbalas* in March 1906, and declared the policy of the Government to be that of the minimum of interference consistent with the maintenance of peace and with the prospect of reconciliation in the future. In pursuance of this policy the resolution sanctioned certain rules for the observance of the *Ashra*, *Chehlum* and *21st Ramzan*, which were accepted without controversy.[6]

Paragraph 10 of the resolution, which prohibited the recitation of *charyari* verses on these days was unsatisfactory to Shias and obnoxious to Sunnis and differentiated in between the essential features of the rival claims. The whole of the controversy centred round it, and the history of subsequent events is one of reiterated complaint and repeated agitation on the part of the Sunnis demanding its alteration. The two Shia members of the Piggott Committee contended in their minority

---

[4]Ibid, para 2.

[5]Government Resolution No. 14/III-591 dated 7th January, 1909.

[6]Home Political B Proceeding No. 67 dated August, 1911.

report that their grievance was that this rule should be extended to the whole period from the 28th of *Zilhij* to the 8th of *Rabi-ul-awwal*. But the Shias as a body saw no reason to be dissatisfied with the resolution of 1909. They received it with gratification and their subsequent actions on the whole were directed towards conciliation. It was otherwise with the Sunnis, who contended that this paragraph amounted to an arbitrary restraint on the part of the Government on their religious liberties, and as such was a violation of the Government's accepted policy of neutrality.[7]

The promulgation of the resolution was followed by the adoption on the part of the Sunni community of an attitude of "sullen discontent."[8] By the advice of their maulvis they took little or no part in the *Ashra* ceremony of that year, both as a protest against the regulating orders issued by the district superintendent of police on the basis of the resolution and as an argument for its reconsideration by the Government. The situation at this time is explained in Mr. Radice's remarks to the Commissioner of the Lucknow Division, in which he points out that the Shias, for whom the resolution of 7 January 1909 was a virtual triumph, had adopted at the inspiration of their *mujtahids* an attitude of studied abstention from expressions of jubilation calculated to provoke the other party. As regards the Sunnis Mr. Radice was of opinion that the future rested very much in the hands of Maulvis and the opinion they might have of their power over the people. He also said: "This class is enlightened and reasonable and holds aloof from what they consider corruptions of a pure religion and have always discountenanced Muharram celebrations," and added that "they will not hesitate to follow the people if the people will not follow them".[9]

It is clear that amongst the Sunnis the worse counsels prevailed, for on the *Chehlum* day, 13 March, a large Sunni procession started for the *karbala*, and *charyari* verses were sung

---

[7].Sunni Memorial dated 24th December 1908, para 8.
[8]Report, Lucknow No. 6 of 5th February, 1909.
[9]Mr. Radice's letter to the Commissioner of the Lucknow Division dated 12th February 1909.

in such a manner as to show a deliberate intention to challenge the orders that were issued.[10]   The police interfered and very skilfully arrested without violence the whole procession numbering nearly 1,000 persons, against whom criminal proceedings were subsequently taken.[11]   Of these, twenty-three comprising the ringleaders for the most part were convicted by the city magistrate on 29 March and sentenced to three months' rigorous imprisonment, the legality of the conviction being subsequently upheld in the Judicial Commissioner's Court. On the same day seven others were convicted. Fifty more were subsequently convicted on 3 May, 141 on 10 May, and 161 on 24 May: sentences varying from three months' rigorous imprisonment to a fine of Rs. 5 being passed.[12] After this salutary vindication of the authority of the law, at the instance of Mr. Radice, who advocated the wisdom of an act of grace in consummation of an act of justice, the Government decided to exercise its powers[13] and substituted fines varying from Rs. 25 to Rs. 5 for sentences of rigorous imprit onment or unexpired portions of such sentences with imprisonment in default of payment.

The situation at Lucknow at the end of March and the beginning of April was a source of much anxiety to the authorities.   The animosities of both parties had been stirred by the events of 13 March and it needed only a spark to kindle a conflagration.   On the Sunni side disaffection seems to have been accentuated by a misconception, deliberate or otherwise, of the meaning of the orders contained in paragraph 10 of the draft appended to the resolution, and it was persistently asserted that the Government had prohibited all praises of the Caliphs absolutely and at all times.[14] With the object of dispelling this erroneous idea Mr. Radice issued a manifesto

---

[10]Extract from Sir John Hewett's speech in Council dated 3rd April 1909.

[11]Under Section 143 (read with Section 188) of the Indian Penal Code.

[12]Proceedings Judicial Commissioner's Court No. 55 of 1909, criminal application register.

[13]Under section 402 of the Cose of Criminal Procedure; 1898.

[14]Demi-official letter from Commissioner, Lucknow Division dated the 23rd March, 1909.

on 26 March in which he explained in a manner to remove all doubt the nature and scope of the provisions of that paragraph.[15] The effect of this explanation was to cut the ground away from the ignorance of the masses or the duplicity of their leaders. The activities of disaffection were still further quelled by the warning contained in the salutary punishment of the participants in the procession of 13 March, followed by the reasonable application of the principle of grace. Moreover the action of the Sunnis formed the subject of the severe criticisms of the Lieutenant Governor in his speech made at the United Provinces Council meeting of 3 April 1909. His Honour, after reviewing the reasoned and impartial considerations which had prompted the resolution of 1909 and the adoption of paragraph 10 of the draft appended thereto commented on the refusal of the Sunnis to take out their *tazias* on the *Ashra* day and condemned the spirit and practice of the *Chehlum* procession of 13 March, which could only be regarded as a challenge. His Honour regretted also that rumours had reached him of proposed retaliation by the Shias, in which however they were anticipated by the action of the police and subsequently restrained by their good sense. He ended by appealing to the better feeling of both parties to merge their petty animosities in the reconciliation which time and wisdom would effect.[16]

The Lieutenant Governor's comments became known in Lucknow on 6 April and combined with Mr. Radice's explanation and the exemplary treatment of the demonstrators of 13 March (involving as it did their temporary incarceration and enforced inactivity) in allaying the forces of disorder.[17]

In the ensuing hot weather the Sunni leaders appear to have debated among themselves a means of evading the provisions of paragraph 10 of the rules appended to the resolution,

---

[15]Paragraph 7, Sunni Memorial dated December 1910.

[16]Extract from Sir John Hewett's speech made at the United Province Council meeting of 3rd April 1909.

[17]Demi-official letter from Commissioner, Lucknow Division dated the 6th April 1909.

and it was agreed in consultation between Sunni leaders of standing and Maulana Abul Khair of Ghazipur, who had come to Lucknow with the idea of effecting a settlement by mediation that no permanent solution of the differences existing between the two communities was possible until the Sunnis were allowed to carry out a separate *Ashra* ceremony accompanied by *Charyari* recitations.[18] The disaffection of the masses was accordingly directed through the secret propaganda of the maulvis to this end: and Maulana Abul Khair was granted an interview by Sir John Hewett at Benares in November, in which however His Honour positively declined to consider the new proposal as being altogether inconsistent with paragraphs 9 and 10 of the draft appended to the resolution.[19]

This further failure left the Sunnis in a very truculent frame of mind, and although the *Muharram* celebrations of 1910 passed off without any actual breach of the peace, the Deputy Commissioner reported that feeling was as strong as ever, and that peace was only kept by the police.[20] Evident indications of this are to be found both in the attempt of the Sunnis at Bara Banki to get permission to recite *charyari handas* in Lucknow on 23 January, on the ground that the 22nd and not the 23rd was the *Ashra* day for Shias, and in the numerous Sunni gatherings which met together in private houses in the convenient proximity of Shia meetings to indulge in vociferous *charyari* recitation.[21]

In the following April however the futility of resistance and the advantages of compromise appeared to have weighed in the counsels of the respective parties. A movement for conciliation was started, which, in spite of Sunni opposition at first, appears to have met with support from both sides. A notice was issued by Saiyid Shahanshah Hussain and the Hon'-ble Mr. Muhammad Nasim announcing the formation of an association called *Anjuman-e-ittihad* directed towards concilia-

---

[18]Lucknow No. 39 dated 25th September 1909.

[19]Ibid.

[20]Fortnightly demi-officials from Commissioner, Lucknow Division dated the 11th and 26th January 1910.

[21]Ibid, dated 8th and 22nd March, 1910.

tion, and inviting the respective parties, the Sunnis to a *milad sharif* and the Shias to a *majlis*, at which their respective *alims* would preside.[22] The *milad sharif* was held in the great hall of the Husainabad Imambara on 17 April, and the *majlis* in the same place on the following day. The account of the procedings pictures on both occasions a representative and enthusiastic gathering of both parties, numbering some 10,000 people, who listened with emotional attention to the exhortations to union enjoined by leading Muslims on all true followers of the Prophet. It can scarcely be doubted that some significance attaches to these events as indicating more conciliatory counsels on the part of the respective communities.[23] It is noteworthy however that the Commissioner places the number at 6,000 of whom only 200 were Sunnis; and that a Sunni *alim* was not forthcoming to recite *milad sharif* at the meeting of the 17 April—a fact which brings into question the disposition of the Sunnis; and that no great results were obtained from these meetings is proved by the renewal of discord in the following July.[24]

Apparently a Hindu Pandit Jagat Prasad was constituted arbitrator, and the arguments submitted before him on behalf of the conflicting parties were published in a pamphlet entitled the *Karrawai mubahisa Shia wa Sunni* and distributed throughout Lucknow on 2 July. The controversy as recorded in the pamphlet ranged mainly between Maulvi Abdus Shakur (Sunni) and Muhammad Sajjad (Shia), and the former seeks to prove that Shias having altered the Koran, or rather having failed to abide by its teachings, have thereby forfeited their claims to be considered Muslims at all.[25]

The publication of this pamphlet was followed a few days later by a Sunni demonstration. A congregation of about a

---

[22]Fortnightly demi-officials from Commissioner, Lucknow Division dated the 19th April 1910.

[23]Account undated of proceedings of April 17-8, 1910.

[24]Fortnightly demi-official from Commissioner, Lucknow Division dated the 19th April, 1910.

[25]Lucknow No. 32 of 6th August, 1910.

thousand people assembled on the *Shahmina Maidan* and
emphasized their dissociation from their Shia coreligionists by
vociferous *milad* and *charyari* recitations.[26] Pursuing their
policy of ill-concealed hostility to the resolution of 7 January,
1909, the Sunnis in the following December presented a memorial through the Deputy Commissioner of Lucknow petitioning
for a reconsideration of the orders contained in it.[27] The
memorial was signed by a large number of persons of little
individual importance and made three principal representations
as the cause and excuse of the prayer for remedial action:-

first, that the inferior social position of the Sunnis as
compared with the Shias had prejudiced their representation
on the Piggott Committee.[28]

second, that paragraph 10 of the notice appended to the
resolution (prohibiting *charyari* recitations on the *Ashra*, *Chehlum*
and *21st Ramzan*) is logically and actually a violation of the
Government's accepted principle of religious neutrality.[29]

third, that the encouragement extended to the Shias had
produced an exultation on their part offensive to the Sunnis
and taking the form of such acts of insolence and provocation
as the exclusion of the Sunnis from the *Tal Katora Karbala*, the
celebration of *Bazm Firoze* and the repetition of the *bila fasl*
formula.[30]

The first of these grievances is discountenanced by the
facts disclosed in paragraph 1 of the resolution of 7 January,
1909, and the third, based on the bare assertion of the memo-
rialists and unsupported by any evidence is dealt with by the
Deputy Commissioner of Lucknow in his letters to the
Commissioner of 8 and 17 December 1910.   Paragraph

---

[26]Ibid.

[27]Letter from Mr. Abdul Aziz dated the 5th December 1910, letter No. 1316
    dated 8th December 1910 from the Deputy Commissioner of Lucknow to
    the Commissioner Lucknow Division.

[28]Ibid, paragraphs 1, 6.

[29]Ibid, paragraphs, 3, 8, 9.

[30]Ibid, paragraphs 11, 12, 13, 14.

11 of the memorial alleges that Sunnis have been excluded by restrictions framed by the authorities in concert with Shias from the practical use of the *Tal Katora Karbala*; but Mr. Way showed that the allegation was unfounded, as no orders had been passed by the local Government or the district authorities which were possibly susceptible of such interpretation.[31]

Paragraph 13 states that "to annoy the Sunnis the Shias have recently taken to celebrate *Bazm Firozi* in honour of one Firoz Abul Lulu, who had never been recognized by them even as a religious head or hero, but was the murderer of Omar, the second *Caliph*".[32] This question had been raised before Mr. Piggott's committee, and the evidence then given went to show that *Bazm-i-Firoze* celebrations had been started by the Shias as a counter-move against the *Bazm-i-Siddiqi*, *Bazm-i-Faruqi*, and *Bazm-i-Usmani* celebration of the Sunnis in honour of Abu Bakr, Omar and Usman respectively.[33] The committee had to consider not so much the question of the existence of such meetings, which were for the most part conducted in private, as the matter of their offensive advertisement in a manner calculated to wound religious feelings, and it was agreed that the subject was one which had been and might well be left successfully to the operation of the criminal law.[34] Mr. Way took the same view, adding that no occasion had arisen for the issue of any special orders in regard to these practices.

As regards the *bila fasl* fromula, which contains in the words "*khalifatuhua bila fasl*" [he is the (Prophets) *khalifa* without any one intervening] the Shia credo in the direct succession of Ali, the son-in-law of the Prophet, the report of the Piggott Committee remarks that "the words in themselves are a mere assertion of the Shia faith that Ali was the rightful and immediate successor of Muhammad; but they contain no such imprecation on those holding an opposite belief as has justified

---

[31]*See also* letter of 15th December 1910 from Commissioner Lucknow Division to the Chief Secretary.

[32]Ibid.

[33]Letter from Deputy Commissioner Lucknow to Commissioner Lucknow Division dated the 17th December, 1910.

[34]Committee's report, paragraph 22.

the suppression of the public utterance of the Shia *tabarra*. We must refer the parties to the terms of section 298 of the Indian Penal Code. We are not prepared to lay it down that the utterance of the words, '*bila fasl*' even in public is in itself necessarily and presumably an offence, any more than the public assertion by a Christian preacher of the doctrine of the Trinity. Either might be an offence under particular circumstances, if uttered with the deliberate intention of wounding the religious feelings of any person, or the facts were such that the speaker's conduct was not covered by any of the general exceptions to the Indian Penal Code".[35] Mr. Way dismissed the matter by showing that there was no ground for the assertion that the public use of the formula had increased and no need of any further orders on the subject.

In the second representation is contained the *fons et origo* of the whole controversy. The Sunni argument is supported by *istiftas* of Sunni *ulamas* declaring it to be the religious duty and positive obligation of devout Sunnis first to recite the praises of Abu Bakr, Omar and Usman before proceeding to commemorate the martyrdom of Hussain and the incidents of Karbala.[36] On this assumption they contend that the prohibition of *charyari* recitations on the three principal days of the *Muharram* amounts to the prohibition of the *Muharram* itself and is therefore an infringement by the Government of the religious liberties of Sunnis.[37]

The situation in Lucknow in the middle of December 1910 was full of elements of anxiety.[38] A Sunni maulvi of the Farangi Mahal by name Abdul Mughni issued in the form of

---

[35]Ibid, paragraph 20.

[36]Ibid, paragraph 10.

[37]The answer to this contention is contained in paragraph 5 of a letter from the Commissioner of the Lucknow Division to the Chief Secretary dated the 15th December 1910 and in paragraph 11 of the resolution of the 7th January 1909; it speaks for itself and needs no comment. The Government accordingly refused to reopen the question and an official intimation to this effect was sent through the Commissioner of the Lucknow Division dated December 30, 1910.

[38]Lucknow No. 51 dated 17th December 1910.

a pamphlet.[39] a collection of *fatwas* attested by Sunni *ulamas,* which declare it to be incumbent on all devout Sunnis first to recite the praises of the first three Caliphs before taking part in the commemoration of Husain.[40]   This statement of the religious duty of the Sunnis is based mainly on the authority of the *Jame-ur-rumuz,* in which it is written "*At the moment one intends to recite the murder of Hussain it is proper to recite first the murder of the first three Caliphs, so that there may not be similitude with the dissenters*".[41]

These *fatwas* are the same as, or similar in character to, the *istiftas* mentioned in the Sunni petition[42] and their public circulation was regarded by the Deputy Commissioner as an indication of renewed intentions on the part of the Sunni maulvis to promotethe exacerbation of the masses. All possible precautions were accordingly taken to prevent disturbances at the approaching *Muharram.*[43]   Mr. Way interviewed two of the authors of the provocative *fatwas,* and at his suggestion they published a further *fatwa* declaring it to be unlawful to oppose the orders of the Government.[44]   The dispositions of the police were made with the fullest care on the lines laid down in the notice appended to the resolution ef 7 January, 1909.[45]   Thanks to these precautions the first day of the Muharram (10 January) passed off quietly, and on 14 January Mr. Saunders writes: "Tazias were taken out by Sunnis, but Way reports that many of them understanding their maulvis to have prohibited *tazias* made very small ones and concealed them under their clothes. He thinks the opposition is now only kept alive by a few interested maulvis".[46]   The report does not indicate the motive of the

---

[39]Entitled *Fatwa-i-wajib-ul-mal.*

[40]Collection of *Fatwas* forwarded by Commissioner.

[41]*Raw a fiz* i.e. Shias.

[42]Paragraph 10.

[43]Letter from Commissioner Lucknow Division dated the 4th January 1911.

[44]Lucknow No. 1 of 7th January 1911.

[45]Letter from .Commissioner, Lucknow Division to Under Secretary, dated the 14th January 1911.

[46]Letter from Commissioner, Lucknow Division to Chief Secretary, dated the 14th January 1911.

maulvis in prohibiting the carrying of *tazias*, but in the absence of evidence to the contrary it seems clear that their action disclosed a desire to pursue the same policy of sullen resistance which greeted the promulgation of the resolution of January 1909.

Indeed this is evident from the subsequent course of events. Although the *Chehlum* (February 20) passed off quietly without demonstration, a report was spread, inspired apparently from Sunni sources, that the Shias were going to recite *tabarra*, or the denunciation of the first three *Caliphs* petitions for minor concessions were made to Mr. Way; and His Honour refused an interview to Maulvi Abdul Bari of the Farangi Mahal.[47]

A final unpleasantness occurred on 28 February, the date which in 1911 marked the double anniversary of the deaths of the Prophet and Imam Hasan. The Shias take out on this day a *tabut* or funeral procession, which is recognized as being for Imam Hasan. This year it was announced to be for the Prophet. The Sunnis resented this, and after a conference had been held the *tabut* was taken out without any declaration as to whose it was. There was no disturbance. The bearings of this incident are somewhat obscure, but it may be attributed with certainty to the continued existence of the friction between the two communities.[48]

The controversy remained in abeyance until 1935 when on the day of *Chehlum* some Sunnis defied the order and recited the *Madhe Sahaba*. In 1936 a much stronger and more troublesome Sunni movement developed and attempts were made to take out processions. This state of things continued for more than three months and a considerable number of arrests were made. In the meantime, in an effort for an amicable settlement, the Sunnis called off their movement and those who were in prison

---

[47] Extract from fortnightly demi-official letter of Commissioner, Lucknow Division dated the 21st February, 1911.

[48] Demi-official letter from Commissioner, Lucknow Division dated the 7th March, 1911.

were released. The expected amicable settlement having proved a failure, the Government appointed the Allsop Committee, the general effect of whose report was that, while reasserting the theoretical right of the Sunnis to recite the Madhe Sahaba, in the circumstances that existed in Lucknow it was a provocative action and should not be allowed.[49]

Eventually, on 18 March 1938, the Government published the Allsop Committee's report and stood by it. The Sunnis were dissatisfied with this decision and were continually bringing pressure to bear on the Government to allow the recitation of the *Madhe Sahaba* under threat of civil disobedience movement. This, however, started about the beginning of March 1939 and met with a very considerable and growing degree of support. Large numbers of Lucknow Sunnis were arrested and *jathas* were organised from many other districts. The Sunni agitation was encouraged by the knowledge that the Government was in favour of making a concession to them, and the district authorities felt that they were fighting a losing battle which would end in the granting of the Sunni claims after the agitation had got out of control. They, therefore, pressed for some definite decision of policy. The Governor accordingly raised the question at a meeting of the Council of Ministers on 22 March 1939, when it became clear that the Ministers were considering a concession to the Sunni demand and held themselves committed to giving the Sunnis an opportunity to recite the *Madhe Sahaba* publicly some time during 1939. The upshot of this decision and further negotiations with Sunnis was the issue of a communique by the Government stating that the Sunnis will, in any circumstances, be given the opportunity of reciting the *Madhe Sahaba* at a public meeting and in a procession every on the *Barawafat* day, subject to the condition that the time, place and route thereof shall be fixed by the district authorities. The communique was issued in some haste, and the intention which had previously been expressed that the Shias would be informed beforehand of what was intended, was not carried out.[50]

---

[49]Note by J.W. Ewart dated 4.5.1939 on Shia-Sunni controversy, para 3.
[50]Ibid, para 4.

The result of the communique was that within a year or two, the Sunnis called off the civil disobedience movement, but the effect on the Shias was far greater than had been anticipated. It appeared to have been an overwhelming blow to them. Their view was that they had the authority of two separate committees and the practice of 30 years in support of their position. They had also been recently ingrating themselves with the Congress in order to make their position stronger. The sanction of the *Madhe Sahaba* had set up among the Shias conditions of intense emotional hysteria. It was particularly strong among the women. Civil disobedience was at once started and very large numbers of Shias, including many members of the most respectable families of standing, had already gone to jail. It was reported that if the *Madhe Sahaba* was actually recited, purdah ladies of high families will come out into the streets, recite the *Tabarra* and go to jail. Shias from and outside Lucknow and even from outside the Province seemed to be seriously disturbed.[51]

It is difficult to know exactly how far politics had played a part in this accentuation of the *Madhe Sahaba* controversy, but there is no doubt that the trouble, to begin with at any rate, was in fact encouraged by the Congress in order to split the Muslims. It must also be remembered that the Congress Muslims were mainly Sunnis and that this agitation was greatly encouraged particularly by the *Ahrars* who were under the influence of the Congress. It is well known that Maulana Hussain Ahmad Madni, who had been a leading figure in the movement for a long time, was in the pay of the Congress, but it is difficult to believe that it was unable to control him.

While the Sunnis agitation was going on, the Shias took great pains to conciliate the Congress and the Muslim political movement on the whole apparently weakened.[52] The effect of the orders in the past about the *Madhe Sahaba* was to swing over Shia opinion in the most violent way against the Congress. The Shias felt that they had been betrayed and that a gross injustice had been perpetrated on them. At the same time, the Sunnis,

---

[51]Ibid.

[52]Ibid, para 5.

other than Congress Sunnis, did not appear to be the least grateful to the Congress and there were even traces of a feeling that the whole matter had gone too far and that something ought to be done on the part of the Sunnis to waive their rights in view of the tremendous strength of opinion shown by the Shias.[53] The Government felt petrturbed as a result of their orders about the *Madhe Sahaba* and wanted to relax the tension but no definite solution appeared within sight.

---

[53]Ibid.

7

Tanzim and Tabligh Movements

It is well known that with the passing away of the Turkish Caliphate and the expulsion of the Caliph from Turkey, much ground was out from under the feet of the Muslim agitators, who had hitherto utilized their pro-Turkish sympathies in exciting the Muslim masses to anti-British feelings and in characterizing all actions of Government in relation to Turkey as interference with religion. The absence of any sympathetic response from the Angora Government in answer to their appeals in favour of a Turkish *Khalifah* demoralised the organizers and promoters of the *Khilafat* Movement in India, who were further discredited on account of exposure in connection with the misplaced trust and misadventure, despite good intentions on the part of the Muslim leaders, of Khilafat funds while in the custody of the Central *Khilafat* Committee, but invested in the Hindu mills. The whole of the money was lost. New ways and means were, therefore, called for to reassure the public and to enlist its aid and sympathy. With this end in view, Dr. Kitchlew, a prominent member of the Central Khilafat Committee, issued, in May 1923, a long memorandum pointing out the necessity of readjusting the "national programme" because the unsettled state of affairs with regard to the

Khilafat had resulted in a setback; and he suggested that a
"new and more dynamic programme" embracing the whole
phase of the life of the community should be considered jointly
by the *Jamiat-ul-Ulema* and the Central *Khilafat* Committee
so as to enable the community to take its proper place in the
country and in the struggle for Swaraj.[1] The proposals outlined
included *inter-alia* organisation of Muslim *jathas* (volunteer
corps) under the control of a permanent committee which
would also be in charge of the Central organisation. The
scheme was formally laid before a meeting of the Central
Khilafat Committee held at Delhi on 24 and 25 June 1924: and
in explaining it Kitchlew urged the need for the establishment
of an *independent* Muslim organisation, firstly because the
Muslim leaders had become hardened to protect their interests,
and secondly because the Hindus and Sikhs were perfecting
their own organisations.[2] It was therefore necessary for the
Muslims not only to organise Muslim *jathas*, but also to open
their own primary schools in mosques, prepare textbooks for
schools, issue *Khutbahs* (sermons) to be read in mosques, etc.,
enforce punctuality in prayers, establish technical and commercial colleges, supervise *Waqfs*, collect *Zakah*, arrange for
relief of widows and orphans, and start Muslim cooperative
societies and banks. Some of the '*Ulema*', however who were
present took exception as they were not previously consulted,
but after slight modifications the scheme was passed and the
Working Committee of the Central *Khilafat* Committee was
asked to correspond with the Muslim League, the *Jamiat-ul-
Ulema* and other Muslim associations on the subject.[3]

What the Tanzim movement, founded in June 1924 aimed at

In furtherance of this scheme, Dr. Kitchlew started an
Urdu daily, the *Tanzim* (Organisation), at Amritsar, and lost
no time in carrying on propaganda which resembled *Akali*
methods. Speaking at Ludhiana on 22 July, he praised the
Sikhs for fighting a great battle with the Government and asked

---

[1]Home Department (Political Branch) Note dated 4-10-1924, para 1, p. 12,
[2]Ibid, para 1, pp. 12-13,
[3]Ibid., p. 13.

the Muslims to emulate their example.   At Lahore he enlisted
the assistance of a few local workers and the Punjab *Khilafat*
Committee issued a circular letter urging local committees to
take up the work and to collect subscriptions.   A deputation
then visited several districts in the northern Punjab, and
Kitchlew planned to devote his entire time to the *Tanzim*
movement.[4]

The efforts made by the organizers met with no appreciable success.   According to a report received in the middle of
July 1924 some well-placed Muslims in the Punjab kept themselves aloof from the movement and it is stated that a section
of the *Maulavis* (religious leaders) was definitely antagonistic to
it.   The latter held the view that part of the scheme which
related to control of mosques encroached upon their own rights.
On the other hand, it is significant to note that by the middle
of September 1924 the movement had irritated the Hindus and
aroused their suspicions.   This is proved by the fact that C.R.
Das, Moti Lal Nehru and Malviya not only protested but also
asked Kitchlew to stop the movement.   These apprehensions
on the part of the Hindus were not altogether unjustified.   According to a newspaper report, at a meeting held at Lahore on
9 August Kitchlew made a forcible speech against the Hindus
and indignantly referred to the malicious and narrow-minded
attacks of the *Arya Samajist* journals against the Muslims.   He
appealed to them to "forget Haqiqat Rai fables" (story of a
Hindu "martyr" for religion).[5]

The activities of the Central *Khilafat* Committee in this
connection were far less prominent and mainly confined to
addressing Provincial Committees, which were asked to furnish
lists of Muslim associations, schools and orphanages.   Shaukat
Ali, however, toured in Kathiawar to collect subscriptions.
His speeches were not objectionable.   The tour terminated on
11 September and a sum of Rs. 25,000 was said to have been
promised.[6]

---

[4]Ibid.

[5]Ibid., para 2, p. 14.

[6]Ibid, para 3, p. 14.

The *Tanzim* Movement was full of potentialities but it remained in its infancy and failed to excite public feeling. It therefore did not prove to be a source of danger to the Government. But if this movement had perfected itself it would have then gone against the Government as well as the Hindus and fulfilled the aspirations of its organizers.[7]

The Tabligh Movement and its aims

The *Tanzim* Movement was not anti-Hindu. It was the Muslim antidote to the Hindu *Sangathan* Movement: organization on communal lines.[8] The *Tabligh* Movement, on the other hand, was anti-Hindu[9] besides being a purely militant proselytizing effort on the part of the Muslims to counteract the *Shuddhi* movement which was started in 1923 by the Arya Samaj in certain parts of the Punjab, United Provinces and Delhi for the conversion of Muslim Rajputs. Within a short time it produced ill-feeling between the two communities throughout the country and culminated in riots in several places.[10]

The *Tabligh* Movement among the Muslims was not entirely a new effort at the propagation of Islam in India. From time to time various sections carried on proselytizing work and there is no dearth of evidence to show that while engaged in such work in support of their respective religions, Hindus and Muslims often came into conflict with each other. The relations between the *Arya Samaj* and the Muslims remained bitter because the former made violent attacks on Islam and the Prophet and elicited counter attacks. These relations remained unimproved although subsequently the nationalist movement in India attracted a greater attention of many of those who had hitherto devoted their energies to religion. A remarkable instance of this is to be found in the case of Lal Munshi Ram, a prominent member of the Arya Samaj, and for a long time Governor of the Guru Kul College,

---

[7]Ibid, para 5, p. 15.
[8]Note by C. Kaye, dated 12-10-1924.
[9]Ibid.
[10]Home Department (Political Branch) Note dated 4-10-1924 para 4, p. 15.

Hardwar, who subsequently assumed the role of a *sanyasi* under
the name of Shradhananda. During the disturbances of 1919 in
Delhi he had identified himself so much with the political
agitation that he was acclaimed a popular hero and was taken
to the Jumu'ah Mosque at Delhi, where he was allowed to sit
on the pulpit and address his countrymen—the blood of the
"martyrs" had indeed united the nation![11]

Hindu militant anti-Islam movement of the Hindu Mahasabha

Swami Shradhananda's pretensions were however short-
lived. He had identified himself with the cause of the Congress,
but after the session held at Gaya in 1922 he discovered that he
had no place among either the followers of Mahatma Gandhi
or the seceders, viz., the *Swarajists*. The Swami, therefore,
reverted to religion again.[12] About this time the slackening of
activities among the Muslims in connection with the Khilafat
movement afforded them leisure to turn their attention to
affairs nearer home. A movement, to revive the Muslim
League to look after purely the Muslim political interests, was
started. This gave a further impetus to Swami Shradhananda
who found it very opportune to organize a purely Hindu
movement under the auspices of the *Arya Samaj* primarily to
gain influence and bring people under his own banner, but in
reality to strengthen the Hindu element to retain the balance
of advantage in political matters when *Swaraj* came into
existence!

Early in 1923 a session of the Hindu *Mahasabha* was
held in Benares at which resolutions were passed among others
one being in support of removing untouchability. This greatly
strengthened Shradhananda's hands, who, notwithstanding
the fact that not much love was lost between the orthodox
Hindus and the *Arya Samaj* owing to religious differences,
utilized the opportunity to his advantage. He began by con-
verting the *chamars* (an untouchable class of Hindus) to the

---

[11]Home Department (Political Branch) Note dated 10-10-1924, para 1. p. 16.
[12]Ibid., para 2.

Arya Samaj and urged that Hindus should allow them the use of all wells and places of worship without any let or hindrance. This was soon followed by a campaign of reclaiming the Malkana Rajputs (Muslims), Jat and Gujar Muslims of Meerut Agra, Muttra, Mainpuri, Etah, Etawah in the United Provinces, and Karnal, Ambala, Rohtak and Hissar in the Punjab. Swami Shradhananda and his lieutenants threw themselves into the struggle with great zeal to bring back the non-Muslims in Agra to the fold of the Hindu religion. It was stated that as many as 300 converts had been obtained from one village alone. There was a belief that the Maharaja of Kashmir, as well as some of the Rajput Hindu princes in Rajputana, rendered invaluable help and support in this conversion (*Shuddhi*) movement. On the other hand the Hindus took objection to an old *farman* (edict) extant in Bhopal which declared that apostasy from Islam was a penal offence. The controversy for some time created a great stir among Muslims. The Muslim press, notably that of the Punjab, took up the matter in great alarm.[13]

Animosity between the Muslims and the Hindus grew apace

The *Arya Samajists* for some time claimed great success and to a keen observer it was obvious that this success would not leave the Muslims unmoved. The Muslim theologians of Deoband and others soon showed signs of resistance. Preachers and propagandists of the *Arya Samaj* and Islam met at Achnera in Agra in April 1923 and started the rival campaigns to reconvert the Malkana Rajputs. The open resistance on the part of the Muslims evidently forced Shradhananda to make his movement an all-India movement. He therefore appealed for funds and himself undertook an extensive tour in India. His visits to different centres and his speeches created widespread enthusiasm amongst Hindus. Subscriptions came in thick and fast. The Punjab Hindu press published fabulous figures of conversions to Hinduism. The Muslim public received a rude shock and reproached the

---

[13]Ibid., 2, 17.

Muslims for their apathy. The *Ahmadiyyah* section of Muslims readily lent their powerful support and were the first to come into the field. They soon claimed easy victories. Khwaja Hasan Nizami of Delhi, a well known *pir*, and a crazy, but experienced pamphleteer, contributed a series of articles attacking the *Arya Samaj* and Swami Shradhananda. It is interesting to mention that he also invited Mahatma Gandhi to embrace Islam. The recriminations between Shradhananda and Khwaja Hasan Nizami became so acute that the lives of both were threatened by the followers of the other[14]. In April 1923 the situation became so tense in a group of villages in Agra that additional police were posted[15] to watch the situation.

The Punjab C.I.D., in its report dated 31 March 1923, wrote : "The outstanding feature of the present political situation is the growing tension between the Hindus and Muslims over the conversion of Muslim Rajputs in the United Provinces. The Khilafat leaders were being urged to permit their organizations to be used to counteract the movement and if they refused to take part in the controversy they would undoubtedly lose many of their supporters".[16]

The Tabligh Movement founded in April 1923 to counteract the Shuddhi Movement

In April 1923 the Muslims of Aligarh, under the leadership of Kunwar 'Abdul Wahhab Khan, a Muslim Rajput, formed a society known as *Tabligh-ul-Islam* to counteract the Arya influence at Agra. At one of the meetings of this Society, a boycott of Hindus was urged. In July 1923 a central *Jamiat-t Tabligh-ul-Islam* was formed with headquarters at Ambala. Syed Ghulam Bhik Nairang, a leading lawyer of Ambala, was appointed organising secretary and Kunwar 'Abdul Wahhab Khan and Haji Sir Rahim Bux of Karnal took a leading share in its organization. In September 1923 a general meeting of this *Jamiat* was held at Ambala, to

---

[14]Ibid., p. 18.
[15]Under Section 144 Criminal Procedure Code.
[16]*See* para 139.

which preachers from all parts of India were invited.[17]   The movement had already spread to certain parts of the Punjab. Muslims of all shades of opinion agreed on the necessity of taking counter measures, the only notable exceptions were a few extremists, such as Abul Kalam Azad, and the 'Ali Brothers, who, though themselves ardent Muslims, refrained from taking part in the movement, for fear of losing the sympathy of Hindu nationalists. Strong contingents of Maulavis and paid preachers were sent to the affected areas. Charges of unfair means were levelled by both parties and the Muslims complained that the Hindus were making offers of money and material help to secure conversions.   This open warfare caused the authorities great apprehension, and not only were the relations between the two communities estranged in the United Provinces and the Punjab, but the movement reacted on the Hindu-Muslim relations throughout India, resulting in rioting in several places, for example, at Nagpur, Ajmer, Amethi, Lucknow, Shahjahanpur, Meerut, Delhi Lahore, Kohat and Gulbarga. The Hindu-Muslim relations, were seldom so strained as at this time, and it may safely be mentioned that the *Shuddhi* and *Tabligh* movements were the most important contributory factors leading to this situation.[18]

The Muslims feared that there was a serious danger to their existence in the future. This was indicated in an article entitled "The Neo-Hinduism — A Political Cult", which was published in 1924,[19] and regarded as an authoritative pronouncement on the subject. I am giving below the main ideas contained in this article:—

The Hindu faith had now assumed a new aspect and taken a new turn. This new inspiration was derived rather from politics than from iis ancient literature. Nationalism was the motor-lever in its modern formation. An imaginary Home Rule with all non-Hindu elements

---

[17]Home Department (Political Branch) Note dated 10.10.1924, para 3, p. 19.
[18]Ibid.
[19]See The Islamic Review, October 1924,

— religions that had their origin from outside India like
Christianity and Islam — was the basic principle on which
the new cult was built up. The various Hindu sects under
the old faith were diametrically opposed to each other in
their tenets. For example, the old Sanatan-Dharma and the
new-fledged Arya Samaj, the two well-known Hindu sects,
always remained at daggers drawn, but the Neo-
Hinduism aimed at ignoring these bitter divergences.
It intended to obliterate all that kept a Hindu of any
colour or class separate from the rest.[20]

The Arya Samaj and its Origins

The curious feature of this new campaign of conversion
to Hinduism, was the choice that was freely given to every
new convert on leaving his old faith, to identify himself with
any of the existing creeds that originated within the frontiers
of India. For example, the *Arya Samaj,* a modern Hindu
sect of recent growth, proved to be instrumental in this programme of conversion. Till now they took pride in their
notoriety for denouncing every other creed in the world, never
sparing even the other sects of Hinduism. They assailed
brother Hindus, and non-Hindus as well, in their abusive
writings. Prophets and teachers were scurrilously libelled
and grossly slandered. In a word, they would not suffer so
much as the sight of any other religion or sect within the
four corners of India, and wished to see the soil of India
purged of all foreign plants.[21] They were a political body

---

[20]Buddhism and Jainism are, admittedly, not sects of, but two different
religions from, Hinduism. They have been so treated for centuries by others
as well as by the their respective followers. They differ from Hinduism in
their basic principles. The only common bond between them and Hinduism
is that India is the birth-place of the three religions. This community of
local origin has now been declared as the only article of faith necessary
under the new dispensation, and the new cult would claim every such
religion as part and parcel of itself. Again, proselytizing is a thing unknown
in Hinduism, but the political needs of the coming Hindu rule in India
would allow and adopt it, though contrary to all ancient writings and usage.
Numerical strength is the chief thing to be attained. They must have it at
any cost.

[21]The Islamic Review, October 1924.

from the very beginning, disguised in a religious garb, though so threadbare was the garment that the form beneath was easy of detection. Their activities now, at last enticed the cat from the bag. They now carried on the campaign of conversion which they called *Shuddhi*; but with changed tactics. Before this, they had hated with a malignant and genuine hate all other sects of the Hindus, but now they willingly allowed the fruits of their labour to be claimed by any other creed that came under this new definition of Hinduism. *Sanatan-Dharma*, the most ancient Hindu sect, and the most implacable enemy to the *Arya-Samaj*, from the very genesis of the latter, now also evinced signs of sympathetic cooperation with the latter in the movement. The new political aspirations, in fact, levelled down all religious differences, and transmuted enmity into amity.[22]

The *Sanatan-Dharma's* aversion against the admission of converts into its ranks — as was the case with the Israelites on the clear authority of the Scriptures — was now totally set aside. The *Samajist*, now willingly, allowed him to go to the *Sanatan-Dharma* section. It is well known that the latter class consisted of idolators and stone-worshippers; while the *Arya-Samajists* claimed to be monotheists, and took pride in image-breaking. This, in fact, had always been the great cause of animosity and discord between the two. But now the whole atmosphere was changed. Religion had been sacrificed on the altar of politics. The whole *Samaj* exertion till now had been towards abolishing idolatry, but now, when the *Samajists* succeeded in changing the faith of a non-Hindu, he allowed his new convert to go to the camp of the idolators.[23]

---

[22]Ibid.

[23]The reason idolatrous, and that class takes a lively interest in political activities. The motive of all these exertions is purely a political one, i.e. to increase the number of Hindus in India, and to use this numerical strength, when attained, to their political advantage.

Swami Shradhananda and other Hindu visionaries of Shuddhi benefits to Hindu India observed the tables turning on them when they found that the untouchables, whose sense of dignity of human nature had been murdered by the Hindu religion, started embracing the World Brotherhood

Suffice it to say that the imminent danger, foreseen by the writer of the article, diminished as soon as Swami Shradhananda announced his resignation from the presidentship of the *Shuddhi Sahabha* and pledged to devote the rest of his life to literary work. But so long as such movements, which were only symptomatic of the chronic disease of Hindu-Muslim differences, continued to manifest themselves, they remained a source of anxiety to the British authorities in India and threatened the peace of the country.

---

of Islam in very large numbers, and realized that instead of losing one third of India to the Muslims they would have to lose half of it if the 70 million untouchables became Muslims. They withdrew from this field and asked the political leaders to take over, who were watching anxiously the outcome of this gamble. So Mahatma Gandhi set out to keep the untouchables within the Hindu fold and to beguile them he declared himself to be a Harijan, the name he gave to the untouchables. But Muslims failed to do their duty in this direction.

8

The Khaksar Movement

It is well known that the Muslims, after having lost their "Empire, wealth, property, honour and organisation"[1], led an easy life.[2] This resulted in serious consequences for them. They suffered from a "sense of inferiority"[3], and took pride in laziness, craving for pleasure, ease and safety. This feeling of inferiority took roots particularly in the minds of the educated middle class people. Young men who were coming out of the colleges to seek employment were not sure of their abilities, and seemed to be dependant in every phase of life. This attitude towards life had entirely changed their national character.[4] The *Khaksar* movement was brought into existence to launch a crusade[5] against the cherished easy way of life and to regenerate that simple and courageous spirit of early

---

[1]Note by the Director, Intelligence Bureau, regarding the publication of pro-*Khaksar* editorial in the Urdu monthly *Tula-i Islam* dated July, 1941.

[2]*The Radiance Weekly*, Vol. III, No. 34 dated Friday, September 24, 1943.

[3]Ibid., Vol. III, No. 33, dated Friday, September 17, 1943.

[4]Ibid.

[5]Ibid., Vol. III, No. 29, dated Friday, August 20, 1943.

Muslims which had given them the leadership of the world.[6]
Its aim was to purify the national life and remould the personality of the people[7] to bring back Islam to its pristine glory.[8]

Inayatallah   Khan   popularly   known   as   'Allama
Mashriq,'[9] was the founder of the *Khaksar* movement.   He
was born on 25, August 1888[10] at Ichhra—a village about five
miles from Lahore.   At the age of 18 he established a new
record[11] in M.A. in mathematics.   Then he went to Christ
College, Cambridge and became a Wrangler.   Next he was
appointed a member of the International Congress of Orien-
talists.   Thus he had a very eminent academic career both in
India and England.   On returning to India he accepted
Government service and served as Assistant Secretary in the
Department of Education and Lands from 1918 to 1920.   Later
in Peshawar he worked as Principal of a college and retired.[12]
In 1924[13] he published a book entitled *Tadhkira*[14] a commentary
on the *Quran*, based on his own researches.   The interpretations given by him clashed with the explanations given
earlier by some of the universally acknowledged religious
divines and were, therefore, objected to by the orthodox
sections of both Sunnis and Shiahs.   But his interpretations
were deliberately moulded in order to fit in with his own
conception of the lines on which he wanted to bring about the
political and social regeneration of the Muslims, and had a

---

[6]Ibid., Vol. III, No. 33, dated Friday, September 17, 1943.

[7]Ibid.

[8]Home Political, F. No. 74/1/1941-Part I I.

[9]Statement by Sir Saiyid Rada 'Ali in the Assembly Chamber of the Council
House at New Delhi, on Tuesday, September 2, 1942.

[10]Home Department (Political, Secret) F. No. 74/4/1940.

[11]Ibid.

[12]Statement made by Sir Saiyid Rada 'Ali in the Assembly Chamber of the
Council House at New Delhi, on Tuesday, September 2, 1942.

[13]Home Department Political (Intl.) F. No. 231/1941-Pol. (I).

[14]The book was to be completed in tene volumes, but only the first volume
appeared.

special appeal for his young followers.[15] The fervour of Islamic zeal which permeated through the book enabled them to look upon the doctrine of Mashriqi as a living force to enable the Muslims to organise themselves and help each other as a united body.[16]

Khaksar is a compound Persian word made up of *Khak* and *sar*. *Khak* is 'dust' and *sar* is 'like', that is to say, one who is a *Khaksar* must be as humble as dust. So in 1931 Mashriqi, the founder of the movement, named it after the word *Khaksar*[17] and devoted all his energies to its propagation. Some of his chief supporters were Sir Saiyid Rada Ali, Dr Sir Diya al-Din Ahmad, Agha Ghadnafar Ali Shah, Sir Sikandar Hayat Khan, Maulawi Saiyid Murtada, Khan Bahadur Shaikh Fadl-i Haqq Pirach and Maulana Zafar Ali Khan.

The *Khaksar* movement was not limited to the Muslims alone. It embraced all.[18] It was open to every Jew, Christian, and Brahmo Samajist—in short, to every man who believed in his Creator.[19] The idea was to attain 'Elysian Bliss' or perpetual happiness by unification of the human race irrespective of caste, creed, religion, nationality or birth.[20] It was dedicated to the service of mankind and to social service with just a touch of spirituality to give it force.[21] The motto of this movement was discipline, its line of action social service, and its aim peace—the essence of Islam and every other

---

[15]Note by Maj. Shah (Ext. Affairs Dept.) dated July 1I, 1941. Home Political, F. No. 231/1941-Pol. (I).

[16]Ibid., P. 7, Para 2.

[17]Statement by Maulawi Murtada Sahib Bahadur in the Assembly, Chamber of the Council House at New Delhi, on Tuesday. September 2, 1942.

[18]Statement by Maulana Zafar 'Ali Khan in the Assembly Chamber of the Council House at New Delhi on Tuesday, September 2, 1942.

[19]Statement by Sir Saiyid Rada 'Ali in the Assembly Chamber of the Council House at New Delhi, on Tuesday, September 2, 1942.

[20]*The Spirit of the Khaksar Movement* by Agha Saiyid Ghadnafar 'Ali Shah. M.A., LL.B., Advocate, *Hakim-i A 'la* of the Burma Province. Home Dept. (Pol. Section), F. No. 74/4/1040-Political.

[21]Ibid.

religion. The organisation was a non-political and non-communal one and had among its votaries a large number of non-Muslims. It aimed at the improvement of physical and spiritual health, development of individual and collective character and the ending of all controversies through extensive social service, strict discipline and all-embracing love.[22]

The *Khaksars* did not believe in taking violent action to achieve their ends. They used to say تفنگ آمد یہ جنگ آمد meaning, when one isdriven to the necessity of resorting to violence, one will take to it. By creed they were not violent. As such they should not be looked down upon as mischief-mongers because there may be an occasion to find out a real master ruler from that dust. This is clear from the following Persian couplet also:

خاکساران جہاں را بہ حقارت منگر
تو چہ دانی کہ درس گرد سوارے باشد[23]

It is interesting to note that the *Khaksars* were opposed to the raising of subscriptions for their organization. Such collections raised from a demoralized nation, demoralized it further. According to the *Khaksars,* most of the noble movements in the past had perished on 'its rock'. In India also this virus had sapped the political life and made it devoid of all energy and vitality. But in order to remove this evil the *Khaksars* imposed upon themselves a self-denying ordinance solely to render social service in a way that it did not involve any money or expenditure.[24]

But in order to carry out this great task of regeneration and remoulding[25] the people, the *Khaksars* laid down certain fundamental principles. These have been described by Agha Ghadnafar Ali Shah, as follows:

[22]Note by Khan Bahadur Shaikh Fadl-i Haqq Pirach. Home Department Political (Internal) F. No. 24/10/1942-Poll. (I).

[23]Note by Sir Cowasji Jehangir. Home Dept. Political (Internal), F. No. 24/10/1942-Poll. (I).

[24]*The Radiance Weekly*, Vol. III, No. 38, dated Friday, October 22, 1943.

[25]Ibid., Vol. III, No. 33, dated Friday, September, 17, 1943.

Basic and Fundamental Principles

(1) *Explicit belief and implicit trust in the Almighty,* be he Jehovah of the Jews, the Param-Atma of the *Puranas,* the Lord-God of the Christians, the Phaya of the Buddhists or Allah of the Musalmans. This Omnipotent Being should only sway the existence of the *Khaksar* and he should drive away all the gods who have taken possession of his heart, soul, mind, and body, *viz.,* the gods of pride, passions, malice, vengeance, satiation, sloth, intemperance, revelry, corruption, debauchery and so on. A *Khaksar* beiieves that the Omnipresent Eye is always watching him and he is accountable for every action of his...He knows that a particular time has been fixed for his departure from this transient world which can neither be postponed nor prolonged and consequently he is not afraid of anything, even of the Angel of Death...Every evil which befalls a *Khaksar* is the consequence of his own shortcoming and every advantage which he derives is a reward for his good actions. A predominating faith in his Creator pervades the very existence of the *Khaksar.* He worships Him, communes with Him, loves Him and is afraid of Him. He is confident that the entire world, with everything in it, is made only for him and there is nothing which he cannot achieve provided he has the character untarnished. (2) *Unrestricted obedience to the Prophet of his faith, be he Krishna, Buddha, Moses, Christ or Muhammad...* To be a *Khaksar* is not only to follow literally his behests, but to imbibe within himself the teachings, the action and the *deeds* of his Prophet to such an extent as to make him the very fascimile of the Redeemer he believes in. He treads on the sublime footsteps of his Preceptor which leads him to a simple, courageous, devotional, pure and lofty life. (3) *The third characteristic of the Khaksar is his staunch loyalty, his unstincted, unresisting and unquestioning obediench to his superior officer.*[26]

---

[26]*The Spirit of the Khaksar Movement* by Agha Saiyid Ghadnafar 'Ali Shah. Home (Political) F. No. 74/4/1940-Political (Secret).

Essentials

(1) A *Khaksar* should lead a pure devotional life consistent with his religion and deny himself every kind of temptation. (2) He must always wear khaki dress. This will bring about uniformity in the rank in all respects. It will be cheap and available for all. It will be simple and unpresuming. A man in khaki will not lag behind when called upon to do public or social service. (3) A *Khaksar* must always carry a shovel or a *belchah*. Apart from being an emblem of labour this instrument is useful in many ways. You can bake over it. You can dig, cut and clean with it, in short there are one hundred and thirty one ways in which this instrument has been found to be useful. (4) The badge of *Ukhuwa* should always conspicuously be stuck on the right upper arm of a *Khaksar* on his khaki dress. *Ukhuwa* means brotherhood. This indicates that the person carrying it belongs to a universal brotherhood which conscribes and intermixes them into a united compagination. (5) The *Khaksars* of the same locality should, under their commander, parade, march and exercise for at least fifteen minutes every day to keep them fit, trained and ready for service. (6) Every *Khaksar* should necessarily perform some sort of public or social service everyday and report to his commander about the same.[27]

Rules

(1) A *Khaksar* should try to make as many friends as he can. (2) He must be humble in his ways and should always be ready to humiliate himself to win friends. (3) He must never discuss with anyone religion or politics. (4) He must avoid quarrels and disputes. (5) He must never be prejudiced against or feel animus towards anybody. (6) Wastage of time and that of money is not permissible to a *Khaksar*. He must feel himself accountable for every second lost and every pie spent. (7) He

---

[27]Ibid.

must develop within himself martial qualities and soldiery attributes. (8) A *Khaksar* should always be honest, punctual and truthful. (9) The mutual salutation between the *Khaksar* should be in the military fashion. (10) A *Khaksar* should always try to make his purchases from a brother *Khaksar* and he in return should make the least profit. (11) A *Khaksar* must be silent, calm and watchful. (12) He must listen and obey. (13) A *Khaksar* should not be a partner or a talky-talky but a practical patient worker. (14) He should never expect or accept any return for his public or social service. (15) He should try to avoid all obligations, so much so, that with the exception of his close relatives, his equal soldiers, or superior officers, he should not take anything without paying for it.[28]

This work of regeneration and remoulding the people was to be carried out every day in the *mahallas* and circles but in this way people got fewer opportunities of meeting each other and still fewer of knowing each other. In order to develop their personality it was necessary to live in the midst of friends and co-workers, and this opportunity was provided to them by organizing camps.[29] The camps were the real schools for teaching unity, discipline and fraternity, and social service provided a lesson in humility and spiritual greatness.[30] They were the real abode of progress and reform and had their own life, their own laws and their own traditions.[31] Everybody was given a field of activity and thereby acted as a keen worker in the movement. The independent work assigned to the people inculcated in them the qualities of leadership.[32]

The *Khaksars* did not like the ordinary customary education. It revealed its weaknesses, particularly during the war because it had completely failed to provide any practical training to the students. It had merely encouraged book know-

---

[28]Ibid.
[29]Home Political (I) F. No. 33/59/1943 & K.W.
[30]*The Radiance Weekly*, Vol. III, No. 38, dated Friday, October 22, 1943.
[31]Ibid., Vol. III, No. 34, dated Friday, September 24,1943.
[32]Ibid., Vol. **III, No. 33**, dated Friday, September 17, 1943,

ledge. But to the *Khaksars* it was personal experience that was true knowledge, and book-knowledge only helped in that experience. Experience showed that almost all great leaders of the world were uneducated or barely educated men, but responsibility created self-confidence in them and it helped them to become leaders.[33] The *Khaksars* thus gave a secondary place to education and laid more emphasis on providing opportunities for civil defence, helping evacuees and refugees, attending to the injured, protecting property and women, and distributing food-stuffs during the war. That was the real education for them.[34]

The *Khaksar* movement was unlike the political movements of India. It depended on the intrinsic value of its programme, changed with the time, pointed out the mistakes of its workers, and punished them; they depended on the opportune moment and diplomatic exploitation of the sentiments of the masses, moved with the time, feared to point out the mistakes of its workers and gave them garlands. Its workers spent their own money for organisational work, burnt their boats for the sake of the *Jamaat* on joining the organization and believed in the calm planning of a businessman; they got travelling allowances for the work done by them, filled their boats with individual fame and property on joining the organization and believed in the joy of a spendthrift. Its workers regarded the present as dark but the future bright; they counted on the immediate present no matter howsoever dark was the future. It depended upon God, righteous action and constant efforts; they depended upon money and loud talks. It maintained that the reform of the people was more necessary than the fear of their displeasure and believed in greater efforts for success; they believed in flattering the prejudices of the people and in greater pomp and show for attaining success.[35]

The *Khaksar* movement was not confined to India alone but commanded a considerable following in Burma, Ceylon,

---

[33]Ibid.

[34]Home Department Political (Internal) F. No. 28/5/1942-Political.

[35]Home Political (I), F. No. 117/4/1943.

Bahrein, South Africa etc. It was, however, in India, and particularly among the Muslim masses, that it had won most of its adherents.[36] The reason for its success is not far to seek. For the dispirited and disorganised Muslims of India the *Khaksar* movement provided many of the attractive characteristics of early Islam, *viz.*, simplicity, discipline, self-sacrifice and a burning desire to serve the community in all walks of life. The military drill and uniform reminded every *Khaksar* that he was a soldier in the service of Allah.

It would now be necessary to examine the progress of the movement from year to year to assess properly to what extent it succeeded in achieving its aims and objectives.

1939.

The *Khaksar* movement started in 1931[37] but it was in 1939 that the *Khaksars* first came into conflict with the authorities of the United Provinces over the Shiah-Sunni dispute. Mashriqi went to Lucknow to bring about a settlement, but by the instigation of the Congress the *Ahrars* did not welcome this move. This greatly annoyed Mashriqi and he ordered his followers to use *belchas* against them contrary to the orders of the Government.[39] He was immediately put in prison but was released shortly afterwards.

1940.

In March 1940, when serious disturbances broke out at Lahore, on the eve of the session of the All Muslim League, the *Khaksars* marched in a procession through the main streets and came into conflict with the Punjab Government which objected to the use of 'shovels' and 'military formations'

---

[36]Speech by Khan Bahadur Shaikh Fadl-i Haqq (North West Punjab) in Council House, New Delhi, on September 2, 1942.

[37]Speech by Khan Bahadur Shaikh Fadl-i Haqq in Council House, New Delhi, on September 2, 1942.

[38]They were pro-Congress Muslims and wanted to maintain their position in the Congress by securing seats in its Working Committee.

[39]Speech by Sir Saiyid Rada 'Ali in Council House, New Delhi, on Tuesday, September 2, 1942.

although it permitted the Sikhs to use the *kirpans*. This was
resented by the *Khaksarss* and Muslims in general, but Jinnah
and other leaders of the League did not take any initiative at
this time to settle the affair. The *Khaksars* therefore, organised
defiance of authority by taking shelter in mosques in Lahore.
The police thereupon opened fire and in the process 32 *Khaksars*
were killed and 1700 arrested and sentenced to imprisonment.
Of the policemen injured, one was Beatty, Deputy Superintendent of Police, and the other was Gainsford, the Senior
Superintendent of Police.[40] Mashriqi bitterly criticized the
Government's action. He was arrested, therefore, on the night
of March 19 at Delhi and removed to Vellore Jail[41] in Madras.
But it was only in the beginuing of June that the *Khaksar* movement was declared unlawful by a number of provincial
governments. Notifications were also issued banning the
performance of military drill and the wearing of a dress resem-
bling a military uniform in public. This action was taken in
order to prevent the growth of 'private armies' in India and
to stop military activities on the part of non-official volunteer
organizations which disturbed the public peace and interfered
with the security of the country.[42] But in August 1940, when
the *Khaksars* assured the Government that they would abide
by the law, notifications declaring them to be an unlawful
association in Delhi and Punjab were withdrawn.[43] This was
followed by agitations[44] in U.P., Dera Ismail Khan[45] and

---

[40]Note on the *Khaksar* Movement in the Punjab, Home Political F. No.
5/10/1942.

[41]Speech by Sir Saiyid Rada Ali in the Council House at New Delhi on
September 2, 1942.

[42]Home Political (I) F. No. 28/3/1944.

[43]Speech by Sir Richard Tottenham in Council House at New Delhi on
September 2, 1942. *See also* Home Political (I), F. No. 28/2/1942.

[44]Home Department Communique dated June 5, 1941. Home Political (I),
F. No. 26/2/1942—Political.

[45]The Muslim associations of Dera Ismail Khan passed the following resolution : "This representative meeting of the Mussalmans of Dera Ismail
Khan vehemently demands from the Government of India the immediate
release of their beloved great leader Hadrat 'Allama 'Inayatallah Khan
al-Mashriqi and in very strong words demands from the Government of the

Ahmedabad[46] for the release of their leader. But the Government had written evidence to prove that he never ceased to carry on unauthorized communication with the outside world and spread entirely false rumours about his health in order to gain public sympathy. He also gave exaggerated figures regarding the number of *Khaksars* arrested and convicted.[47] The Government, ruled out, therefore, his release at this stage.

1941.

In May 1941, the *Khaksars* contemplated concerted action to bring pressure on the Government to secure the release of their leader and proposed to adopt the same tactics as they had adopted at Lahore—entering into mosques armed with the *belchahs* and making those mosques the bases of operations or demonstrations. This was followed by a representative meeting of leading *Khaksars* in Peshawar to finalize the plan. The organizers of this meeting were officially warned not to proceed with it but they decided to ignore the warning.[48] The results were obvious. The *Khaksars* were then declared to be an unlawful association by all the Provincial Governments in India at the beginning of June, 1941.[49]

Mashriqi's first move in the campaign to secure his own release from jail was to start a 'potential fast', or partial hunger-strike, on 16, October 1941. This news produced much excitement among the *Khaksars*. Miyan Ahmad Shah, who was at this time the acting head of the movement, advised the *Khaksars* to refrain from having recourse to unlawful agitation so long as negotiations for their leader's release were in progress, but recalcitrant elements amongst them accused him of

---

Punjab that it should forthwith remove the charge of violence from the *Khaksars* so that in the present regime of war the atmosphere may become pacified." *See also* Home Political F. No. 74/8/1940-Poll. (I).

[46]Home Political (I) F. No. 74/7/1941.

[47]Home Dept. (Government of India) Communique dated Simla, June 5, 1941. Home Political (I) F. No. 28/2/1942.

[48]Resolution regarding ban on the *Khaksar* Movement. Home Department Political (Internal) F. No. 24/10/1942.

[49]Ibid.

cowardice and inefficiency and many instances of disobedience to his instructions came to light as the duration of the fast lengthened.[50] This agitation manifested itself in different parts of India.[51]

In Delhi a number of meetings were held urging the *Khaksars* to make every sacrifice to secure the release of their leader. On 26 November, two *Khaksars* courted arrest by parading in uniform. Earlier they observed a fast in a mosque for four days, and before leaving it one of them had delivered an inflammatory speech for which he was prosecuted under the Defence of India Rules. Local *Khaksars* thereafter agreed to suspend the agitation temporarily because the action taken by them was contrary to the advice given by Miyan Ahmad Shah.[52]

A substantial section of the Muslim public in the Punjab also favoured the demand for Mashriqi's release.[53] In U.P. also there was growing restlessness among the *Khaksars*. By the instigation of some professors of Muslim University at Aligarh, about a dozen students observed a fast on 30 Novermber as a protest against the Government's failure to release the *Khaksar* leader and looked forward to defy the ban on the organisation.[54]

Meetings were also organised at Peshawar and Bannu to demand his release.[55] A proposal to organise protest demonstration by shouting objectionable slogans in mosques on Fridays was successfully opposed by the saner element because they considered such demonstrations to be inopportune. The *Jamiyat al-Ulama* (non-Congress), the Frontier Muslim Associa-

---

[50]Note on the *Khaksar* Movement. Home Department (Political—Internal), F. No. 74-4/1941.

[51]It illustrates the degree of support that existed for the *Khaksar* Movement.

[52]Note on the *Khaksar* Movement. Home Department (Political—Internal), F. No. 74/4/1941.

[53]Ibid., para 2 (3).

[54]Ibid., para 2 (2).

[55]Ibid., para 2 (4).

tion (a non-political organization) and the Mardan Muslim League adopted, however, resolutions supporting the demand for Mashriqi's release.[56]

In Sind a new movement sprang up, ostensibly for Muslim unity but based on the recognition of Mashriqi as the leader of the Muslim community. Persons who signed the pledge to become its members were instructed to wear a black badge on the right arm as a mark of resentment at Mashriqi's detention. The followers of the new party called themselves *Fida in-i Islam* (Devotees of Islam) and designated Mashriqi as *Amir-i Sharia* (leader of the community) but the number of persons who signed the *Fidai* pledge did not exceed even fifty.[57] In Hyderabad,[58] some *Khaksars* who went on a sympathetic fast were persuaded by Nauwab Bahadur Yar Jang to discontinue it. Some agitation for his release was also reported from the Bhopal State.[59]

These developments placed the question of the removal of restrictions on the *Khaksars* in a favourable light. The Central Government invited opinions on this issue, and a number of Provincial Governments expressed their agreement to the removal of the ban. On 23, September 1941, the Central Assembly also accepted a motion by Sir Saiyid Rada Ali recommending the lifting of the ban on the *Khaksars*. The Punjab Government also agreed to the removal of the ban provided a clear, unambiguous statement was made by the *Khaksar* leader that as long as the war lasted social service would be performed in an individual capacity and there will be no drilling and no use of uniforms, badges or symbols.[60]

1942.

Mashriqi agreed to this proposal and on 16, January 1942, issued the required instructions to his followers to abandon the

---

[56] Ibid.

[57] Ibid., para 2 (5).

[58] Ibid., para 2 (6).

[59] Ibid.

[60] Ibid., para 3.

military side of the movement entirely for the period of the
war. These were:

> (1) The period of half-an-hour's drill previously prescri-
> bed for *Khaksars* to be replaced by half-an-hour's *isha*
> prayer.   (2) *Khaksars* to assemble at the summon of a
> bugle at fixed times and to stand in a row, but not to
> take in any drill; to remain smart and disciplined, and
> obey the orders of caution given to them by the *salar-i*
> *mahalla;* to wear khaki dress occasionally and a red badge
> equal in size to a rupee and, to use *belchah* for social
> service only.   (3) Social service, without discrimination
> of caste or creed, to be performed after prayers. (4, Every
> *Khaksar* to march, rather walk, to salute his acquain-
> tances in a military style and to perform exercises of a
> military nature for at least two minutes a day. (5) *Khaksar*
> camps to continue at a distance from inhabited area and
> (6) leaders to enlist two thousand followers each to raise
> the strength of the movement to 25 lakhs by 15, September
> 1942.

In short, the new programme aimed at the development among the *Khaksars* of a military sense in every walk
of life, but at the same time it avoided public drilling to
remain within the law.[61] Mashriqi was released from jail
on 19 January but the ban on the movement continued
to be in force. He was given complete freedom to meet the
Khaksar leaders but was not permitted to leave the Madras
Presidency[62] or to make any communication to the press.   This
was done to prevent him from acting in a manner prejudical
to the defence of British India.[63] As regards the removal of
the ban, the Government agreed to lift it provided Mashriqi
furnished the undertaking that it would not again result in any
danger or risk to the security of the country.   From that day
onwards he tried to bargain with the Government of India

---

[61]See F. No. 74-4/41-Poll. (I), Part III, p. 4. *See also* F. No. 37/8/1942-Poll.
(I), pp. 2-4.

[62]Home Political (Internal) F. No. 8/12/1952, p. 2.

[63]Ibid.

instead of convincing it that his instructions would be obeyed by his followers.[64]

While doing so Mashriqi issued inconsistent statements. What he told the Goernment was very different from what he told his followers. He violated as well the conditions on which he was released. The Government proved these charges by displaying a circular signed by Mashriqi which clearly stated that everything possible must be done to maintain the military spirit of the *Khaksars* even though dilling, wearing uniforms, and the use of arms were suspended temporarily. Similarly, another circular in its possession showed that he had issued instructions for recruiting a large number of the *Khaksars* and made arrangements for their military training in order to bring the Government to terms. On being confronted with these circulars Mashriqi himself did not deny that they were issued by him. On the contrary, he sent to the Government a long letter of an argumentative nature which confirmed the opinion that "he was not a very easy person to do business with."[65] It thus becomes quite apparent that the Government's attitude towards him was neither unreasonable nor arbitrary.[66] It is apparent from the instructions issued by him that he wanted to preserve the identity of the organisation, although the ban on military drill applied equally to all the other volunteer organisations also.[67]

In spite of such contradictions, Mashriqi's new instructions led to the revival of the *Khaksar* activities in Delhi, Punjab, North Western Provinces and United Provinces, but in other provinces it was non-existent.[68] Everywhere in Delhi the *Khaksars* appeared in khaki shirts and *shalwars* and wore

---

[64]Speech by Sir Richard Tottenham dated September 2, 1942. Home Department Political (Internal) F. No. 24/10/1942.

[65]Ibid.

[66]Ibid.

[67]Addendum to the Note on the *Khaksar* Movement. Home Political Department (Internal), F. No. 74-4/1941-Poll. (I), Pt. III.

[68]Home Department (Intelligence Bureau), Note Dated October 20, 1942, para 3.

the prescribed armed badge.[69]   In Punjab there was a revival of their activities in a modified form in spite of the fact that the actual working of the new programme was hampered by the existing ban on the organisation.   Such activities consisted mainly of attendance at small gatherings and congregational prayers and the performance of social service.[70]   Efforts were also made by Muhammad Aslam Chishti to enrol more *Khaksar* students in the movement.   But the success[71] was not appreciable.   Only students of the M.A.O. College at Amritsar and the Zamindar College in Gujarat volunteered to become its members.

The new programme was, however, carried out with varying degrees of enthusiasm in U.P. There was a substantial enrolment of persons in the movement, particularly the students. Camps with moderate attendances were organised at various places and workers who did not report for duty were whipped. Although as a general rule *belchahs* were not usually carried, they were frequently seen with students in Lucknow and Kanpur.   But in other districts the movement was non-existent[72].   It is interesting to point out that on 23, October 1942 *al-I lan*, a *Khaksar* newspaper of U.P., threatened the Government to withdraw the restrictions imposed on the organistion.[73] It went on to say:

> The Goxernment of India may well labour under the delusion that they can end the *Khaksa*r movement through a policy of complete taciturnity which they have been adopting for sometime past. The paper reminds the Govern ment that no moveiment has fizzled out in this way; on the other hand it has gained momentum gradually. The efforts made by the Government of India in 1940 to crush the

---

[69]Ibid.

[70]Ibid., para 4.

[71]Note on the *Khaksar* Movement, Heme Dept. (Political-Internal), F. No. 74-4/1941-Poll. (I), Pt. III.

[72]Ibid.

[73]Intelligence Bureau (Home Department) Note dated October 20, 1942. Home Department (Political-Internal) F. No. 28/5/1942-Poll.

movement have failed, because instead of weakening it, it has in fact considerably strengthened the movement much as the *Khaksars* have, by making valuable sacrifices, become hardy soldiers imbued with an unconquerable spirit of achieving their goal.[74]

This threat proved to be of no avail. The paper was sternly warned by the U.P. Government not to indulge in such criticism in future. The *Khaksar* organisation thus remained an unlawful association.[75]

In the North Western Frontier Province, the new programme took the form of assembling at prayers, wearing khaki clothes and performing social service. The prescribed red badge was also worn.[76] On one or two occasions disciplinary action was taken publicly against the defaulting *Khaksars*. There was but little success because large numbers of people did not join the movement.[77]

The total number of the *Khaksars* at this time was 16 lakhs.[78] Owing to public pressure, the Government wisely lifted the ban on the organisation on 28, December 1942, and also cancelled orders confining Mashriqi's movements to the province of Madras.[79] But it sternly warned Mashriqi to abolish the essential features of the organisation if he planned to reorganise the movement at this stage.[80]

---

[74]Home Political F. No. 8/7/1942-Poll. (I).

[75]S.J.L. Oliver, Esq., I.P. Under Secretary to the Government of India, to the Chief Secretary to the Government of Punjab dated New Delhi, November 19,1942. Home Political (1) F. No. 28/7/1942-Poll. I.

[76]Note on the *Khaksar* Movement, Home Department (Political-Internal) F. No. 74-4/1941, Part III.

[77]Intelligence Bureau (Home Department) Note dated October 20, 1942. Home Department (Political-Internal), F. No. 28/5/1242-Poll.

[78]Home Department (Political-Internal), No. F. 74/4/1944-Poll. (I) Pt. III, para 6.

[79]Activities of Allama Mashriqi and his followers after the lifting of the ban on the *Khaksar* Organisation, Home Department (Political-Internal) F. No. 74-4/1941-Poll. (I), Pt. III.

[80]Addendum to the Note on the *Khaksar* Movement (1943-45). Home Department (Political-Internal), F. No. 28/5/1943-Poll. (I), and K.W.

1943.

Mashriqi evaded the restrictions imposed on him and his organization. This was confirmed by a press statement[81] which he issued on 3 January from Madras. Fresh orders were now issued by him for the recruitment of 1,000 *mujahidin*[82] and the enrolment of 100,000 ordinary members. But in June, when the *Khaksars* organised a 'military camp'[83] at Bhuch, the Punjab Government urged the Government of India to reinforce restrictions on them. This was not done but Mashriqi was "finally warned"[84] on 19 July to stop unlawful activities. This had the desired effect, because three days later he issued orders to the *Khaksars* to remove the red badges from their arms at once. He also directed them not to wear the headdress[85] but only to cover their heads with white handkerchiefs at the time of prayers, and prohibited military display at camps which were "exclusively reserved for congregational prayers, religious and social lectures and sports."[86] Objectionable activities thus ceased for some time, but Mashriqi continued to complain that "a most determined campaign"[87] was being waged against the *Khaksars*. This very much disheartened him

---

[81]This statement repeated the assurances previously given by him, but stipulated that the *Khaksars* might use *belchahs* at the time of genuine social service, might wear round red-cloth badges of the size of a rupee. Instructions to this effect were also given by Mashriqi to the *Khaksar* leaders from the Punjab, Delhi and United Provinces who met him at Delhi on January 2, 1943.

[82]The orders defined a *mujahid* as "one who was regular in his soldierly prayers, who was devoted to social studies irrespective of creed or colour, who wore khaki dress, including the red *Khaksar* insignia, and carried a small edition of the *Qur'an* under his arm, and who had a *belchah* and the uniform of his rank ready and complete at his home."

[83]Note on the *Khaksar* Movement, para 2. Home Department (Political-Internal), F. No. 28/5/1943-Poll. (I) & K.W.

[84]Ibid.

[85]The prescribed head-dress consisted of a white piece of cloth, one yard and a half square, worn in the Arab or *Hajji* fashion and secured by a 3/4 inch thick cord, the colour of the cord varying with the rank of the wearer. *See also* Home Department Political (Internal) Branch F. No. 28/5/1943-Poll. (I) & K.W.

[86]Note on the *Khaksar* Organisation dated April 8, 1943. Home Department Political (Internal) Branch F. No. 28/5/1943-Poll. (I) and K.W.

[87]Ibid., para 3.

and he expressed willingness to even suspend the organisation.[88]

In U.P. attempts were made ro revive the movement by organising *Khaksar* Military Training Camp at Lucknow on 28 May. It was attended by 460 *Khaksars* mostly from U.P., Punjab and Bengal, but broke up in two days owing to inadequate boarding and lodging arrangements.[89] Meetings were also held at Kanpur asking the *Khaksars* to emulate the martial spirit of the Sikhs. An unpleasant incident was, however, narrowly avoided in Lucknow on *Barawafat* day when a number of *Khaksars* with uniforms and *belchahs* moved about freely in the city contrary to the orders of the Government. Eleven of them were arrested and this was followed by a protest demonstration.[90] A clash seemed imminent, but better sense ultimately prevailed and the *Khaksar* leader ordered his men to march. Thereupon the Government released the arrested *Khaksars*.[91]

In Punjab there was some increase in the *Khaksar* activities.[92] On 19 March *Khaksar* Day was celebrated in most of the towns. About a month later, on 18 April some *Khaksars* with *belchahs* hidden in bedding-rolls, proceeded to a tomb a mile outside the town of Karnal, spent the night there and planned to repeat similar expeditions every month.[93] A

---

[88]Ibid.

[89]Ibid., para 2.

[90]Some 300 *Khaksars*, of whom 75 were in uniform and carried *belchahs* while the rest carried sticks, gathered. Some of them then marched to the bungalow of Deputy Commissioner but were stopped by the police. The *Khaksars* very much resented this.

[91]Note on the *Khaksar* Movement, para 6. Home Department (Political-Internal) F. No. 74/4/1941-Poll. (I), Part III.

[92]Ibid.

[93]As a result of orders mentioned above, more *Khaksars* were seen wearing khaki shirts and shorts and red badges, and by June the *Khaksar* strength in this province was approximately 4,000. Mashriqi then issued a circular asking a limited number of *Khaksars* in various provinces to be ready to go out of India within one month if so required. Twenty-one *Khaksars* were selected for the purpose from Punjab, but the orders were apparently issued only with a view to testing the loyalty of his followers as nothing more was heard of the proposal.

Khaksar camp[94] was also held at Shaikhupura from 16 to 18 June on the occasion of Bhuch Cattle Fair. The posting of sentries, the employment of buglers, the hoisting of flags and the punishment for breaches of discipline indicated that this camp was organized purely on military lines. The Government, as such, took a serious note of it and on 12 September instructed Mashriqi to state clearly that in future no such camps would be organised.[95] *Khaksar* prestige had now come to 'a low ebb,'[96] and hence subsequent efforts to recruit more persons in the organisation were not marked with much success in N.W.F.P.,[97] Sind[98] and Bombay.[99] The policy of distributing offices to wealthy *Khaksars* brought further discredit to the organisation. Mashriqi himself admitted it at a private meeting that this "movement had collapsed."[100]

1944.

But in June 1944 yet another attempt was made to reorganise the movement. A new *Mujahidin-i Khaksar* Department was opened under a *Nazim-i A'la* whose office was called the *Bab al-nizam*. He worked directly under the *Khaksar* Headquarters and controlled Provincial, Divisional and District *Salars*. Provincial offices were called *Bab-al-imam*. The *Mujahidin* consisted of experienced *Khaksars*[101] who could do constructive work and enlist new recruits. Another sinister feature of the *Khaksar* reorganisation was the opening of a *Khaksar*

---

[94]About 350 *Khaksars* from various districts of the Punjab attended, all of them wearing khaki clothes and red badges and nearly all carrying *belchahs*. In addition five *Khaksar* officers wore cross-belts during the first two days of the camp although they removed them on the last day, while 9 daggers and 16 swords were carried by others.

[95]Home Department (Political-Internal) F. No. 74-4/1941-Poll. I (Part III).

[96]Note on the *Khaksar* Organisation dated November 8, 1943. Home Department (Political-Internal) F. No. 21/5/1943-Poll. (I) & K.W.

[97]Ibid.

[98]Ibid.

[99]Home Department (Political-Internal) F. No. 74-4/1941-Poll. (I), Part (III).

[100]Home Department (Political-Internal) F. No. 28/5/1943-Poll. I & K.W.

[101]They had all participated in *Khaksar* work on different 'fronts' and could set an example to others.

Cutlery Works and the appointment of two knife-makers as *Salars*.[102]

Soon after this reorganisation, Mir Ghulam Qadir, the newly appointed *Hakim-i A'la* of N.W.F.P., toured the various districts and it resulted in the revival of some *Khaksar* activity outside Peshawar. But in 1944 when he attempted to force an issue with the authorities over the holding of a camp the *Khaksar* High Command prohibited it, because he did not want Mir Ghulam Qadir to get credit for it. Mir Qadir, in disgust, resigned from the organisation and accused Mashriqi "of following a policy which only added to his prestige and glory but not of other party members."[103]

Certain other factors also brought disrepute to the organisation at this stage. In Bombay, the *Khaksars*, who always carried copies of the *Quran* with them, greatly annoyed the Muslim masses because they considered it disrespectable to the Holy Book.[104] In Punjab a *Khaksar*, who objected to flogging for misappropriating funds, was assaulted by six of his co-workers in a Lahore mosque on 25 July on Mashriqi's orders, but he cleverly managed to escape and reported the matter to the police. The police registered a case and arrested the accused. The *Khaksar* complainant was thereupon denounced as a traitor but at the same time the six accused were also sentenced to a year's rigorous imprisonment and a fine of Rs. 100 each.[105] In another case, 30 *Khaksars* who marched through the Lahore city and contravened orders prohibiting parades and drills of a military nature were arrested and sentenced to imprisonment varying from one to two years. This greatly lessened the *Khaksar* enthusiasm for reorganising the movement afresh. The all-India strength of the *Khaksar* further dwindled from 23,000 in 1943 to 20,000 in 1944.[106]

---

[102]Home Department [Political-Internal] F. No. 28/5/1943-Poll. [I] & K.W.
[103]Ibid.
[104]Ibid.
[105]Under Rule 56/58, Defence of India Rules.
[106]Home [Department Political] F. No. 28/5/1943-Poll. [I] & K.W.

1945.

The *Khaksars* were now greatly confused and made the last bid to reorganise the movement by altering the basic ideology of the movement. Accordingly, a Department of Politics, known as *Bab al-siyasat*, was opened with headquarters at Bombay to lay down a policy for the attainment of "immediate and right sort of independence for India."[107] Saiyid Allah Bakhsh Shah, who was previously entrusted with the task of carrying on a campaign to promote Hindu-Muslim unity, was to head it. This Department instructed the *Khaksars* to keep contacts with local political leaders of Congress, Muslim League, the Hindu Mahasabha and the Communist Party and explain to them the importance of the movement. It also advised the Muslims to stop cow-sacrifice but at the same time stopped and confiscated the distribution of 24,000 copies of a pamphlet on the subject. This clearly showed that the *Khaksars* were confused about their future programme and the movement therefore completely collapsed shortly afterwards.[108] It was followed by resignations of its important leaders.[109]

1946.

Finally, after the Great War was over, Mashriqi wrote to the Government of India that "his undertaking to them ceased with the cessation of hostilities and that he should be permitted to resume pre-war activities."[110] The Government of India conveyed its decision to Mashriqi on 30 March 1946, in these words:

> As regards your request you do not appear to understand the position. While there is even now no objection to the *Khaksars*, as a legal organisation, indulging in such activities as do not offend against the law, your statement obviously could not have meant that the *Khaksars*, would be at liberty to resume illegal activities after the war.

---

[107]Ibid.
[108]Ibid.
[109]Like Dr Muhammad Ismail Nami and Ghulam Mustafa Bhurguri.
[110]Home Department Memorandum No. 28/4/1945-Poll. [I], dated March 16/19/1946.

Government of India notifications...prohibiting drilling and the wearing of uniforms of a military type are still in force, restricting the holding of camps and parades by political and communal organizations and banning altogether any such camps or parades held for the purpose of performing drills or movements of a military nature. These apply to the *Khaksars* as much as to any other organisation. The Government of India therefore cannot agree to the proposed statement forwarded with your letter dated the 17th August, 1945. Any statement you may wish to publish must make it perfectly clear that the activities of the *Khaksars*, must remain *strictly within the law.*[111]

This letter containing the Government's policy towards the *Khaksars*, was widely circulated throughout India,[112] and sounded the death knell of the *Khaksar* movement.

Khaksar Currency

We shall now discuss some specific but interesting issues relating to the *Khaksars*, such as their currency, famine-policy, approach towards political parties, and publicity arrangements. Contrary to the ideology of the movement, Mashriqi, in order to raise donations and draw attention towards the *Khaksar* organization, issued currency notes to his followers and promised to make the repayment on the liberation of India.[113] This becomes clear from a letter reproduced below. It was written by one Muhammad Ashiq of Mahalla Sarai Kala Khan in Peshawar City and published in a Lahore Weekly called *Jatistian* on 7 October 1942:

I enlisted myself in the *Belcha Fauj* (Army of Spades) on being led astray by the slippery talks of 'Inayatallah

---

[111]Extract from a Letter No. 28/4/1945-Poll. [I] dated September 6, 1945, from the Government of India, Home Department to 'Inayatallah Khan Mashriqi, P.O. Ichhra, Lahore.

[112]Ibid.

[113]F.C. Burne, Esq., C.I.E., I.C.S., Chief Secretary to the Government of Punjab, to the Secretary to the Government of India, Home Dept., New Delhi, dated October 17, 1942, Home Political (I), F. Ne. 28/9/1942.

PLATE 1

PLATE 2

Mashriqi, and was made a *Salar*, and remained as such
for a long time. At last I studied the true state of affairs,
and it became clear to me that this movement was frivo-
lous and meaningless. So I segregated my connexion
with it. The army under my control melted away also
out of disgust. I am sending to you testimonials of my
training and currency notes issued by Inayatallah. You
please publicize the fact that this man issues currency
notes as well and deceives people by giving out that these
are bills of exchange to be cashed on sight.[114]

These notes were generally issued to *Salars* on the promise
that hard cash will be given to them in exchange for these notes
from the mint of Inayatallah Khan on the auspicious occasion
of his coronation. This was to take place on the eve of India's
independence.[115] The impression of these currency notes
contained the map of India with crescent, star, numbers etc.
(*See* Plates I and II).

These were issued under Mashriqi's orders and the
Government of India banned and forfeited.[116] this currency in
the interest of maintaining law and order in the country.

Famine policy

The Bengal famine offered an opportunity to Mashriqi
to boost his organization[117] as the agonies of people had protracted over an unconsciously long period of time and yet the
end was not in sight. *The Radiance Weekly* wrote:

Men showed their courage by committing suicide and
women their kindness by killing their infants. Husbands
drove away wives and wives drove away ailing husbands;
children had forsaken aged and disabled parents and
parents had also left home in despair; brothers turned
deaf ears to the entreaties of hungry sisters and widowed

---

[114]*Jatistan*, Lahore, dated October 7, 1942.

[115]Home Political (I), F. No. 28/9/1942, p. 2.

[116]Ibid.

[117]Home Department [Political-Internal] F. No. 28/5/1943-Poll. [I] and K.W.

sisters maintained for years together departed at the time of direct need. Corpses were frequently seen lying by the side of roads in the towns. Such grim and ghastly sights were not even seen in those countries where war was actually going on and taking its own toll of life.[118]

Mashriqi sought prior permission from the Bengal Government to serve the suffering people and devised a scheme to serve the 600,000 Bengal destitutes during the famine. In obedience to his orders, officers of the *Khaksars* organisation reached Calcutta from various parts of India. They started the work of collecting and despatching destitutes to various centres outside Bengal but chiefly to places in Punjab, U.P. and Sind. Here they were maintained as their guests but no distinction of caste or colour was made in the choice of destitutes. The Bengal Government cooperated with the *Khaksars* by paying railway fare plus Rs. 5 each to cover the incidental expenses of the destitutes.[119] Altogether 800 destitutes, 200 of them Hindus, were benefited by the relief measures. But the Hindu Mahasabha expressed resentment at such concessions being allowed to *Khaksars* and requested the Bengal Premier to take steps to ensure that they did not remove any more Hindus from Bengal.[120]

Mashriqi, on knowing this, made it clear that his organisation was not communal, and as such he had authorized Pandit Amar Nath Joshi and two other *Khaksars* from Punjab and Sind to deal with Hindu destitutes. Nevertheless, this created communal difficulties and on 20 December 1943, the Bengal Premier directed the *Khaksars* to close down the camp on Jinnah's advice. This was done and the destitutes in the *Khaksar* camp were made over to the Government three days later on 24 December 1943.[121] Mashriqi felt greatly annoyed over it and closed the incident by issuing a telegram to Jinnah in which he criticized the order of the Government of

---

[118]Vol. III, No. 36, dated Aligarh, Friday, October 8, 1943.
[119]Home Department (Political-Internal) F.No. 28/5/1943-Poll.(I) and K.W.
[120]Ibid.
[121]Ibid.

Bengal and making a "token present"[122] of the dead bodies of six hundred thousand of destitutes to Jinnah on the occasion of his birthday.

The Bengal famine[123] affords another illustration of Mashriqi's violation of the basic principles of his movement because he ordered the collection of subscriptions from his followers on the pretext that "the situation was grave".

Policy Towards Political Parties

Contrary to their ideology of rendering social service, the *Khaksars* persuaded the leaders of various political parties "in most emphatically demanding complete independence of India".[124] They urged the Congess and the Muslim League to resolve their differences and offered to place a million *Khaksars* at their disposal to achieve their goal on the condition that their leader alone should be entrusted with the task of securing independence. They reiterated that "we do not get entangled in political controversies which hold up the progress of the nation. We are not a political party. We keep aloof and yet we are with all."

The *Khaksars'* relations with the Muslim League need separate notice because it was the only authoritative and representative political organisation of the Muslims in India. The Muslim League received support not so much out of genuine sympathy as from the motive of consolidating its position *vis a vis* the other political and communal parties.[126] That is why its leaders like Jinnah, Sir Nizam al-Din and Hasan Isfahani persuaded the *Khaksars* to join the party and offered to associate them with the Executive Committees of its various provincial

---

[122]Ibid.

[123]Mashriqi to Nauwab of Murshidabad, No. 10549, Idara-i 'Aliya, Ichhra, Lahore dated October 2, 1943. Quoted in the Radiance Weekly, dated Friday, October 8, 1943.

[124]Home Department (Political], F. No. 74-4/1941-Poll. [I] Part III, para.4.

[125]'*Khaksars and the Political Goal of India.*' Home Political (I), F. No. 33/5/1943.

[126]Speech by Saiyid Rada 'Ali in Council House, New Delhi, dated September 1941. Home Poll. [I], No. 74-4/1941.

branches. Mashriqi was even tipped to be a Member of its Working Committee.[127]

As a result of these overtures Mashriqi agreed to join the League provided the *Khaksars* were (i) allowed to maintain their fundamental individuality, (ii) exempted from taking part in Muslim League subscriptions and dinners and (iii) offered the offices already promised to them. But the gap between Jinnah's offer and Mashriqi's response was too wide to be bridged.[128] Later on, the League once again persuaded the *Khaksars* "to adopt the Muslim League as their political body and to work under its flag with the Muslims, all of whom wished to lead an honourable life in India"[129]. Nothing substantial came out of this offer until Mashriqi promised that his followers would fill the need of a national army if and when *Pakistan* materialized. Jinnah thereupon readily supported the *Khaksar* demand for the lifting of the ban on the organisation. But unluckily when negotiations started between the two leaders Mashriqi changed his mind and announced that his organisation would continue to maintain its separate identity and render social service[130] to all political parties. Negotiations thereafter completely broke down. The Muslim League got furious. In 1943 it passed the anti-*Khaksar* resolution because they had now entered into 'politics' contrary to the original programme of rendering social service to the humanity. The League argued that "the moment they entered into politics they were a separate body".[131] But the *Khaksars* criticized this action as "strange and monstrous" as the League had failed to realize that the life of an individual or of a nation could not be divided into two watertight compartments by separating religion from politics.[132]

[127]'*Khaksar-Muslim League Negotiations.*' Home Department [Political-Internal], F.No. 28/5/1942-Poll.

[128]'*Khaksars and the Muslim League.*' Home Department [Political-Internal], F.No. 74-4/1941-Poll. [I], para. 5.

[129]Ibid.

[130]Ibid.

[131]The Radiance Weekly, Vol. III, No. 44, dated Friday, December 3, 1943.

[432]Activities of Allama 'Inayatallah Khan Mashriqi, Leader of the *Khaksar* Organization and his Followers. Home Department [Political-Internal] F, No. 28/5/1943-Poll. I and K.W,

The Muslim League was further annoyed when a *Khaksar*, Rafiq Sabir of Mozung, Lahore, who was touring India for organisational work attacked Jinnah on 26, July 1943 in Bombay. Some *Khaksars* now seriously thought of disbanding the movement while others became critical of Mashriqi's leadership. Many left the organisation to join the Muslim League. Mashriqi himself agreed that the movement was greatly discredited as a result of this assault. But in order to cover up the lost prestige he carried on the propaganda that Rafiq Sabir had been expelled from the movement but it had no effect. He also denied responsibility for this assault because the Unionist Party in Punjab had abetted this outrage. This led to strained relations between the *Khaksars* and the Muslim League. But the publication of an Urdu Booklet entitled *Hamla*[133] (*Attack*) in 1944 proved that this attack was the result of a deeply laid conspiracy between the Government of India and Jinnah himself to disrupt and destroy the *Khaksar* movement and that the alleged attempted murder was a 'put-up shot'.[134] Jinnah's assailant was consequently sentenced to five years' rigorous imprisonment. This development occurred probably because Jinnah was convinced that Mashriqi had turned pro-Congress and would ultimately place the organisation at the disposal of its leaders.[135]

Party Organs

Al-Islah was the official organ of the *Khaksar* organisation. It started its publication from Lahore in October, 1934. Between 1935 and 1940 it was warned[136] for publishing objectionable articles like '*Khaksar Movement and Silence*'[137] and '*Last and Final*

---

[133]Ibid.

[134]Ibid.

[135]Home Political [I] F. No. 17/4/1943.

[136]D.O. letter No. 2790-C.D.S.B. dated April 20, 1940, from Saiyid Ahmad Shah, I.P.S B.I., Punjab, Lahore, to Calcutta Special Branch, Home political [I], F. No. 33/8/1940-

[137]The gist of this article, containing pro-*Khaksar* propaganda, is given below: A silent nation is in reality the only powerful nation. Silence is the first and last sign of strength. All the biggest powers of nature remain silent and do practical work quietly. The German nation was defeated during

Orders of the Salar-i Khas Hind'[138] and was therefore banned. Attempts were made in 1942 to revive its publication from Karachi but these proved to be of no avail. The *Khaksar* policies were then supported by *Iqbal* which was published from Rawalpindi and the daily *Sultan* from Bombay.

The first issue of *al-Akthariyat*, a weekly, came out from Lucknow in April 1943. Its tone was threatening and decidedly anti-government but when security was demanded from its editor it stopped its publication. Towards the end of 1943 two weeklies, *viz.*, *The Radiance Weekly* and *al-I-lan* started their publication. They encouraged and emphasized the militant aspect of the movement[139] in a balanced tone.

The *Khaksars* also published a *Camp Number* after the famine relief work in Bengal. It came out in the form of an Urdu booklet printed under the title *Musibat Zadagan-i Bengal aur Khaksaron ki Khidmat*. It does not give the name of the author or publisher or even the place where it was printed, but it is clear that it was issued under the orders of 'Abd al-Rashid Quraishi, *Hakim-i Ala*, Bengal, and edited by Dr Abu Zafar Muhammad Tahir, *Bab-i Ali, 31/109,* Chitpur Road,

---

the Great War as it did not observe silence and spread true and false news of every kind among the masses which resulted in disorganisation. The Britishers though involved in greatest difficulties remained silent on account of which they remained firm upto the last with the spirit of victory among them. Even the persons in constant touch with them did not kow as to what was in the minds of the Britishers,
See also al-Islah, Vol. 1/7, No. 10, dated August 7, 1940.

[138]In this article the *Khaksar* leader made a stirring appeal to its followers in the following words:
O Soldiers of God ! If the movement is going to die after 10 years why should not every faithful [Muslim or *Khaksar*] die by cannons and guns respectfully so that those bodies may not live which have in any case to die some day.
O Soldiers of God ! The Holy Quran is demanding sacrifice from you.
See also Home Political [I] F. No. 83/8/1940.

[139]The Government of India drew the attention of the United Provinces Government to the veiled incitement to violent action which was contained in some articles, against which, however, the Provincial Government did not consider any immediate action.
See also Home Political [I] F. No. 28/5/1943 and K.W.

Calcutta. The booklet contained *Khaksar* propaganda and praised the work done by them during the Bengal famine.[140]

The task of carrying on *Khaksar* propaganda outside India and particularly in Muslim countries bordering India was entrusted to Arbab Sher Khan.[141] It would be particularly interesting to note in this connexion that he made systematic efforts to stop the publication and restrict the circulation of those newspapers which published anti-*Khaksar* or anti-Islamic articles.[142]

The Bible of the Khaksars

No account of the *Khaksar* movement would be complete without a critical examination of *Tadhkira*. Its study is essential because it throws a flood of light on the religious conceptions[143] of Mashriqi. Mashriqi was greatly influenced by western sciences and philosophy and talked much about state and sovereignty. His views and conceptions about authority were materialistic. There was no transcendental reality in his writings. Under the influence of western thought he found fault with everything that was Islamic. He had strange notions of course unpuritanic—about religion. To him disbelief meant

---

[140]Home Political [I] F. No. 28/5/1943 and K.W.

[141]He was appointed as Hakim-i A'la of 'Outside India'. Along with this order a number of appointments were also made in the *Khaksar* organisation as follows:

'Abd al-Ra'uf Khakwani	*Hakim-i A'la*, U.P.
Muhammad Akram Khan Jalis	*Hakim-i A'la*, N.W.F.P. and Kashmir
Bashir Ahmad Siddiqi	*Nazim-i A'la*,
Muhammad Aslam Khan	*Hakim-i A'la*, Sind
Hajjit Kahim Bakhsh	*Nazim-i A'la, Mu'awinin-i Hind*
Nauwab Bahadur Yar Jang	*Nazim-i A'la, Maulavian-i Hind.*
Wahid al-Din Haidar	*Hakim-i A'la*, Madras.
Ghulam Mustafa Bhurguri	*Hakim-i A'la*, Baluchistan.
Mir 'Ali Ahmad Khan Talpri	*Hakim-i A'la*, Punjab.

[142]Note on the *Khaksar* Movement. Home Political F. No. 74-4/1941-Poll·[I], Part III.

[143]An Exposition of the *Tadhkira* by Prof. M. Ai-Fadl. Home Department [Political-Internal], F. No. 231/1941-Poll. [I], p.2.

lack of power and faith stood for material strength and domination. Muslim rulers according to him were not only unsympathetic but dictatorial and despotic.[144]

Islam's conception of life was extensive but that of Mashriqi was a limited and narrow one. This was owing to the fact that he largely borrowed from the writings of Darwin, Bacon, Hobbes, Machiavelli, Bentham, Mill and other leaders of Hedonism and misunderstood the meaning of personal liberty and authority. He failed to appreciate that Islam was not only a moral code but a perfect social organisation and that there was a great difference between the institutions of Islam and those of other riligions. In Islam religion was not a private concern and its vitality had to be maintained but not at the cost of personal liberty. Islam aimed at the sovereignty of the *Shari a* and not at dictatorship[145].

The *Tadhkira* was described by its author as the '*Bible of the Khaksars*'[146] and a 'permanent reality'.[147] To make it effective its author adopted an oratorical style and used charming words to illustrate the domination of Islam and God's Kingdom. But in reality he was under the influence of the western philosophers and scientists and his criterion of judgement was un-Islamic. According to him everything that succeeded was good and everything that failed was evil. This he had borrowed from Machiavelli. His conception of Islamic Caliphate was based on Laski's materialism. Spiritualism had no place in his theory of state.[148]

Referring to the Caliphate, Mashriqi lamented the downfall of the Muslims and shed tears at the deplorable state of the Muslim community. He criticized them for not following his ideology and called them hell-bound, worthy of disgrace and insult, perverted and wrong. Influenced by the teachings of

---

[144]Ibid., p. 3.

[145]Ibid.

[146]'Allama Mashriqi' : *Isharat*, pp 2.6,19.

[147]Ibid.

[148]'An Exposition of the Tadhkira' by Prof. M. Al-Fadl. Home Department [Political-Internal] F. No. 231/1941-Poll. [I] p. 4.

Hobbes, Mashriqi bowed before every material power. This sort of conception was absolutely against the teachings of Islam.

Mashriqi's way of interpretation of *Quranic* verses was novel. For example a well-known verse is :

Ye shall have the upper hand if ye but be believers.[149]

It is easy and clear in its sense and means that success follows belief and faith. But Mashriqi formed a new theory that where there is success there is belief. Every prosperous and successful man is a believer whether he follows Christianity or Hinduism.[150]

Mashriqi was a messenger of materialism. He counted everything in terms of matter. His criterion of judging right from wrong depended not so much on the intrinsic value of a thing as on the power and strength gained through it. According to him the world was governed by the law of nature and there was no power to control and manage it.[151]

He supported the view that every religion aims at worldy superiority and domination.[152] This is absolutely against the teachings of Islam. No doubt, power comes in the wake of Islam but this is not the object of Islam. Islam aims at inner cleanliness and purity of heart. A student of Islam cannot fail to find out the real mission of the Prophet of Islam. He was a true Muslim and the first Muslim when he claimed prophethood in Mecca. For full eleven years he preached Islam and conveyed the revelations to the Meccans under unfavourable circumstances. He was tortured and ridiculed by the polytheists. During this period he had no land to rule, no forces, no worldy power. Was that not an Islamic period of his life? Was he not then a true Muslim?[153]

---

[149]Ibid., p.6.
[150]Ibid., p.6.
[151]Ibid., p.7.
[152]Tadhkira, Arabic Part, p. 30.
[153]Prof. M. Al-Fadl, Op. cit., p. 8.

Mashriqi was so horrified with the scientific inventions of his age that he seemed to have lost his mental equilibrium. He did not consider the Great Book of Islam—the *Quran*—as a miracle and interpreted words like 'angels', 'genii' and 'Satan' in his own materialistic[154] way. To him God's blessing was a palpable thing. It had nothing to do with spiritualism.[155] Similarly, lawful or unlawful things were connected with men's social and worldly life and the Straight Path meant only a social programme to achieve a wordly goal.[156]

Mashriqi's conception of God's unity (*tauhid*) was un-Islamic. He did not believe God only in words but wanted to follow His programme of work and endeavours. As the idolaters carried out this programme he regarded them as unitarians but criticized the Muslims as *kafirs* because they failed to make any attempts for the advancement of their community. This strange conception of *tauhid* left no scope for Islamic spiritualism and real unity of God as taught by the Holy Prophet. It led Mashriqi away from the spirit of Islam theoretically as well as practically.[157]

Mashriqi and the Hereafter

Mashriqi's conception of the Paradise and Hell was quite different from that of Islam. According to him, ruling nations lived in Paradise and the down trodden in Hell. This showed that he had no faith in the Hereafter and this was the reason why he did not discuss such an important topic in the *Tadhkira*. He failed to realize that belief in the Day of Judgment[158] is one of the most fundamental teachings of all the Prophets. To believe in it is an essential condition for being a Muslim. The whole structure of religion rests upon it and on its foundation is also built the great edifice of Islam. Man's attitude about

---

[154]Tadhkira, Arabic part, pp. 87, 99.

[155]Ibid., Urdu part, pp. 215, 217.

[156]Ibid., p. 225.

[157]Prof. M. Al-Fadl, Op. cit., p. 9.

[158]It forms the fifth article of faith and without it, faith remains incomplete in Islam.

an action is decided by his belief in the Day of Judgment.[159] Such a belief looked not only reasonable but also important and necessary to maintain peace and order in the society. But it found no place in Mashriqi's writings, though he later on included it in his Ten Articles of Fath.[160]

Unorthodox views in Tadhkira

The *Tadhkira* shows Mashriqi's strange and unorthodox views. It is asserted that the European Christians are the true believers in the *Quran* who act righteously in our age. It is they who are pious and who will prosper.[161] Materialism is the only means to be dearer to God.[162]

To the author of the *Tadhkira* faith is nothing, and action everything. He wants scientific exactness in religion and gives mechanical interpretation of Islam. According to Mashriqi the Christians, Jews, Muslims and Hindus are all alike. He who obeys God is a believer and a Muslim. Here is a total disregard of the articles of faith enunciated by the *Quran*. Mashriqi discards the divine five articles of faith and introduces ten new articles of his own. To a Muslim the Five Articles of Faith are : (i) Belief in the Oneness of God, (ii) Belief in the Angels of God, (iii) Belief in the Books of God, (iv) Belief in the Prophets of God and (v) Belief in the Day of Judgment.[164] But Mashriqi enumerates the following as the Articles of Faith : (i) Unity of action, (ii) Unity of the nation, (iii) Obedience to a ruler from amongst the people, (iv) *jehad* against the enemies with wealth, (v) *jehad* with sword and

---

[159]It is a great determining factor in man's life. Islam declares that one day the world will end. God will destroy and annihilate the existing physical system, and in its place will evolve another higher and better cosmos. Man will again be given life. God who created man in this world will revive him. Actions and deeds of man will be judged. Full justice will be done. Good-doers will be rewarded and evil-doers will be punished.

[160]'An Exposition of the Tadhkira by Prof. M. Al-Fadl. Home Department [Political Internal], F. No. 231/1941-Poll, [I], p. 11.

[161]Tadhkira, Arabic Part, p. 85.

[162]Ibid., Arabic Part, p. 31.

[163]Ibid., Arabic Part, p. 52.

[164]Ibid., Arabic Part, p. 56.

person, (vi) Travels to foreign countries, (vii) Perseverance and constancy in endeavours, (viii) Nobility of character, (ix) Acquisition of science and learning, and (x) Belief in the world to come.[165]   The author of the *Tadhkira* does not attach much importance to the five daily prayers, and likens them to the sharpening of the chisel by a carpenter to do his day's work.[166] He condemns the religious leaders and books on jurisprudence.[167]   In the opinion of Mashriqi, to obey any religious leader, *imam* or *wali*, dead or alive, is to pave a way to hell.[168] He denounces the dress of the *ulama* and calls them deceits. Lip faith is nothing to Mashriqi.[169]   It is all idolatory to be called Christians, Jews, Hindus, and Muslims.[170] Mashriqi believes that all sects, *viz.*, Shiahs, Hanafis, Shafiis, Sufis, Wahabis etc. are but hell-bound.[171]   To perform the pilgrimage in old age is no devotion, no worship.[172]   Mashriqi strongly condemns the exegetical (*tafsir*) literature. To him the commentaries on the *Quran* are full of irrelevant matter.[173] To keep the fast, to offer prayers, to perform the pilgrimage and to pay the poor rate is not at all worship and devotion unless they spur one on to *act*, to uphold God's magnificent system of law.[174]

The *Tadhkira* was not a 'master-piece'.[175]   It was rejected by a large section of the Muslims. The *Jamiat-i Ulama* even issued a *fatwa* and condemned it as anti-Islamic.[176]   At heart,

---

[165]Ibid., Arabic Part, p. 80.

[166]Ibid., Urdu Preface, pp. 91, 91.

[167]Ibid., Urdu Preface, p. 65.

[168]Ibid., Urdu Preface, p. 61.

[169]Ibid., Urdu Preface, p. 83.

[170]Ibid., Urdu Preface. p. 110.

[171]Ibid., Urdu Preface, p. 60.

[172]Ibid., Urdu Preface, p. 97.

[173]Ibid., Urdu Preface, p. 55.

[174]Ibid., Urdu Preface, p. 98

[175]Note by Sir R. Tottenham, Secretary, Home Department, dated March 3. 1943. Home Political [I] F. No. 131/1941-Poll. I.

[176]Note by Maj. Shah dated July 11, 1941.   Home Political [I], F. No. 231/ 1941-Poll. [I].

Muslims on the whole did not want the *Tadhkira* to elucidate the *Quran*.[177] They contradicted Mashriqi's views by widespread publicity throughout India and the Middle East.[178] The *Khaksars* themselves accepted its defective interpretations. The British Government considered this evidence sufficient enough to discredit[179] Mashriqi whenever it wished to do so.

Government's Policy towards Khaksars

The *Khaksars* presented a difficult and rather baffling problem before the Government. There were conflicting views about the nature of their organisation. One school of thought regarded them as a communal or political organisation and adherents of a new creed or mode of life, while another looked upon their activities as a movement which designed to meet temporal power. The Government judged the *Khaksars* not by what they said or by what they wrote but purely by what they did and how they acted. They regarded them as no less than "a private army in India" or an association organised on military lines under military discipline. In pursuance of this policy they declared drilling and wearing of semi-military uniforms to be illegal and succeeded in placing themselves in an unassailable position.[180]

The disturbances of 1939 and 1940 had convinced the Government that the *Khaksar* organisation interfered with the maintenance of law and order and constituted a danger to the public peace.[181] Their occupation of selected mosques not only implied a gross misuse of religious edifices for non-religious purposes but also caused serious inconvenience to genuine

---

[177]Eastern Times, dated June 6, 1941.

[178]Home Political [I] F. No. 231/1941-Poll. [I].

[179]Note by Sir R. Tottenham, Secretary, Home Department, dated March 3, 1943. Home Political [I], F. No. 231/1941-Poll. [I].

[180]Speech by Sir R. Tottenham, Secretary, Home Department, in Council House, New Delhi, dated September 2, 1942. Home Department [Political-Internal] F. No. 24/10/1942-Poll. [I].

[181]Ibid.

worshippers as the mosques were converted into "bases of unlawful operations."[182] The Government, declared, therefore, the *Khaksar* organisation as 'unlawful,[183] This step created a good impact. The *Khaksars* thereafter failed to establish themselves in mosques and there was no disturbance of peace.[184] Still, strict vigilance was kept on the organisation of camps to forestall any move to challenge the authority of the Government.[185] The *Khaksars* thus failed to exploit Islamic sentiments to obtain recognition as the only organised body able to protect and further Muslim interests.[186]

The *Khaksars* possessed, no doubt, some characteristics of a military movement, but they justified it in the midst of a world-wide conflict in which the fate of India and of all freedom-loving countries was at stake. They were astonished if anyone condemned their organisation because they wanted to awaken the masses to their responsibilities by instilling martial instincts in them.[187] On the other hand, they criticized the Government for following a policy which emasculated subject nations, killed their sense of life, denied them the right to organise themselves, the right to strive for a disciplined brotherhood, and the right to love and serve their brotherhood.[188]

The *Khaksars* wanted to help the Government in their own way by offering the services of fifty thousand volunteers[189]

---

[182]Home Department Communique dated June 5, 1941. Home Department [Political-Internal], F. No. 28/2/1952-Poll. [I].

[183]Ibid.

[184]Home Political F. No. 74/1/1941 [I]

[185]Ibid.

[186]Ibid.

[187]Speech by Khan Bahadur Shaikh Fadl-i Haqq Pirach at Council House, New Delhi, dated September 2, 1942. Home Department [Political-Internal F. No. 24/10/1942-Poll. [Ij

[188]Ibid., p. 16.

[189]It is interesting to quote here a telegram which 'Allama Mashriqi sent to Sir Stafford Cripps on March 23, 1942:

"I committed the crime of offering the Viceroy October 6, 1939, when every political party was irreconcilably hostile, 50,000 *Khaksars* unconditionally, to defend India to last drop of blood. Also published

at the disposal of the Government. But this offer was repeatedly rejected in 1939, 1940, 1941 and 1942 on the ground that they wanted to retain their own identity in the army. Instead, the Government asked them to join the army or the police force as ordinary recruits,[190] but this did not suit their convenience. The Government sought, therefore, the required help from the Allies but did not lift the ban on the organisation. This policy made the *Khaksars* utterly useless and harmless.[191]

It is often contended that the *Khaksars* were 'fifth-columnists'[192] and 'in touch with the Nazis', but these allegations appear to be untrue because they were loyal to the Government[193] and did not help the Congress or the Muslim League in the dislocation of administration. Throughout, they remained hostile to the Axis dictatorship and as such did not follow the Nazi methods. This is proved by the fact that Mashriqi drew up the constitution of the *Khaksars* in 1924, but at that time Hitler was neither heard of nor had prepared any scheme of the Nazi organisation. The similarity between the two

---

pamphlet exhorting everybody to help British utmost. Result was: pamphlet confiscated, myself jailed, organization banned, 2,000 *Khaksars* arrested forty murdered in cold blood, my *purdah*-house thrice raided, eldest son aged sixteen jailed, my women children thrown to winds, other son aged thirteen murdered, my entire money—several lakhs—confiscated, my family twelve starved, my daughter refused dowry, myself forced to pay Rs. 1,000 personal expenses, jail threatened with lashes, lashes, locked, tortured, kicked by Superintendent, solitarily confined, smoking disallowed, servants removed during fast, my invalid pension 300 monthly arrears 12,000 confiscated, my wife, children, brother, friends disallowed interview altogether, until after twenty-two months detention without trial I secured my release after fasting eighty days and am still ordered to remain in Madras till settlement...."[7]

[190]Speech by Sir Richard Tottenham ar Council House, New Delhi, dated September 2, 1942. Home Department [Political-Internal] F. No. 24/10 1942-Poll. [I].

[191]Ibid.

[192]Speech by Dr Diya al-Din Ahmad at Council House, New Delhi, dated Ssptember 2, 1942. Home Department [Political-Internal] F. No. 24/10/ 1942-Poll. [I].

[193]Home Political F. No. 74/4/1940 Poll.

is a matter of chance or accident. If anyone copied the other, it was Hitler who copied Mashriqi.[194]

The fact remains that the *Khaksar* movement showed infinite capacity for harm[195] not only in the heyday of its activities but also during the period it was declared unlawful by the Government. But in spite of this, it cast a powerful influence on the people by inscribing on its banner the words 'Action and Glory' which created a magical appeal among the Muslim youth. In India, too as in post-war Germany, the young educated generation was utterly desperate with the existing state of affairs[196]. A university graduate, if he was not one of the lucky few who won a Government post, sold his talents for Rs. 35 a month. In Madras, graduates joined the police force for even less. In U.P., they started going to post-offices. The Bachelor of Arts training made them nothing more than clerks. The universities' cultural simulations kept them dissatisfied with an empty life[197]. It was because of this discontent that the *Khaksar* movement appealed to the people for its ideals of physical fitness, social service, inter-communal harmony and the like and won a large number of adherents. Students who came under its influence, particularly at Aligarh, were "straight-forward, confident of themselves, and uninferior".[198] They wanted this spirit to permeate through the masses to change the face of the country. But owing to its internal contradictions and its worship of violence the movement came to grief.[199] The Government could have made a better use of these virtues by providing the young men with "a programme of real glory and action" because these were essential for their recuperation from an excess of frustra-

---

[194]Speech by Dr Diya al-Din Ahmad at Council House, New Delhi, on September 2, 1942. Home Department [Political-Internal], F. No, 24/10/1942-Poll. [I].

[105]The Hindu, Madras, dated September 19, 1941.

[196]Ibid.

[197]The Indian Journal of Social Work, vol. II, No. 2, dated September, 1941, pp. 185-202.

[198]Home Political F. No. 74/6/1941-Poll. [I].

[199]Ibid.

tion. But instead of curing this discontent they suppressed the subversive movement by force.[200]

Mashriqi officially announced the disbandment of the movement after independence[201] and spent the remaining years of his life in Pakistan to carry on his political activities afresh.[202] He died of cancer at Lahore on 27 August, 1963, after a protracted illness at the age of 75 and was laid to rest in Idara-i Aliya Hindia, the headquarters of the *Khaksar* movement at Ichhra, Lahore, in the presence of thousands of his admirers and relatives.

---

[200]The Indian Journal of Social Work, vol. II, No. 3, September 1941, pp. 185-202.

[201]Pakistan High Commission Letter No. Inf: 6 [2]69 dated February 4, 1969.

[202]He founded Islam League in 1948 and vehemently opposed the principle of parity between East and West Pakistan till all units in West Pakistan emerged into one single unit on the basis of solidarity of West Pakistan. He wanted East and West Pakistan to be one unit and pleaded for one common language—Urdu—and one common culture—Islamic—for the whole of Pakistan. He also denounced western democracy and communism and demanded establishment of Islamic democracy in the country. On April 2, 1957, he was expelled from Islam League by a decision of the Council of Islam League on the plea that he miserably failed to liberate Kashmir due to the loss of mental equilibrium.

9

Red Shirt Movement

The *Red Shirt Movement**, started in 1929 under the leadership of Khan Abdul Ghaffar Khan with the object of uplifting and improving the people of the Frontier and of preparing them for the attainment of independence. It collapsed in 1947 but no account of this movement can be properly understood without a background of the history of the North Western Frontier Province. It would be interesting to note that although hundreds of books have been written on Indian National Movement few of them throw sufficient light on the Red Shirt Movement.

The Background

It is well known that after the Durranis British rule was established in the province which was annexed to Punjab in 1849. But again in 1901 it was separated because anti-British Pathans in Punjab had begun to look upon the British as their enemies because they introduced new and brutal laws in the province.[1] These laws were embodied in the Frontier

---

* The Red Shirts of Khan Abdul Ghaffar Khan were better known as *Khudai Khidmatgars* or Servants of God, a volunteer corps of Frontier Pathans organised on the basis of non-violence and passive resistance.

[1] "The *Naujawan Sarhad*", Peshawar, dt. January 1930,

Crimes Regulation Act. This was such a brutal and savage act and the British enforced it in such an atrocious manner that it created communalism, disharmony and mutual enmity among the Pathans. No longer did they live together in harmony and unity. Besides this Act did great damage to the self-respect of women. They were arrested and taken to the courts. Under this abnoxious law the police could start a fictitious case against anyone the British happened to dislike. No proof or evidence was necessary. Of course the person was brought before the Assembly of Elders, known as *Jirga*, but it was not the peoples *jirga*.[2] The British had created their own *jirgas*, of their own people, and a person could be sentenced to twelve or fourteen years imprisonment without any right of appeal. Innocent people were dragged to the courts and put to death while sinners often escaped scot-free.[3]

Under the British the Frontier became an asylum of immoralities where sodomy, prostitution, use of knives, playing with quails and other evil habits had become the necessary occupations of life. *Khans* or tribal *Sirdars* took pride in keeping lads for committing sodomy; daughters were sold in the market and deprived of legacy rights. Cousins regarded themselves as enemies. Seeking revenge was unparalleled.

Government framed many rules for caging and uncaging people. Justice was auctioned in the courts. Magistrates were ignorant; *Munsiffs* were untrimmed logs, *Vakeels* were selfish and shirked work.[4] Agriculturists were considered to be quadrupeds and beasts and bought and sold with the land as the property of the 'big bellies'. No steps were taken to educate the children. The real purpose of the Government was to keep the Pathans illiterate and uneducated and this was the reason that in education the Pathans were most backward in India.

The Frontier province, once considered to be the 'pride of the East' had become the field of 'cunning tricks of the

---

[2]Ibid.

[3]Ibid.

[4]The "*Naujawan Sarfarosh*", dated 25 March, 1930.

West' and an 'asylum of robber capitalists of Europe'. The blood sucking machineries of Lancashire and Manchester began to suck its blood from its veins and the selfish and merciless '*banias*' of Europe took complete possession of its resources and wealth. Industries were thus taken over by them and labourers and peasants were chained in all sorts of restrictions and made helpless.[5]

The events of 1919 infuriated the Frontier people. Lloyd George's false assurances to grant self-government to the people of India and General Dyer's improper action at Jullianwala Bagh (10 April 1919) when in 10 minutes his troops killed 379 innocent persons and wounded 1208 roused the greatest indignation among the people. They got ready to get rid of the worst servitude of the British Raj so as to relieve themselves of the curse of capitalism because labourers had been oppressed and peasants killed by the ruinous action of the Government.[6] They were dying of hunger and reduced to the worst position by restrictions imposed by Frontier laws. The Government held the view that men deserved worse treatment than animals, justified tyranny and violence on the peasants and aimed at the extinction of the spirited tribes who once had the fate of India in their hands.[7]

It was therefore no surprise that in 1927 when the Simon Commission went to the Frontier, it refused to give Reforms to the people on the ground that the place was a '*Powder Magazine*',[8] and therefore its people should not be allowed any freedom. It was argued before them that in the neighbouring country, Afghanistan, even though the people were much more backward, King Amanullah granted them parliament and so they were also fit for reform. The result of this was that during the absence of Amanullah, the British Government after spending crores of rupees secretly sowed seeds of

---

[5]Home Political File No. II/III of 1930.

[6]'*Naujawan Sarfarosh*', dated 25 March, 1930.

[7]Communique on Peshawar dated 3 May, 1930 by H.W. Emerson, Home Political File No. II/III of 1930.

[8]Speech by Abdul Ghaffar Khan dated 7.10.1934 at Suja Musjid at Comila, Home Political File No. 1/1/34.

revolution in Afghanistan. When Amanullah came back he was driven away from the country and another man was made King. It thus becomes quite clear that the British government did not at this stage desire to give any Reforms to the people of India.

Beginning of Movement

In January 1929 Ghaffar Khan toured the Frontier province to enlist some support for sending a mission to Afghanistan[9] in order to give some support to ex-King Amanullah. He appealed to Kohat tribesmen to interfere and fight for the ex-King but Government refused permission to this mission to go to Afghanistan because it was not invited by any responsible Afghan authorities. Ghaffar Khan now established a society in Peshawar to carry on propaganda on behalf of King Amanullah.[10] It was known as *Anjuman-i-Naujawanan-i-Sarhad*. The real object of the *Anjuman* was the organization, through the youth of the province, of labourers and peasants against the curse of capitalists and imperialists.[11] Inter-alia it advocated the removal of evil social customs, the extension of primary education, and combating of communalism to bring about peaceful life in the province.[12]

The President of the *Anjuman* was a *Hijrat* refugee, Abdul Akbar, who was trained in Tashkent.[13] The *Anjuman* had a Provincial Central Committee of 49 persons and an executive of 10 persons to control its district, tehsil and village branches. All these branches were known as '*Jirgas*'. The object of these *Jirgas* was to further the objects of the *Anjuman*.[14] But in order to give them power to further these objects Ghaffar

---

[9]Note by M.C. Hallett dated 20.4.1934, Home Political File No. 4/4/1934-Political, para 2.

[10]Ibid, See also Home Political File No. 17/29 of 1929.

[11]Note by M.C. Hallett dated 20.4.1934, Home Political File No. 4/4/1934-Political, para 4.

[12]The Frontier Provincial Youth League and its volunteer organisation of Khudai Khidmatgars, commonly known as "The Red Shirt Organisation", (Peshawar 1930), p. 1, Home Political File No. II/III of 1930.

[13]Telegram No. 1428/1929-S dated 11 June, 1930 from Viceroy Home Department, Simla to Secretary of State for India, London, Home Department File No. II/III of 1930.

[14]Ibid,

Khan established the *Khudai Khidmatgar*[15] organisation[16] and merged the *Anjuman* with it[17]. The *Khudai Khidmatgars* were given complete military training to convert the so called 'magazine' into a 'peaceful house'.[18] The motive for choosing this name was to awaken in the Pathans the idea of service and the desire to serve their country and their people in the name of God, an idea and a desire which was sadly lacking among them[19]. The *Khudai Khidmatgars* wore the prescribed dress i.e., a Red Shirt and paid its cost from their own pockets.[20] The colour was chosen simply because the ingredients of the dye were cheap and easily available.[21] But the British government started calling these *Khudai Khidmatgars*[22] as 'Red Shirts' and that is why this movement has come to be known as Red Shirt Movement.

Upon enrolment the *Khudai Khidmatgars* took the following pledge with the Holy Quran in their hands: "I shall always obey the order of God...In my service for the freedom of humanity, I shall ever remain non-violent in thought and deed and will be absolutely fearless ... I shall never be effected by flattery or abuse... I shall always protect the oppressed from the oppressors... I shall never accept remuneration for my services... I regard all the creatures of God—be they Christians, Hindus, Parsis, Sikhs, Germans, Frenchmen or Englishmen, whoever they may be—as God's creatures and I am the servant of those creatures."[23] They thus believed in universal brotherhood. That was true religion. Christ had come to the world to help the poor and to release them from

---

[15]Khudai Khidmatgar means a servant of God, and is the name by which by the volunteers of the Frontier Province call themselves.

[16]H.A.F. Metcalfe's statement in Legislative Assembly, Home Political File No. 24/9/1235.

[17]Dr. Khan Saheb's statement in the Legislative Assembly, Ibid.

[18]Autobiography of Badshah Khan, (New Delhi, 1969), p. 46.

[19]Telegram P. No. 1928/1929-S, dated 11 June 1930, from Viceroy, Home Department, Simla, to Secretary of State for India, London.

[20]Statement by T.A.K. Sherwani in Legislative Assembly, Home Political File No. 22/109/1935.

[21]Hindustan Times, dated 6.8 1935.

[22]Statement of T.A.K. Sherwani in Legislative Assembly, Home Political File No. 24/9/35.

the clutches of the tyrants who oppressed them. Moses came with the same purpose. *Khudai Khidmatgars* also wanted to do the work which all the religions of the world and all those reformers who came to preach them wanted to do.[24]

In 1929 Ghaffar Khan's attention was drawn to the Congress session[25] at Lahore because many people from Frontier were going to attend it.[26] Ghaffar Khan also accompanied them. At this session Congress asked the Pathans to play their part in the service of the country and the nation. The people of the Frontier attending the session then assembled to discuss the idea and decided to work with Congress.[27] Ghaffar Khan then moved a resolution that the "Frontier people shall have the same rights as the people of other provinces of India" and supported another proposed by Hakim Abdul Jalil that "the Frontier Crimes Regulation should be abolished."

After returning from this session people resumed work with great enthusiasm. They went from village to village, talked to the people, founded *Jirgas* and enlisted *Khudai Khidmatgars*. The movement spread to all parts of the province by January 1930. At first when the movement started Government considered it as a joke and used to say "*The Pathans and the non-violent movement are poles apart. Let them alone. They are wasting time.*"[28] But after a few days when this movement gained strength the Government became nervous and asked Ghaffar Khan what was the matter? He said it was simply an organisation for social reformation and we are organising the Pathans for that purpose. Then the Government said "You

[23]This was the pledge that was taken by the Red Shirt volunteers. Unfortunately they hit upon a colour, which was red, and it was really a red rag to the bull.

[24]Abdul Ghaffar Khan's Sepeech dated 27 Oct. 1934 at Nagpada Neighbourhood House, Home Political File No. 4/4/1934.

[25]Note by N.C. Haig, dated 23.4.1934; Also File No. 4/4/1944.

[26]Isemonger Report, 1929-30, p. 8, Home Political File No. II/III of 1930,

[27]Badshan Khan, My Life and Struggle, pp. 100-1.

[28]Abdul Ghaffar Khan's speech dated 2.10.1934 at Abboi Hall, Calcutta, File No. 1/1/1934-Pol.

won't use your organisation against the Government" and Ghaffar Khan replied "Trust us and we will trust you" but Government did not trust us. Ghaffar Khan was arrested in April 1930 along with many of his followers.[29]

This created an uproar. Riots broke out throughout the Frontier province on 23 April 1930.[30] The people refused to pay revenue and frequently cut off the telegraph wires. Villages abstained from reporting cases to the police and referred them to their own *jirgas*.[31] Thus a programme of civil disobedience was carried out. This movement created one good effect.[32] The people no longer feared British Government and were inspired with new hope and courage.

The Government, in order to maintain its prestige crushed the movement.[33] The Indian soldiers were ordered to open fire on people but they refused saying "what have they got"? They have neither stones nor lathis. On whom should we fire? They were thereupon removed and court martialed and sent to jail. The British soldiers were then brought and they opened fire and 200 to 250 persons were martyred.[34] At various places they ruined and looted the houses of people, broke into pieces all the utensils used for drinking tea and eating food. They put phenyl in the flour pots of the people—the poor people.[35] The persons arrested were subjected to various oppressions in the jails. Some were severely beaten, beards of some were shaved or plucked. There was also oppression upon the females. Some were made naked and some were beaten for nothing. Owing to repeated oppressions the people became courageous and reck-

---

[29]Abdul Ghaffar Khan's speech dated 2.10.1934 at Abbot Hall Calcutta, File No. 1/1/34-Pol.

[30]Isemonger Report (1929-30), para 21, Home Political File No. II/III of 1930.

[31]The Red Shirt Organisation, p. 21, Home Political File No. II/III/1930

[32]Note by M.G. Hallett, dated 20.4.1934, Home Political, File No. 4/4/1934, para. 8.

[33]Hindustan Times, dated 29 November, 1934.

[34]Abdul Ghaffar Khan's speech dated 2.10.1934 at Nagpada Neibghbourhood House, Home Political File No. 4/4/1984.

[35]Ibid.

less.[36]   It became crystal clear that the greater the violence was shown by Government the greater was the increase in the national spirit of the people.   Within three months at that time 40,000 persons were enrolled[37] as *Khudai Khidmatgars*.

The *Khudai Khidmatgars* never forget to quote two incidents[38] to show the violent attitude of the Government.   In May 1930 some soldiers went to Utmanzai, surrounded the village, and did not permit the people to answer even the call of nature which they naturally did in the open outside the village.   They did not allow their cattle to go and they also had to starve.   They did not stop here but went and occupied the house in which the office of *Khudai Khidmatgars* was located. The people in the office were thrown out from the first storey and several of them lost their legs and arms.   The office was then burnt to ashes.[39]   The Government offered compensation[40] for the sufferers but that was not accepted as it was contrary to the oath taken by *Khudai Khidmatgars*.   In the other incident which occurred in June 1930 the Government troops surrounded a village, brought out the people and forced them to stand in the sultry sun.   Not only that: they also placed heavy stones on their necks and asked them to carry the stones uphill and pile them there.[41]

The Government, on the other hand, blamed the *Khudai Khidmatgars* for their violent activities and referred to two incidents[42]

---

[36]Abdul Ghaffar Khan's speech dated 7.10.1934 at Suja Kusjid at Comila, Home Political File No. 4/4/1934.

[37]Ibid.

[38]Siatement by Dr. Khan Saheb, Legislative Assembly Debates, Vol. I, No. 8, dated 5 February, 1935.

[39]Statement by Mr. Sherwani, Legislative Assembly Debates, Vol. I, No. 8, dated 5 February 1935. All see Home Political File No. 22/109/35.

[40]Statement of Mr. H.A.F. Metcalfe, Dy. Commissioner, Peshawar, on Resolution regarding removal of ban a Red Shirt Organisation, Home Political, File No. 244/1935.

[41]Statement of Mr. H.A.F. Metcalfe, Dy. Commissioner, Peshawar, on Resolution regarding removal of ban a Red Shirt Organisation, Home Political File No. 24/4/1935.

[42]Express letter from North West Frontier Provinces, Peshawar, to Home, Simla, Secret No. 2146/P-C, dated Peshawar, 12 June 1930. Home Political File No. II/III of 1930 (Secret). See also Home Political File No. 4/4/1934, para 8.

to prove this charge. The first one concerns a very estimable old gentleman who was known for his loyalty to the Government. That old gentleman, who was one of the principal *lambardars* of the village, had the temerity to send his son to a Government school in Charsadda. He was taken by the *Khudai Khidmatgars* and forced to crawl on his hands and knees along the streets of Charsadda in order to teach him that anybody who sent his son to a government school was only worthy of the grossest humiliation. This was one instance.

The second incident concerns a young policeman, Mr. Murphy, in the Mardan sub-division who did not allow a band of *Khudai Khidmatgars* to come into the Mardan Cantonment because he anticipated a disturbance. Therefore he went out with some police and stopped them at a village 3 miles outside Mardan. Troops were present on the occasion, but in order to avoid any bloodshed, Mr. Murphy decided to deal with the situation himself. Those *Khudai Khidmatgars* were given a matter of several hours to go back to their homes but they declined to move. Mr. Murphy was forced to lead a charge himself against the *Khudai Khidmatgars* in order to try and push them back but he was seized and stoned and belaboured to death. His head was beaten in and his revolver was snatched from his belt and used against him. Troops were present on the occasion but no retaliation was done and no shots were fired. Was that non-violence?

The Government propagated that the organisation and method of penetration of *Khudai Khidmatgars* into the villages showed that they followed communist ideology. But this was wrong. Such an impression originated firstly because they wore Red Shirts and secondly because the President of this association had at one time received training in Tashkent but its organisation was only imitative in its communist aspects and did not owe its birth to communist or Soviet direction.[43] The Red Shirts did not at any time receive any financial aid from any foreign country.

---

[43]Note by M. G. Hallet dated 20.4.1934. Home Political F. 4.4.1934, para 8. *see also* Isemonger Report (1929-39), p. 23. Home Political File No. 11/111 of 1930,

Maximum possible efforts were then made by Government to establish other organizations in the Frontier province to minimise the importance and influence of this movement. Accordingly in 1930 the *Khaksar* party was founded with the help of Allama Mashriqi, the Headmaster of Government High School at Peshawar. But by now the *Khudai Khidmatgar* movement had become so popular that *Khaksar* party failed to make much headway though it did spread to other parts of India. Allama Mashriqi ultimately gave way and that was the end[44] of the *Khaksar* party in the Frontier province.

About this time two Committees known as the Sulaiman Committee—appointed by the Government—and the Patel Committee—appointed by the Congress—were asked to report on the April riots. The Sulaiman Committee absolved[45] the Frontier Government from all blame in connection with these riots but at that time it was well known not only in India but even in Britain that the Frontier Government had lost its head. The Patel Committee work was obstructed because Patel was not allowed by Government to go to the Frontier. He was stopped at Attock, but even then after stopping at Rawalpindi for sometime he seriously studied everything about the condition of the Frontier and drafted the report but it was immediately proscribed[46] by the Government.

Ghaffar Khan now extended his activities into the tribal territory. The Afridis who were at the time at war with Government and other trans-border tribes were asked to come and make common cause with the people of Peshawar district.[47] Two meetings were then organised in defiance of the Political Agent's order forbidding all meetings. At one of

---

[44]Badshah Khan, My Life and Struggle, p. 133.

[45]Statement by Mr. B. Das, regarding Resolution on removal of ban on Red Shirt Organisation in N.W.F.P. Home Political File No. 24-9-1935.

[46]Speech by Abdul Ghaffar Khan at Esplanade Maidan dated 22 October, 1934. Home Political File No. 1-1-1934.

[47]Statement issued by the Chief Commissioner, N.W.F.P. on 24 December, 1931. Home Political File No. 31-28-1-1932.

these meetings the *Khudai Khidmatgars* threatened non-payment of water rates if persons arrested were not released.[48]

To deal with this threatening situation Government despatched troops to Dargai to arrest *Khudai Khidmatgars.* The seizure of papers found on them revealed that they had been in touch with anti-Government party in Afridi country.[49] Inflammatory pamphlets were also discovered but these had already been distributed in Swat territory to stir up disaffection against the Wali of Swat. This was considered to be a grave menace to the peace and order of the Province.[50]

Movement declared unlawful

Finally, on 13 May 1930, the Government declared the association of *Khudai Khidmatgars* as unlawful and characterised it as *Red Shirts* or '*Razakaran*',[51] so that it may create such a tremor in the hearts of the people that they may turn against the movement. But in the eyes of the people they remained *Khudai Khidmatgars*, i.e., the servants of the nation.[52] The Red Shirts of the Frontier were thus not like Red Shirts under Hitler in Germany[53] or like those under Sir Oswald Mosley in England[54] because they did not want to promote their welfare at the cost of other nations.[55] They were simple, truthful and broad-minded.[56] Government criticised[57] them because they

---

[48]Statement issued by the Chief Commissioner, N.W.F.P. on 24 December, 1931. Home Political File No. 31.28.1.1932, pp. 2-3.

[49]Ibid, p. 3.

[50]Statement issued by the Chief Commissoiner, N.W.F.P. on 24 December, 1931. Home Political File No. 31.28.1.32.

[50]Abdul Ghaffar Khan's speech dated 30 September at Town Hall, Calcutta, File No. 1.1.1934.

[52]Statement by Mr. B. Das dated 5 February, 1935. Legislative Assembly Debates, Vol. I, No. 8. Home Political File No. 24-9-35.

[53]Abdul Ghaffar Khan's speech at Nagpada Neighbourhood House dated 27 October, 1934, File No. 1.1.1934.

[54]Bombay Chronicle dated 31.10.1934. Home Political File No. 1/1/1934.

[55]Abdul Ghaffar Khan's speech dated 29 October, 1934 at Bombay. Bombay Chronicle dated 30.10.1934.

[56]Statement by A.C. Fryer, Superintendent of Police on Special Duty at 12.9.1933. Home Political File No. 45/17/1933 & K.W.

[57]Ibid, p. 65.

did not tolerate their humanitarian service[58] and thus crushed this organisation which was engaged in the social uplift of the province.

The Red Shirt movement differed from similar movements in other parts of India. This movement was supported by turbulent people who wanted to overthrow the Government but in other parts of India such movements were supported by educated classes. Moreover the urge for personal freedom in Frontier was more deep-rooted and kept alive by contact with tribesmen living across the Frontier where every man counted himself a king. It had a ready following among the rural population. This movement had thus acquired a greater fillip than the *Swaraj* movement in the rest of India.[59]

It is interesting to note how this movement which was originally a social movement assumed a political colour. Government in fact made it political. The policy of terrorism made the people helpless. They went to the Muslim League, the Muslim Conference and to the Muslims of Lahore, Simla and Delhi and requested them to help but they were unwilling to do so. Ghaffar Khan was pained to hear all this and wanted to know, while in jail, whether there was any other body in India willing to save them from ruin and destruction. Congress promised to help them. This made the movement political.[60]

Government agents now contacted Red Shirts and said "We are prepared to concede whatever you want". But there was a condition attached to it and it was that they should give up Congress and Mahatma Gandhi. The Red Shirts refused to do this because when they were in difficulties, neither the Musalmans, nor the Muslim League nor any other Muslim organization helped them. Only the Congress had saved them from ruin and destruction. This obligation could never be forgotten particularly by Pathans. They reiterated "*We*

---

[58]Hindustan Times, dated 29 November 1934.

[59]Abdul Ghaffar Khan's speech dated 27 October, 1934 at the Nagpada Neighbourhood House, File No. 1/1/1934.

[60]Abdul Ghaffar Khan's speech dated 27 October, 1934 at the Nagpada Neighbourhood House, File No. 1/1/1934.

caunot give up the Congress. The Pathans are not an ungrateful people. We shall never desert any one who does us a good turn."[61]

People heaved a sigh of relief when the Delhi Pact[62] was concluded between Lord Irwin, the Viceroy, and Mahatma Gandhi, the leader of the Indian National Congress. Civil Disobedience movement was now called off by Congress which agreed to participate in the Round Table Conferences in London for settling the political issues between Great Britain and India. The repressive ordinances which had been issued since 1930 were withdrawn and all political prisoners arrested in connection with Civil Disobedience movement were released by Government of India.

Revival of Movement

Ghaffar Khan was released on 10 March 1931. He now reorganised the *Khudai Khidmatgars* as an integral part of All India Congress organisation and prepared his followers for the renewal of the struggle. In a series of stirring speeches he exposed the British government and urged the people to disobey its orders. He made village to village tours in the areas adjoining the Peshawar Cantonment.[63] On his arrival at various villages large crowds lined the roads, beat the drums and fired shots to welcome him and thereby also showed their militant spirit.[64] Sometimes the crowds were so huge that general traffic and business had to be suspended for hours and shopkeepers compelled to close shops for fear of disorder.[65] As in other provinces the exploitation of economic distress remained a marked featured of the movement. The campaign for the non-payment of revenue[66] and water-rates and for the refusal to take Government canal water was intensified. Many of his

---

[61]Ibid.

[62]Statement dated 28 December 1932, para 1. Home Political File No. 31/28/1/32 of 1932.

[63]Statement issued by the Chief Commissioner, N.W.F.P. dated 24 December, 1931. Home Political File No. 31/28/1/32 of 1932.

[64]Ibid.

[65]C.I.D. Report for the 2nd half of October, 1931.

[66]In one part of the Peshawar district a 'Red Shirt' tahsil was opened and collections were made from Zamindars. Revenue payers were instigated to refuse payment of their dues on the plea of not being able to pay.

followers were also opposed to the attachment of property and organised boycott of auction sales.[67]　They demanded remission of 75%[68] of the revenue and the payment of the remaining 25% in kind.[69]　Plans were formulated to establish a *Khudai Khidmatgar Tahsil* to collect a cess from the collectors—1/10th of the produce—as a contribution to *Khudai Khidmatgar* funds.　This movement signified a general intensification of the propaganda against the payment of Government dues.[70]

In a memorable but fiery speech Ghaffar Khan said that 98% of the people who lived in villages did not get enough to eat.[71]　They had no good clothes, no hospitals, no schools and *the condition of their houses was such that even the asses and dogs of Europe would not live in them.*[72]　India, which used to be called the golden country, was inhabited by beggars who were dying of starvation although the country was producing more and more. In order to improve this state of affairs he asked people to make full use of the *Charkha* and to work unitedly.　He likened men and women to the wheels of a cart.　Without two wheels no cart could move and so no country without the two wheels of men and women could attain *Swaraj*.[73]

Time showed that this appeal had a remarkable effect. The people realised that the *Charkha* could at least get them one meal whereas earlier they starved the whole day.　Some people said it was sheer waste of time to ply it but Ghaffar Khan's advice to them was that it was valuable.　That is why Mahatma Gandhi also found out time to ply *Charkha* regularly for sometime.　In Bengal besides plying the *Charkha* the people

---

[67]Statement issued by the Chief Commissioner, N.W.F.P. dated 24 December, 1931, p. 2. Home Political File No. 21/28/1/32 of 1932.

[68]Statement issued by the Chief Commissioner, N.W.F.P. dated 24 December, 1931, p. 2. Home Political File No. 31/28/1/32 of 1932.

[69]C.I.D. Report for the 1st half of July 1931, Ibid.

[70]C.I.D. Report for the 1st Half of November 1931, Ibid.

[71]Speech by Abdul Ghaffar Khan dated 24 October 1934 at the meeting of Congress Subjects Committee. Home Political File No. 1/1/1934.

[72]Abdul Ghaffar Khan's speech dated 18 & 19 December, 1934 at Wardha.

[73]Ibid.

who used to sold them yarn to buy machine made cloth were discouraged to do so because the profit of the mill went to one person whereas all people should have shared it.[74] The *Charkha* thus provided the people not only with bread but also created political consciousness.[75] The people henceforth used *Khuddar* instead of foreign machine-made cloth.

Ghaffar Khan convinced the people that the English were the common enemies of Congress as well as the Pathans.[76] He invariably asserted that "India belonged to Indians and not to the English and that the young men of India wanted to turn out the latter bag and baggage."[77] According to him a Government under whose regime corruption and injustice flourished and the rights of the poor classes were ignored deserved to be overthrown.[78] In order to encourage people, he therefore invariably spoke of martyrs like Bhagat Singh, Das and Dutt who had sacrificed their lives for their country and encouraged them to follow their example.[79] Time and again he reminded the people that "*it is shameful that handful of foreigners could govern 35 crore people. Even 35 crore donkeys would not submit so meekly*".[80]

Ghaffar Khan always dinned the following words into the ears of his followers: "Do not rest until freedom is won.

---

[74]Abdul Ghaffar Khan's speech at the opening ceremony of All India Swadeshi Exhibition at Bombay on 2 October 1934. Abdul Ghaffar Khan's speech dated 18 and 19 December 1934 at Wardha.

[75]Abdul Ghaffar Khan's speech dated 24 October, 1934 at the meeting of Congress Subjects Committee.

[76]Abdul Ghaffar Khan's speech at Beki in Mardan district dated 12 December 1931. *See also* Statement issued by Chief Commissioner, N.W.F.P. dated 24 December 1931. File No. 31/28/1/1932-Pol. *See also* C.I.D. Report for 2nd half of November, 1931.

[77]The Naujawan Bharat Sabha of Peshawar 1929-30, Peshawar, 1930, File No. 464 of 1930.

[78]Communique on Peshawar dated 5 May 1930, p. 21, Home Political File No. II/III of 1930.

[79]The Naujawan Bharat Sabha of Peshawar, 1929-30 (Peshawar 1930), Home Political File No. 464 of 1930.

[80]Abdul Ghaffar Khan's speech dated 30 November, 1934, Home Political File No. 1/1/1934.

It does not matter if you are blown up with guns, bombs etc. If you are brave come out into the battlefield and fight the English who are the cause of all our troubles."[81]   He appealed to both the Hindus and Muslims not to quarrel over their respective rights but to unite and lay down their lives for the sake of freedom.   Knowing fully well that Government wanted to keep them apart on grounds of religion, in a stirring speech, he remarked that "true religion meant freedom" and asked people to join Congress because it was fighting for freedom.[82]

Khaffar Khan wanted Muslims and Hindus to read their respective religious books and act on them but not to keep them on the shelves.   Both the religions taught that 'slavery was a curse'.[83] Quoting from Quran he said "O Muhammad, you tell the Muslims that if they left Quran they be under His Wrath, i.e., He will place them under the rule of a foreign nation."[84] Muslims should know that religions came in the world to raise the nations and not to humiliate them. Similarly he advised the Hindus to read Gita because it taught the people to safeguard the rights of the weak and to ruin the oppressors.[85]

Ghaffar Khan criticised the Government for propagating that people's interests would not be safe in the hands of Congress because it aimed at establishing Hindu Raj.   But he did not see anything bad in it because such a rule would at least retain the wealth of the country and provide food to the people. That was the difference between the slavery to whites and slavery to the blacks.[86]

---

[81]Abdul Ghaffar Khan's speech at Beki in Mardan sub-division dated 12 December 1931. Home Political File No. 31/28/1/1932.

[82]Ibid, p. 5.

[83]Communique on Peshawar, dated 5 May 1930, Home Political File No. II/III of 1930, p. 13.

[84]Speech by Abdul Ghaffar Khan, dated 29.8.1934 at Patna. Home Political F. No. 31-28-1-1932.

[85]Ibid, para 5.

[86]Abdul Ghaffar Khan's speech dated 30 September 1934 at Town Hall, Calcutta. File No. P/1/34-Pol.

Ghaffar Khan also attacked the Government's policy of discrimination in social life, police and jails. He said, *"We are not worthy of being called Pathans, as the English people describe us as Black, and think it beneath their dignity to eat and drink with us. They treat us as if we were dogs... Our deplorable condition is due to our being ruled by a tyrannical and unjust English people, who are responsible for all the crime in India and are the enemies of the entire human race."*[87] Comparing the pay of the Police in England and in India, he said that in England where the police was organised in the interests of the English people the police was handsomely paid and consequently was not addicted to bribery. But in India a sub-inspector received only Rs. 80 a month and a constable a miserable sum of Rs. 20, as compared with Rs. 200 given to the English soldier who in addition was provided with whisky and free rations.[88] That too when police in India had to support large families and entertain many friends. Consequently in order to meet their expenses they were forced to practise dishonesty. The Government deliberately underpaid its servants and encouraged Indian officials to take bribes from public in order that ill-feeling and hatred may be ripe among them.[89] In this way the public came to the conclusion that the Indians were bad officers and bribe-takers while Englishmen were not. This was the reason why Englishmen had good reputation and Indians bad. He therefore blamed Government for this state of affairs and for deliberately encouraging corruption.[90] Talking of jails he said that the food and accommodation provided to Indians was inadequate and disgraceful.[91] They were provided with one blanket in severe cold and only one loaf of bread whereas Europeans were given a comfortable home. This sort of civilization

---

[87]Communique on Peshawar dated 5 May, 1930. Home Political File No. II/III/1930, p. 13.

[88]Communique on Peshawar dated 5 May 1930. Home Political File No. II/III 1930, p. 13.

[89]Ibid, p. 6.

[90] *Pakhtun,* dated November 1929.

[91]Abdul Ghaffar Khan's speech dated 14 October 1934, at Rampur Railway Station, Home Political File No. 1/1/1934.

under which one nation was destroyed to benefit another and one nation was shot down with bullets was no better than a *'beastly civilization'*. He therefore advocated equality of treatment with all including *Harijans* and untouchables.[92]

Ghaffar Khan's views on Congress, freedom struggle, secularism, racial discrimination, discrimination in administration, and in other walks of life brought him the reputation of being called *Frontier Gandhi*. But he did not like to be called by this name and said *"I am not Gandhi. There should be one Gandhi. Now if you make two Gandhis they too will fight among themselves and your cause will be injured by this fighting. For the freedom battle there must be one General...... In case there are two, our country will suffer and the third party which is here will feel great relief. Bear this in mind very well."*[93] It is also interesting to remember that Ghaffar Khan's stirring speeches always ended with cries such as *'Zalim Hakumat Barbad' – 'Khudai Khidmatgar Zindabad'-Up, up, Jawaharlal Nehru, 'Down, down, King George'*.[94]

The Government considered Ghaffar Khan's speeches and activities to be of 'a dangerous character' and issued prohibitory orders under Section 144 of the C.P.C. to place a check upon his activities.[95] Besides the Viceroy telegraphed Mahatma Gandhi that he was inciting people to revolution and trying to stir trouble. Mahatma Gandhi in reply said, "If Khan Abdul Ghaffar Khan asserted the right of complete independence it was a natural claim and the claim made with impunity by the Congress at Lahore in 1929 and by me with energy before the British Government in London. Moreover let me remind the Viceroy that despite knowledge on Government's part that Congress mandate contained such

---

[92] Ibid, 16 October, 1934, Ibid.

[93] Abdul Ghaffar Khan's speech at Albeit Hall, Calcutta, dated 2.10.1934. Home Political File No. 1/1/1934.

[94] Hindustan Times, dated 28 November, 1934.

[95] Letter from Government of N.W.F.P. to General Secretary, Congress Parliamentary Board, N.W.F.P., Peshawar No. 2888-P.C., dated 7 August 1936. Home Political File No. 40-3-36-Pol,

claims, I was invited to attend London Conference as a Congress delegate."[96] After receiving such a curt reply Government ordered wholesale arrests of all the Red Shirt leaders. This was followed by the announcement for the first general elections in the Frontier province.

First General Elections

The Montague-Chelmsford reforms were introduced in the province with considerable haste. A special officer was imported from the Punjab who prepared electoral rolls for the whole province in about two months. Elections for the Frontier Legislative Council took place in the second week of April 1932. The province had in the meantime been divided into various constituencies. The administrative district of Peshawar was divided into seven Muslim rural constituencies. Peshawar city and the cantonments and the non-Muslims had their own constituencies.[97] Owing to a shortage of election officers and police, elections in the various constituencies took place on different dates. The first elections were held on 7 April, 1932 and in the last constituency voting finished on 12 April. Thus elections lasted a week.

Franchise was conferred, roughly, on all males above the age of 21 who paid land revenue of ten rupees a year, or owned property worth six hundred rupees or had attained a certain standard of education.[98] Owing to the haste in which the electoral rolls were prepared, there were naturally many mistakes in them and many persons who were entitled to vote were omitted while many without the requisite qualifications had their names on the register. Roughly speaking, on the average, in a village containing a thousand able bodied men about a hundred had their names on the electoral roll.[99]

---

[96]Telegram from Mahatma Gandhi to Private Secretary to H.E. the Viceroy, dated 1st January, 1932.

[97]The First General Elections in the N.W.F.P., Journal of the Royal Central Asian Society, Vol. XXI, January, 1934, Part I, p. 65.

[98]The First General Elections in the N.W.F.P., Journal of the Royal Central Asian Society, Vol. XXI, January 1934, part I, p. 65.

[99]Ibid, pp. 65-66,

The province had never seen an election previously and ninety per cent of the voters had never even heard of such a thing. To them therefore the vote did not convey any intelligible meaning. They could not understand what a vote stood for. The candidates who stood for the various seats, and their agents, had very little time to explain the meaning of a vote to the electors and in any case it was impossible for them to reach the voters, who were scattered about in various villages at considerable distances, in the short time at their disposal. There was no press worth the name and the electors being illiterate, pamphlets and posters were useless. Public meetings were prohibited on account of Red Shirt activities.[100]

There was only one organised political party in the province, namely the Red Shirts, and it had declared the boycott of the elections. Its prominent leaders were clapped in gaol but the rank and file and the smaller leaders remained in the villages. Its organisation could not be broken up and although its members gave up the wearing of Red Shirts in public, yet they continued to hold secret meetings and to carry on a very active propaganda. Its emissaries went from village to village and directed the members of the organisation to prevent the voters from taking part in the elections by every means at their disposal.[101]

Religion plays a very important part in the life of the residents of the province, and the Red Shirt movement had also a quasi-religious hold on the uneducated part of the public. It was therefore the easiest thing in the world to proclaim that elections were against religion and that any person taking part in them would be committing a heresy. The Red Shirts, therefore, took full advantage of this opportunity, and declared that voting was sinful and that it was introduced by the "Satanic" Government in pursuance of its anti-Islamic policy.[102]

Ghaffar Khan was a very popular person at this time and

---

[100]Ibid, p. 66.

[101]The First General Elections in the N.W.F.P., Journal of the Royal Central Asian Society, Vol. XXI, January 1934, part I, p. 66,

[102]Ibid,

was considered a hero by the vast majority of villagers. They were told that whosoever fixed his thumb impression to the ballot paper would be signing the death warrant of Abdul Ghaffar Khan. The counter-foils of the ballot papers had to be signed by the voters and those who could not write had to fix their thumb impressions to them. It was therefore given out that their signatures meant the signing of Abdul Ghaffar's death warrant for which the Government needed a sort of referendum and had devised this method for obtaining the necessary authority. The electors were also told that their signature on the ballot papres would be followed by heavy taxation and other dire consequences.[103]

The Red Shirts had more than three months for this propaganda and when the elections became nearer this propaganda became more intense. Polling stations were fixed at the police stations in the district. It was impossible to send police to the villages and no one had thought beforehand of posting police on the few roads that existed or of arranging flying squads. On election days the voters had to walk several miles, or in some cases, where there were roads, had to go by lorries and horse-vehicles to the polling stations.[104]

The Red Shirts had announced picketing of the police stations and one or two days before the election at each polling station they blocked all the roads and paths leading to them. The villagers from most of the villages joined them because of the religious colour which was given to this work, and the riffraff and all the hooligans naturally took the most prominent part in it. Owing to the propaganda, a major portion of the electors decided not to take any part in the election. Another portion refused to vote on account of timidity. They had no desire to come into conflict with the Red Shirts. There were therefore only about ten to fifteen per cent of the electors who were willing and had decided to take part in the elections.[105]

---

[103]Ibid.

[104]The First General Elections in the N.W.F.P., Journal of the Royal Central Asian Society, Vol. XXI, January 1934, Part 1, p. 67.

[105]Ibid.

According to a voter who had decided to take part in the elections one day previous to the day of polling he was at a village about six miles distant from the polling station. News arrived in the afternoon that the road to the police station was being picketed. The voter went in a motor car and at a distance of about two miles, at the junction of two roads, he found about five hundred persons sitting in the middle of the road, completely blocking it. No argument could persuade the pickets to allow this voter to pass, and he therefore had to return to the village. At midnight this voter attempted again, this time accompanied by a couple of lorry loads of other voters, in the hope that the pickets might have moved away for the night. He however found that their number had doubled and that they had blocked not only the road but all the paths in the vicinity. Some of the pickets were also armed with daggers and pistols which they were displaying with threats. He and his companions had to return once more.[106]

One companion of this voter slipped from the lorries in the darkness and entered the crops on the road side. Some of the pickets discovered this after a short time and began to chase him. A regular hunt began in the darkness and the quarry had to run for his life. He told this voter in the morning that he had to lie for hours in the crops with voices all around him shouting death to him at sight. He managed to reach the polling station at 6 a.m. badly bruised and his clothes torn by the thorns and hedges. He covered the distance of about four miles in six hours.[107]

This voter also started for the polling station once more in the morning, and found a police party proceeding in a lorry to the polling station and decided to follow at close distance. When they reached the pickets they found a huge crowd on the road. The police lorry attempted to pass through the crowd, which gave way but shortly after started a fussilade of brickbats and stones. This voter's car was badly hit and all

---

[106]The First General Elections in the N.W.F.P., Journal of Royal Central Asian Society, Vol. XXI, January 1934, Part I, p. 67.
[107]Ibid.

the glass was broken but he and his companions in the car, however, escaped injury. The police had to open fire on the pickets and it was only after twenty or thirty shots that the crowd gave way and the road opened sufficiently to allow the police and this voter to reach the polling station.[108]

The experience of many others who had to reach the polling station by motor cars or lorries was similar to that of this voter. Many had to return to their villages and many were held up by the Red Shirts and kept under arrest till the end of the day. Those who had to walk to the polling station by country paths or had to come on horseback had most harrowing experiences. A prominent Khan was thrown from his horse near Rustam, dragged on the ground and severely beaten. Another's jaw was broken by a brickbat. Another Khan had to be carried home on a stretcher. Hundreds of others received minor injuries and lost their turbans. The Red Shirt pickets stopped at nothing. They would first stop the voter and endeavour to persuade him to go back. If he insisted on going forward they would threaten him. If that proved of no avail then they would use physical force. Insults and abuses were prolific, and every voter who tried to go to the polling station had a tale to tell in the evening. A number of motor cars and lorries were damaged and all traffic on the roads stopped altogether.[109]

The boycott of the elections was thus enforced with a thoroughness which surprised everybody. At some polling stations only a very few votes were recorded. At one place out of a thousand eligible voters only six managed to reach the polling station.[110] The results of the elections were thus surprising. Candidates with strong following were defeated and others who would have probably forfeited their deposits of the elections found seats in the Legislative Council.[111] The

---

[108] The First General Elections in the N.W.F.P., *Journal of the Royal Central Asian Society,* Vol. XXI, January 1934, Part 1, p. 67.

[109] Ibid, p. 68.

[110] Ibid.

[111] Ibid.

first elections in the Frontier Province will therefore always be remembered. They created such an apprehension in the minds of both candidates and the voters that in the District Board elections which followed a few months later, in many constituencies no candidates were nominated and in nearly all the constituencies elections were uncontested.[112]

Policy of Government

The Frontier province remained quiet from 1932 to 1935 and political life developed on peaceful and constitutional lines.[113] The Government now followed a cautious policy and took such steps which directly or indirectly did not strengthen the hands of the Red Shirts. Thus in 1932-33 when Father Elwin, a celebrated Don of the Oxford University went to the Frontier to see for himself the actual position to ascertain for himself first hand, the actual truth, for a few days he was not interfered with, but when the Frontier authorities found that the gentleman was not going to represent their point of view but the actual facts, and that he was a seeker after truth, he was promptly removed from the province.[114] The second incident is concerned with Miss Wilkinson. When she came with her party to the Frontier, Dr. Khan Saheb's son accompanied her to Mardan. Here a meeting of the Red Shirts was organised so that Miss Wilkinson might see for herself what they were doing. As soon as the police got scent of this they could not tolerate the sight, they did not want that the Red Shirts should extend the facts to her and started shooting and firing practice around the place of meeting. Miss Wilkinson took the opportunity just in time and asked the organisers of the meeting to disperse the meeting. The manner in which it was dispersed was so quiet that Miss Wilkinson spontaneously remarked that "*even in Europe we had never seen such orderly dispersal of a big crowd like this.*"[115]

---

[112]The First General Elections in the N.W.F.P., Journal of the Royal Central Asian Society, Vol. XXI, January, 1534. Part I, p. 69.

[113]Dr. Khan Saheb's statement in the Legislative Assembly, Home Political, File No. 22/109/1935, p. 25.

[114]Dr. Khan Saheb's statement in the Legislative Assembly, Home political Department File No. 22/109/1935, p. 18.

[115]Ibid, p. 19.

The ban which was imposed on Red Shirts in 1931 continued upto 1936 because Government continued to hold the view that it was an organisation which was revolutionary[116] in character. The externment orders against Ghaffar Khan and Khan Saheb too remained in force and Government ruled out the possibility to assimilate the position of the Frontier province with the rest of India.[117] The Red Shirt movement became rudderless. It was now confined to a small body of the poor but fanatically determined persons. Demonstrations were organised on a small scale in such a way as to avoid arrests. Prisoners who were being released[118] were settling down quietly. The movement was changing its character and there was likelihood of its becoming religious or even constitutionally political.[119]

The Red Shirt movement failed because the *"Government regarded the Frontier province as the gate-way of India and its people as the gate-keepers of India"* and openly said, *"How can we give reforms to the gate-keepers? How can we give a share in the administration of the province to the gate-keepers? If we give anything India will be out of our hands."*[120] Therefore every possible effort was made to prevent these gatekeepers to unite with India. It was primarily for this reason that this movement was crushed from the very outset. The Government succeeded in its task by following a policy which was based on "double-method of representation."[121] The Red Shirts were told that they were uncivilized and that if the strong hand of Britain is

---

[116]Legislative Assembly Debates, Vol. I, No. 8, dated 5 February, 1935. See also Note by H.C. Haig, dated 23.4.1934. File No. 4/4/1934.

[117]H.D. Craik to Hon'ble K.B. Mian sir Fazl-i-Husain, Member of Council, dated New Delhi, 8 December, 1934.

[118]Statement by H.C. Froyer, superintendent of Police on Special Duty dated 12.9.1933. Home Political File No. 45.17.1933.

[119]Ibid.

[120]Abdul Ghaffar Khan's speech at Nagda Neighbourhood House, dated 27 October, 1934. D.I.B. F. No. 22. P.F. 1934. *Also See* Home Political File No. 11-12-34-Political.

[121]Statement by Mr. Bhullabhai J. Desai in Legislative Assembly, Home Political File No. 22/109/1935, p. 26.

not there the Hindu Raj would swamp them.[122]   Similarly the
rest of Indians were told that the uncivilized Pathans would
swamp them.[123]

Responsible persons and organs of public opinion throughout India continued to protest against maintenance of the ban
on Red Shirts but it was removed only after the Frontier Legislative Council passed a resolution to this effect by 74 votes as
against 46.   But the Government justifying its policy argued
that the maintenance of ban facilitated the pace of constitutional development of the province because nineteen political
or semi-political associations[124] were formed since its inception.

Ghaffar Khan was released in 1936 but was again forbidden to go to Frontier province.   It was only in August 1937
when the elections for the Provincial Assembly were over, that
he was allowed to return to the province.   Meanwhile in 1936
elections, the Red Shirt party won the majority of seats but in
spite of that the Governor asked Sir Nawab Sahibzada Abdul
Qayyum to form a government.   But after five or six months,
in September 1937, the opposition passed a vote of no confidence against this person.[125]   Dr. Khan Saheb now formed a
Congress government with the help of Red Shirts and did good
work for the welfare of the people.   But in one respect it did
more harm than good.   In actual fact all the power in the
government was vested in Governor, and his subordinate officers took no notice of what Red Shirt Ministers said, nor did
they give them any help or assistance.   They acted on the
advice of the Governor and did as he told them.   *Thus only
fifty paise worth of power was gained but the country needed the whole
rupees worth.*

War and its after-math

War broke out in 1939 and together with the Congress
Ministries everywhere in India, the Frontier Ministry also

---

[122]Ibid.

[123]Ibid.   Home Political File No. 22/100-1936.

[124]Note by M.G. Hallett, dated 24.1.1935. Home Political File No. 24-9-1935.

[125]Badshah Khan, My Life & Struggle (New Delhi, 1969), p. 157.

[126]Ibid., p. 158.

resigned. At a meeting of the Congress Working Committee a resolution was then passed that India would help Britain in her war effort but on the condition that after it was over[127] Britain would grant her freedom. On that occasion Mahatma Gandhi and Ghaffar Khan resigned from the Working Committee because they did not advocate violence to help the British in their war effort. After this meeting individual *Satyagraha* (passive resistance) started in the country but nobody was allowed to take this course of action without Gandhiji's approval. In the case of Frontier Province Gandhiji transferred this authority to Ghaffar Khan. This was followed by a mass movement against British rule and Gandhiji launched the Quit India movement in August 1942.[128] Thousands of persons were arrested. Ghaffar Khan guided this movement in the Frontier province with great discipline. He permitted the cutting of telephone wires or removal of railway sleepers on the condition that the saboteur himself went to the police and told them what he had done. This was done to develop moral courage, provide inspiration to others, and to protect the innocent people from harassment by police. The government severely crushed this movement.

Then came the elections of 1945-46. Government brought large number of students from Aligarh Muslim University and from Islamia College, Calcutta, and workers and leaders of the Muslim League from many parts of India to this province to work in the election campaign. The Britishers also worked enthusiastically on behalf of the Muslim League.[129] The issue at stake in this election—the last general election in united India—was India or Pakistan, Hindu or Muslim, Islam or Kafir, temple or mosque.[130] But by the grace of God the Muslim League was defeated and the Red Shirts won the elections with a large majority and formed a Ministry. This election showed that the majority of the people in the country still supported the Red Shirts. When therefore

---

[127]Badshah Khan, My Life & Struggle (New Delhi, 1969), p. 159.
[128]Ibid, p. 160.
[129]Badshah Khan, My Life & Struggle (New Delhi. 1969), p. 175.
[130]Ibid., p. 176.

in 1947 another referendum was forced upon the people they
considered it to be gross injustice and refused to have anything
to do with it because less than a year ago the election had been
fought on this issue.[131] It is really unfortunate that while
throughout India representative assemblies were asked to
decide whether they wanted to remain in India or go over to
Pakistan, the Frontier Assembly was not given the right to
decide the future of its people. The Congress did not help
the Red Shirts at this critical hour but on the contrary delivered them into the hands of enemies. Sardar Patel and
Rajagopalachari were primarily responsible for this because
they forced the Congress Working Committee to accept the
Mountbatten Plan of 3 June 1947. Both the Congress and
the Muslim League formally agreed to the creation of Pakistan.

Mahatma Gandhi and Ghaffar Khan protested that if a
referendum was to be held at all it should be a referendum on
the question of 'Pakhtunistan or Pakistan'[132] but nobody listened to them and the referendum was forced upon the people.
The Red Shirts refused to take part in this referendum and
so the way was clear for the Muslim League and they used all
the cunning, deceit and force they could command but in spite
of all that, they got only fifty per cent of the votes which is
nowhere enough to decide the fate of a country or a nation.[133]
The British, who ought to have remained neutral in this referendum, openly had the police and the army canvass for votes.
They also posted police and army personnel at the polling
booths and even forged the signatures of people who did not
want to take part in the referendum.[134] The Frontier Province
was thus lost to India and that marked the end of the Red
Shirt movement.

This made Ghaffar Khan very sore because Pathans
had always stood side by side with the Congress in the struggle for freedom but were now thrown before 'the wolves'[135]

---

[131]Ibid, p. 204.
[132]Ibid, p. 178.
[133]Badshah Khan, My Life & Struggle (New Delhi, 1969), p. 179.
[134]Ibid, p. 179.
[135]Ibid, p. 204.

They regarded it as a pronouncement of death sentence upon them.[136]   Strangely enough at this time Maulana Azad advised Ghaffar Khan to join the Muslim League knowing fully well that he believed in constructive work and was opposed to its destructive principles and practices.   Ghaffar Khan wondered over it but henceforth ceased to have any respect for Azad. Only then Azad realised that Ghaffar Khan would never change colour like a chameleon.

Till the dawn of independence in 1947 the Red Shirts served their country and their people as best as they could. They showed bravery and a capacity for suffering with strict adherence to non-violence under the gravest provocations.[137] They owe everything to Mahatma Gandhi because by his *'great miracle'* he had converted the militant Pathans to his creed[138] of non-violene.[139]   A new life grew up into the race. This can be judged from the remark that Abdul Ghaffar Khan had made before a huge audience in 1934.   He had said,[140] "Go to the Frontier and see for yourself what revolution this movement, this non-violent movement has created there.   You must have read regarding our race that we were a people who used to fight amongst ourselves for small things.   To give up life for trivial matters, to shoot one another—this was our profession. Please come and see what a glory this movement has created in us today".

---

[136]Ibid, p. 205.

[137]Dr. Khan Saheb's plea for removal of ban on Red Shirt Organisation. Home Political File No. 22/109/1935; See also Hindustan Times, dated 6. 8. 1935.

[138]In 1945 there was a move to set up a new political party out of the Red Shirts. Its ideology was to solve problems in a violent way aud was to be known as Black Shirt Party.   But C.I.D. enquiries revealed that no such party actually came into existence.   See Home Political [I] File No. 28/8/ 1935.

[139]Statement by Abdul Matin Chaudhury in the Legislative Assembly. Home Political File No. 24/109/1935.

[140]Abdul Ghaffar Khan's speech dated 2.10.1934. Albert Hall, Calcutta, File No. 1/1/1934-Political,

10

All India States
Muslim League and Muslim Majlis

Little information is available on the All India States Muslim League and the Muslim Majlis. The former body though not very active followed some important objectives while carrying out its activities and programme.[1] The later one, the Muslim Majlis was known to have only leaders but no followers and their sole importance lay in their ability to attract newspapermen to their meetings and to obtain space in the Nationalist Press.[2] It gave to the Congress leaders a wholly incorrect idea of the strength of their Muslim supporters and thus retarded reapproachment with the Muslim League. The British Government however regarded it to be an important body only in so far as it reflected some weakening in the repute of the Muslim League.[3]

The All-India States Muslim League was formed in October

---

[1] Home Department (Intelligence Bureau) Note dated 17.3.1943. Home Political (I) F.No. 17-2-43 of 1942.

[2] Mr. V.Sahay's Note dated 27.6.1944 in the Home Department (Intelligence Bureau). Home Political (I) F. No,28-2-44 of 1944.

[3] Ibid.

1939, as a result of consultations which took place between Nawab Bahadur Yar Jung and M.A. Jinnah during the latter's visit to Hyderabad that year. The new organisation was intended to be an "allied body" of the All-India Muslim League and its Constitution, which was formally adopted at the first session of the States League held at Lahore on 23 March, 1940, was drawn up on the lines of the constitution of the All-India Muslim League.[4]

According to the constitution, which was drafted by Kunwar Abdus Samad Rajasthani in consultation with Nawab Bahadur Yar Jang, India was to be divided for the purposes of the States League organisation into three territorial zones, namely:

1. *Himalayan Zone*, consisting of Indian States adjoining Sind, Baluchistan, N.W.F.P., Punjab, U.P., Bengal and Assam and Jammu and Kashmir States.

2. *Vindhyachal Zone*, consisting of Indian States adjoining C.P., Bihar and Orissa and the Rajputana and Central India States.

3. *Deccan Zone*, consisting of Indian States adjoining Bombay and Madras and the Hyderabad and Mysore States.

The constitution referred *inter alia*, to "Greater Hyderabad under His Majesty the Nizam being restored and rehabilitated to its original territorial integrity and entity with complete governance and active jurisdiction over Berar, Northern Circars, Muslipatam, Sholapur and the other Ceded and Administered areas as recognised to be originally and perpetually under the Sovereignty of the Nizam in justification and fulfilment of its alliance of friendship with the British Crown". It further prescribed that "as far as possible, peaceful, progressive and constitutional methods will be resorted to achieve success. It also provided for the organisation of Muslim National Guards" for the preservation of Islamic military spirit."[5]

---

[4]Home Political (I) F. No. 17-2-43 of 1943, para 1.
[5]Ibid, para 2.

The principal object of the States League was the safe-guarding of Muslim interests in Indian States in various ways such as ensuring proper representation of Muslims in State Services and Legislatures. In a representation made to Sir Stafford Cripps by the States League in March, 1942 it was stated, among other things, that "over thirty million Muslims residing in Indian States claimed equal representation with Hindus, in the Councils of all constitutional Princes." The States League also aimed at strengthening Muslim mass contact and alleviating miscellaneous hardships of Muslims in Indian States.[6]

In regard to the war effort, the States League stood for "wholehearted support to Britain for the successful prosecution of the war".[7] In this connexion, Jinnah at that time made it clear that the partial ban on collaboration with Britain in its war effort, which applied to the All-India Muslim League did *not* apply to the States League.

Certain suggestions on the question of relations between the Central Government and the Indian States were put forward by the States League in January, 1941 for the consideration of Princes and their Prime Ministers. These were as follows.[8]

(1) That the future constitution of India should not be acknowledged and accepted by His Majesty's Government if it was not acknowledged and accepted by the States;

(2) That the conferment of Dominion Status on India should not, in any, affect and involve the "independence, integrity and expansion" of the States, and that Paramountcy should not be transferred to any future authority to jeopardize the existence and entity of the States;

---

[6]Ibid, para 3.

[7]Ibid, para 4.

[8]Ibid, para 5.

(3) That the States *en bloc*, should not be deterred from forming a separate confederation of their progressive units of administration and from demanding a separate Dominion Status for a free and equal partnership in the British Commonwealth as well as in an "All-India Central Government;"

(4) That the States should not cooperate with an "All-India Central Government" if the status of equality and independence was not provided in the future constitution of the country;

(5) That the Chamber of Princes should not remain unconcerned in advocating the cause of the States in harmony with the policy and plan pursued by more than two crores of the States Muslims who formed a major portion of the Muslim nation in the country and as such were determined to have an honourable future in any constitutional Government Central or Local.

The first session of the All-India States Muslim League was held at Lahore on 23 March 1940 concurrently with the annual session of the All-India Muslim League. At this session, Nawab Bahadur Yar Jung, who was unanimously elected President of the All-India States Muslim League, said that political awakening among the States peoples and the refusal of the All-India Muslim League to include State Muslims in their organisation had compelled them to organise themselves separately.[9] During the course of his speech, Nawab Bahadur Yar Jung observed: "Hyderabad could not be turned into a democratic state because the State had not been conquered by any non-Muslim power since its establishment and not only the present Nizam but every Muslim was the ruler of that State."[10]

The second annual session of the States League, held at

---

[9] A resoluiton requested the All India Muslim League to grant affiliation to All India Statas Muslim League.

[10] Home Political F.No. 17.2.43 of 1943, para 6.

Madras from 11 to 13, April 1941, was attended by some 500 delegates from States throughout India. Congress interference in the affairs of the States was condemned and resolutions were passed supporting the Pakistan scheme; and urging the Rulers of Indian States, when introducing constitutional reforms, to secure and safeguard the rights of the States Muslims[11].

The third annual session was held at Allahabad, at the same time as the annual session of the All-India Muslim League from 4 to 7, April. Among the resolutions passed at this session were requests to Rulers of certain Hindu States to safeguard the rights of their Muslim subjects.[12]

While the All-India States Muslim League was anxious to secure the independence and integrity of Muslim States in future India, it appeared to have a different solution for Hindu states. At a meeting of representatives of Muslim, in Hindu States held at Aligarh on 17 July 1942, a resolution was passed declaring that Muslims in Hindu States were determined to establish a confederation of India consisting of (1) Northern India Federation, (2) Southern India Federation and (3) Indian Federation (stretching from the Bay of Bengal to the Gulf of Cutch). The reasons for the proposal, as explained in the resolution, were: "The Muslims of the Hindu states have resorted to this as vital differences political and constitutional, exist between the Hindu States and the Muslim States and hence they cannot make any common cause and cannot serve the attainment of the motives of the interested people and parties. In the future political and constitutional adjustment and advancement of India, Muslims in the Hindu States must have their position and prestige acknowledged and accepted."[13]

The relations between the All-India States Muslim League and the All-India Muslim League can best be described in Jinnah's own words. He declared in May 1941 in the

---

[41]Ibid, para 7.

[42]Ibid, para 8.

[43]Ibid, para 9,

course of an interview, that the Pakistan scheme of the All-India Muslim League had nothing to do with the Indian States. He added that the States Muslim League was not under the control of the All-India body, nor was there any question of affiliation of the State Leagues to the All-India Muslim League, as the affiliation would raise many thorny questions such as the constitutional status of the respective States, their relation with the Sovereign Power and many other details which "for the present might well be left out". Jinnah added that though the "parent body" had no direct connexion with the States Leagues, the latter looked to the former for support and sympathy whenever the rights of Muslims of Indian States were ignored or trampled upon. He cited the instances of Jaipur, Rajkot and Hyderabad where the "help" rendered by the All-India Muslim League succeeded in adjusting local differences.[14]

The position of the All-India States Muslim League was thus, strictly speaking, that of an organisation subsidiary to the All-India Muslim League, but not formally affiliated to it. The States League, however, looked up to the All-India Muslim League for instruction and guidance in all matters affecting its policy and programme. In practical politics the States League hardly wielded any direct influence, although it claimed to have been responsible for the amelioration of the position of Muslims in certain Hindu States. It was, indeed, practically a "one man show", Nawab Bahadur Yar Jung being the chief moving spirit and financial backer of the League.[15] The Nawab was a Jagirdar of the Hyderabad State. He was interested in securing the independence of that State in future India and advocated the retrocession to it of the Ceded Territories. He was also an active worker of the All-India Muslim League. Another active worker was Kunwar Abdus Samad Rajasthani, a graduate of the Aligarh Muslim University, who had been responsible for the League's propaganda since its inception. Other members of the present and past Working Committees

---

[14]Ibid, para 10.
[15]Ibid, para 11.

of the League were comparatively unimportant and inactive.[16] The Central office of the States League was transferred from Delhi to Nagpur in July 1942.

---

[16]The Central Office of the States League was transferred from Delhi to Nagpur in July 1942.

Names of memebrs of Working Committee year-wise are given below:-

1941

Nawab Bahadur Yar Jung Bahadur, President of the All-India States Muslim League, has nominated the following to the Working Committee of the League for 1940:-

Mr. Abdul Hasan Syed Ali (Hyd rabad); Mr. Abdul Jabbar Khalil (Mysore, Travancore and Cochin); Seth Mohamad Osman Memon(Kathiawar States); Mr. Patkan Ghulam Rasul (Baroda and Gujarat States); Mr. Mahmudul Hasan Siddiqi of Bhopal, Mr. Manzar-a-Alam of Gwalior and Mr. Mohamad Yakub of Indore (Central India States); Mr. A.S. Khan Rajasthani of Jaipur and Maulana Mohamad Bahlol Khan Dena of Jaipur (Rajputana States), Mr. Solat Ali Khan of Rampur (U.P. States); Mr. Mohamad Ishaq (Jammu); Abdur Rahman (Jammu); Mr. M.A. Hafiz and Mr. M.A. Abdul Aziz (Kashmir) and Syed Ali Mohammad Rasdi of Khairpur (Sind, Baluchistan and Frontier States).

1942

The Propaganda Secretary of the All-India States Muslim League says that Nawab Bahadur Yar Jung, President of the League, nominated the following persons to its Working Committee :—

Kunwar A.A. Rajasthani of Jaipur, Khan Bahadur Dewan Shokat Ali and Mr. Mahmudul Hasan Siddiqi of Bhopal, Sahibzada Manzar-a-Alam Ansari of Gwalior, Sahibzada Kutabuddi Khan of Indore, Hakim Nisar Ahmed, Jagirdar of Jodhpur, Sahibzada Abdul Majid Rahmani of Bahawalpur, Begum Ross Masoaod of Patiala, Rais Solat Ali Khan of Rampur, Mr. M.A. Hafiz of Kashmir, Mr. Ghulam Abbas of Jammu, Pathan Rasool Khan of Baroda, Bhai Osman Memon of Rajkot, Shan Ali Hasan of Junagadh, Mr. Abdul Hasan Syed Ali, Mr. Abdur Raof, Begum Sughra Humayun Mirza of Hyderabad, Deccan, Mr. Abdul Jabbar Khalil of Mysore, Haji Essa Haji Abdus Sattar of Cochin and Mr. K.M. Bijli of Travancore.—A.P.I.

1943

The Secretary of the All-India States Muslim League announces the following as the personnel of the Working Committee of the League for the year 1942-43.

Nawab Bahadur Yar Jung Bahadur, (Hyderabad), President; Mr. Mahmud-ul-Hasan Siddiqi (Bhopal), Secretary;

Maulvi Abdul Hasan Syed Ali (Hyderabad), Mr. Abdul Raof (Hyderabad), Khan Bahadur Diwan Shaukat Ali (Bhopal), Mr. Mahmud Sharif (Mysore), Mulla Fazal Bhai (Ujjain), Syyed Fakhar-ud-Din Ahmed

All India Muslim Majlis

Early in May 1944 Dr. Shaukatulah Shah Ansari, a Congressman and Secretary of the Azad Muslim Board, announced in the Press that a meeting of Nationalist Muslims would be held in Delhi on 6, 7 and 8 May and that invitation had been sent to prominent leaders of the Ahrar Party, the Jamiat-ul-Ulema-i-Hind, the Momin Conference, the Krishak Praja Party of Bengal, the All-India Shia Conference, the Muslim Majlis (a Bengal organisation of no importance), the Khudai Khidmatgars of the North-West Frontier Province, the Anjuman-i-Watan of Baluchistan and other independent Muslims *"to discuss the present political situation in the country and to decide upon what lead to give to Indian Muslims."* The Board was the Executive of the *Azad Muslim Conference* which itself was described as a federation[16*] of the

---

(Indore), Pathan Rasool Khan (Baroda), Ali Abbas Sahib (Alwar), Mr. M.A. Haffez (Jammu), Manzar Alam (Gwalior), Hakim Nisar Ahmed Sahib (Jodhpur), Ghulam Abbas Sahib (Srinagar), Hatim Bhai (Palampur), Usman Bhai Sahib (Rajkot), Mr. Mohi-ud-Din Sahib (Cochin), Maulvi Abdur Rahmeen (Kolahapur) and Kunwar A.S. Khan Rajasthani (ex-officio).

The women representatives are : Atiya Begum Sahiba (Janjira), Begum Sughra Hamayun Mirza (Hyderabad), Miss Bilquis Ahmad Hasan (Bhopal) —A.P.I.

[16*]The Azad Conference and the Congress, the League and the Maha Sabha in a word all political and economic movements in India proclaim independent federated India as the goal, but here their agreement ends. Congress aims at a federation of autonomous units in which defence, external affairs, communications and customs, shall be subject to the unitary control of the federation. The League wants a confederacy of two federations where also these shall be subject to the control of each of the federations but there must be no single directing agency over them. The conception of the Hindu Mahasabha is diametrically opposed to that of the League, for it aims at a central government which should be so powerful that the constituent units are reduced to the status of mere subordinate provinces. The Azad Conference has adopted the scheme formulated by the Jamait-ul-Ulema and holds that there can be only one Indian federaration but its federating units should be conceived as independent sovereign states rather than mere autonomous provinces. The Praja Party accepts this general scheme but believes that the federating units as well as the federal centre must be republics organised peasants of India. *See also* Muslim Politics 1906-47 and Other Essays by Humayun Kabir (Calcutta, 1969), pp. 33-34.

various parties mentioned above. Some fifty Nationalist Muslims who responded to the invitatinon included S.A. Brelvi, editor of the "Bombay Chronicle"; Hafiz Mohd. Ibrahim, ex-Minister, Bengal; K.B. Mohd. Jan of Calcutta; Sheikh Abdul Majid Singhi; Kh. Abdul Najid, Bar-at-Law of Allahabad, Dr. K.M. Ashraf and Sajjad Zahir, communists; Dr. Abdul Latif of Hyderabad; Maulana Ahmed Said and Mufti Kafait Ullah of the Jamiat-ul-Ulema, Delhi; and Mohd Ahmed Qazmi, M.L.A.; of Saharanpur. The President of the Majlis-i-Ahrar refused to participate in the meeting (in spite of Hafiz Mohd Ibrahim's personal request to Mazhar Ali Azhar) on the ground that the discussions will only lead to further dissensions in the Muslim community. Mr. M.A. Kazmi was present in his individual capacity and not as an Ahrar representative. No Khudai Khidmatgar from the North-West Frontier Province attended the meeting. A.K. Fazlul Haq, ex-Premier of Bengal, did not attend the meeting but wrote to Shaukatullah Shah Ansari stressing the need for setting up a "rival organisation" to the Muslim League designed "to draw all the Muslims into it." He went on to say that to start such an organisation was a "tremendous task" but that "something should be done and the policy of drift which has been our characteristic in the last few years must be definitely given up". He significantly added: "Your Azad Muslim Conference exists only on paper. The Ahrar organisation has got some life in it, but it is confined to the Punjab and some part, of the United Provinces and possibly also to Delhi City. The Khaksars are popular in many places; but as a matter of fact in Bengal none of these organisations is universally popular. In these circumstances you have to consider very carefully the steps you should take to bring about the Muslims under one organisation. We must be prepared that our organisation should be ready for fighting the elections which will take place soon, as the war is soon coming to an end."[17]

During the discussions at the meeting the communist group led by Dr. Ashraf, in consonance with the communist principle of "self-determination" for all nationalities, voiced

---

[17]Home Political F.No. 28.2.45-(I) of 1944, para 1.

its support of the Pakistan ideal and went so far as to suggest that Nationalist Muslims should join the Muslim League to facilitate a Congress-League understanding. Among others in favour of this course was Dr. Latif of Hyderabad (the pro-pounder of Pakistan scheme) who urged that Nationalist Muslims should work for their ideals from within the Muslim League.[18]   In the end, however, this suggestion was rejected and a compromise formula was agreed to. A number of reso-lutions were passed.

Two of the more important resolutions,[19] were as follows:

Resolution I

"This meeting of Nationalist Muslims views with great concern the hardships to which India has been subjected in the present phase of the war and the suffering borne by the Indian people under the existing system of Government. The evidence of which is to be found in the intolerable rise in prices, burden of taxation, scarcity of certain essential commodities and the total absence of others.

"In the opinion of this meeting, experience has shown that the present Government is not capable of saving the people from this distress, that no satisfactory solution is possi-ble until a real national Government exercising full authority is formed at the Centre.

"This meeting further declares that all Indians, irrespec-tive of creed or community, and all patriotic organisations with out exception are deeply interested in the defence of India. They are inspired with a real patriotic urge and a true spirit of sacrifice which can be directed most effectively, under a natio-nal Government for the protection of the country against foreign invasion and aggression by Fascist Powers.

"This meeting deplores the fact that the British Govern-

---

[18]Ibid, para 2.

[19]*See Appendix* A Home Political (I) F.No. 18.2.44 for copy of important resolution passed at the Session of the Azad Muslim Conference at Delhi on May 6, 7, and 8, 1944.

ment, in spite of its knowledge that the Indian people are opposed to Fascism, is still unwilling on account of its short-sighted policy, to transfer power to them through a national Government.

"This meeting now declares that the formation of a national Government is no longer a political issue but has become a first-rate military question in view of the exigencies of the present phase of war. The victory of the democratic forces, the defence of India and resistance to Japanese aggression, all these considerations demand the immediate establishment of a national Government and the transfer of power to the Indian people.

"This meeting, therefore, urges the British Government to start negotiations with the leaders of India without any further loss of time so that a real national Government wielding effective authority should be established in the country".

Resolution II

The second resolution states "This meeting of nationalist Muslims considers, in the best interests of the country, that a Hindu-Muslim settlement should be brought about without any delay. It appeals to both Hindus and Muslims that having regard to the urgent need of such a settlement, they should take necessary steps towards this end, and considers that the release of Gandhiji offers an excellent opportunity of which advantage should be taken. In the opinion of this meeting a solution of the communal problem satisfactory to all parties concerned can be secured on the following fundamental considerations, and such a solution will satisfy the needs and aspirations of Indian Muslims:-

(1) India should continue to remain a united country.

(2) The Constitution of India should be framed by its own people;

(3) There should be an All-India Federation.

(4) The units of the Federation should be completely

autonomous and all residuary powers should be vested in them.

(5) Every unit of the Federation should be free to secede from it as a result of a plebiscite of all its adult inhabitants.

(6) The religious, economic and cultural rights of minorities should be fully and effectively safeguarded by reciprocal agreement."

Explaining the background of the resolutions S.A. Brelvi, Hafiz Mohd. Ibrahim and Dr. Shaukatullah Shah Ansari told Press Correspondents that the first resolution sets out the immediate programme which Nationalist Muslims proposed to popularise. They added that, with Gandhiji's release the process of attempting a settlement with the Muslim League would be resumed and that means had been suggested in the second resolution of hastening that settlement.[20]

For implementing the resolution on Hindu-Muslim settlement and other resolutions, the meeting also resolved that Nationalist Muslims should organise themselves under the aegis of a new body to be called the All-India Muslim Majlis with its headquarters at Delhi and branches throughout India. A.M. Khwaja[21] accepted the Presidentship of the Majlis and

---

[20]Home Political (I) F.No. 28.2.44 of 1944, para 2.

[21]Abdul Majid Khwaja of Aligarh and Allahabad was born in 1883. He was educated at Aligarh and went to England in 1904. He obtained his degree at Cambridge and was called to the Bar. Returning to India in 1907 he became a member in turn of the Home Rule League, the Congress and the Muslim League. Early in 1921 he gave up legal practice and figured prominently in the Khilafat and non-cooperation agitations. Was convicted in December, 1921 under Sec. 17, Criminal Law Amendment Act, and sentenced to 6 months S.I. On release he was appointed Secretary of the Provincial Khilafat Committee. In 1923 he stood unsuccessfully for election to the United Provinces Legislative Council and presided at the Provincial Khilafat Conference. In 1926 he started a sectarian organization named Khadim-ul-Musalmin (Servant of the Muslims) at Aligarh and attended the Khilafat Conference at Delhi in the same year as a delegate. In 1930, he spoke at a Congress meeting in favour of joint electorates but took no part in the civil disobedience movement. Withdrew from active public work in 1936 when the

was authorised to nominate a Central Working Committee and an Organising Committee for the Provinces. Dr. Shaukatullah Ansari was placed in charge of the Central office at Delhi. K.B. Mohammad Jan, M.L.C., Bengal, and a supporter of Fazlul Haq, was appointed as one of the general secretaries. In his first statement as President, Khwaja Abdul Majid gave the reasons which led Nationalist Muslims to form a separate party of their own. He said that most Nationalist Muslims belonged to one or the other of the political organisations opposed to Muslim League, and several of them were content to be members of Congress ; in 1940 the Azad Muslim Board was formed consisting of the representatives of these organisations, but the experience of the past four years had convinced them that it was a mistake merely to form a "Federal Board" which could neither approach the masses nor enlist members ; it was, therefore, decided to form a "distinct party". He added: "For the peace of mind of all concerned, I may add that the Majlis would not stand in the way of any leader or any party and would not obstruct any settlement that they might wish to arrive at, but we shall not accept for ourselves as true Muslims any settlement which does not recognise the principles that we stand for".[22]

The aims and objects of the Majlis as stated by the President were:

1.　to awaken the Islamic spirit of the Muslims of India and to "persuade them to act upon the same";

2.　to obtain full freedom for India;

3.　to cooperate with all organisations whose interests were in no way contrary to the objects of the Majlis; and

4.　to work for the attainment of the objectives set out

Muslim members of the Unity Board in the United Provinces decided to seek election on the Muslim League ticket. In July 1937 at a meeting at Anand Bhawan, Allahabad, presided over by Pandit Jawahar Lal Nehru, he was elected as one of the joint secretaries of the Allahabad branch of the Civil Liberties Union.

[22]Home Political (I) F.No. 28-2-44 of 1944, para 3.

in the Delhi resolutions in collaboration with the other political parties.

Membership of the Majlis was open to Muslims of all shades of opinion and the membership fee was 2 annas per annum (same as in the case of members of the Muslim League). The real object of Nationalist Muslims in setting up the Muslim Majlis was to bring indirect pressure to bear on Jinnah and the Muslim League to come to terms with Congress with a view primarily to capturing power at the Centre during the war. Failing this, it was their intention to expand the organisation and, wherever possible, to challenge the claim of the Muslim League that it was the only representative organisation of Muslims.[23]

The President of the Majlis then nominated a working Committee.[24] According to a Press report, the President and his colleagues had tested public response in the United Provinces

---

[23]Ibid, para 4.

[24]President: A.M. Khwaja, Bar-at-Law, Allahabad.
  General Secratary: Dr. Shaukatullah Shah Ansari, Delhi.
  Secretary: K.B. Muhammad Jan, M.L.C., Calcutta.
  Treasurer: Halim Jung, Delhi.
  Members: Hafiz Muhammad Ibrahim, Congress ex-Minister, U.P. Nisar Ahmed Khan Sherwani, U.P.
    Syed Ali Zaheer, President of the All-India Shia Political Conference.
    Syed Turail Ahmed of Aligarh (father of M.A. Kazmi, M.L.A.)
    Maulvi Abdul Majid, A silk merchant and Momin leader of Benares.
    Maulana Bashir Ahmed, General Secretary, Jamiat-ul-Ulema.
    Maulana Shahid Mian Fakhri, a Khilafatist of Allahabad.
    Mufti Ziaul Hasan Hindi of Ludhiana.
    Maulvi Zaheeruddin of Ambala, President of the All-India Momin Conference.
    Fan Mohammad, Bar-at-Law, a Congressman of Bannu.
    Abdul Qaiyum Khan, deputy leader of the Congress Party in Central Legislative Assembly.
    Sheikh Abdul Majid Sindhi, ex-Minister in the Allah Bux Cabinat.
    Abdul Samad Khan of Quetta, leader of the Anjuman-i-Watan, Baluchistan.
    Syed Abdulla Brelvi, editor of the "Bombay Cronicle".

and Bihar and felt convinced that their programme appealed to Muslims—a claim which was hardly substantiated by
facts. The office of the Majlis was located in Hameed Manzil,
Daryaganj, Delhi.[25]

The Majlis consisted essentially of the same elements as
the Azad Muslim Conference. The fact that Gandhiji's release
synchronized with its inaugural meeting at Delhi appears,
according to the statement of an organiser, to have "profound-
ly affected the proceedings". The inspiration behind the
Majlis was undoubtedly that of Congress; its principal organisers were present or past members of Congress or otherwise
associated with that body, and its activities received a measure
of publicity in the Congress Press out of all proportion to their
importance. The following of the Majlis consisted of its office-
bearers, members of the Working Committee and a handful
of sympathisers. Rifts were common in the new organisation. A
communist Muslim associated with Majlis asked Shaukatullah
Ansari to "clear up the confusion" created by the Press statements issued by the chief organisers and to declare publicly
that the Majlis "stands for unity on the basis of self-determination and does not hinder a Congress-League settlement".[26] He
also told Ansari that this declaration "must come either from
you or Hafiz Muhammed Ibrahim, if you do not want us to
start a controversy right from the beginning". The Majlis
made an attempt at re-organising Muslim anti-League forces
but did not make a deep impression on the Muslim community
generally. Leaders of the Muslim League treated the new
organisation with unconcealed contempt.

Suffice it to say that the Majlis attracted wide
notice from its very foundation but could not for obvious
reasons achieve success commensurate with its promises.
When different institutions seek to work together while
maintaining their separate entity, differences in programme
and outlook must necessarily reveal themselves and hamper
progress. Compromises are inevitable and compromises

---

[25]Home Political F. No. 28-2-1944, para 5.
[26]Ibid, para 6.

always lack the force and intensity of single-minded and unitary action. In spite of this inevitable weakness, it cannot be denied that the Majlis achieved two things. It's establishment was itself a challenge to the Muslim League and threatened the position of Mr. Jinnah and his satellites. It also checked the lying propaganda of British imperialists who sought to represent to the world outside the opinion of the League as the voice of the Musulmans of India.

Glossary

AFRIDI	Name of one of the tribal groups into which Pathan people are divided.
AHIMSA	Hindu (also Buddhist and Jain) doctrine of non-violence.
AHRAR	Free. Freeman. Militant pro-Congress Muslim political and religious organisation founded in 1928.
AKALI	Worshipper of the eternal one. Particularly strict devotee of the Sikh faith. In modern usage, the principal Sikh political party.
AMAN SABHA	Peace Committee.
AMIR	Commander, Prince, ruler; title of ruler of Afghanistan till 1926.
ANJUMAN	An Assembly.
ANNA	Unit of money of the value of 1/16th of a rupee.
AZAD	Free.
AZADI	Freedom.
BRAHMAN (Brahmin)	The highest caste of the Hindu world orginally a priestly caste.
BEGUM	A feminine Muslim title, originally of princesses and noble women.
CRORE	100 lakhs or 10 million.
DARBAR (Durbar)	Court, ceremonial assembly; government of a princely state.
DAR-UL-ULUM	University.
DIWAN (DEWAN)	Minister, in Princely States, Chief Minister; also Council of State. The titles DIWAN SAHIB and DIWAN BAHADUR were conferred by the Viceroy in the name of the British sovereign on distinguished South Indians.
FAQIR	Poor, Needy; thence Muslim religious mendicant.
GURDWARA	Sikh temple.
HARIJAN	The people of God. Term coined by Mahatma Gandhi for untouchables. Title of Mahatma Gandhi's newspaper.
IMAM	A head or chief in religious matters, whether he be the head of all Mohammedans. as the Khalif,

	or the priest of a mosque, or the leader in the prayers of a congregation.
INAM	A gift.
JAGIRDAR	Holder of a Jagir, a tenure under which public revenues of the land were assigned to the tenant either in return for services or unconditionally. The tenure frequently became an hereditary property.
JAMIAT-UL-ULEMA-I-HIND :	Association of learned men of India pro-Congress Muslim organisation.
JAIN	Believer in religion differing from Hinduism founded by Vradhamand Mahavira in sixth century B.C.; numerous among bankers and merchants in central and northern India.
JATHA	Group of demonstrators.
JEHAD	A secred war of Mussalmans, against the infidel.
JIRGA	Council of Elders.
KHAKSAR	Like the earth, humble. Volunteer organisation of Muslims.
KHAN	Ruler, Sovereign. Muslim title; commonly on adjunct to Afghan or Pathan names.
KHILAFAT	Deputy ship. The office of Caliph, the title adopted by successors of Prophet in the leadership of Muslim world.
KORAN	The sacred book of the Muslims the supposed revelations made to Mohammed, and delivered by him orally, collected and committed to writing by the Khalif Omar.
KOTWALI	Police Station.
MAHATMA	Great Soul.
MAULANA	Our Master. Title of respect accorded to Muslim judges, heads of religious orders, and persons of great learning.
MOHTAMIN	An Officer.
MOMIN	Muslim weaver.
MUNSIFF	Judge of lowest court with civil jurisdiction; summary civil court of first instance.
MULLAH	In Muslim countries, a learned man, teacher, doctor of the law; in India, the term is applied to the man who reads the Koran and also to a Muslim School teacher.
NAWAB (NABAB)	Originally a Governor under the Mughal Empire, thence a title of rank conferred on Muslim nobles.
PANDIT	A Hindu title. In its strict sense applied to those versed in the scriptures, but used commonly to denote a member of the Brahman community.
PARGANA	A fiscal area, a sub-division of a Tahsil (Northern India).
PATHAN	Generic name given to pushto speaking people

inhabiting North West Frontier of India and Afghanistan.

PIR A holy man Muslim religious leader; a spiritual guide.

QADIANI Unorthodox Muslim sect properly termed Ahmadi after their founder, Mirza Ghulam Ahmad, but also known as Qadian after the Punjab town of Qadiyan from which he came.

RAJ Kingdom, rule, sovereignty.

RAJA King, prince.

SARDAR (SIRDAR) Chief, leader. Title borne by Sikhs, sometimes also by Hindus and Muslims.

SARKAR State, Government. Originally a treasury, revenue district or territorial division; in the latter sense often spelt CIRCAR.

SANGATHAN Tying together. Adherents of the movement aiming at Hindu Unity.

SATYAGRAHA Holding on to truth. Total self-giving integral to Mahatma Gandhis' whole concept of victory achieved through non-violent resistance.

SHASTAR The law books or sacred writings of the Hindus.

SHAH (SHIA) Sect. The name given by other Muslims to those who believe that Ali, cousin and son-in-law of the Prophet, was his rightful successor.

SUNNI Way-Practice, One who follows the practice of the Prophet; the term generally applied to Muslims who acknowledge the first four Caliphs equally as his rightful successors.

SWARAJ (SWARAJIYA) Self-rule. Independence.

THANA Police Station.

ZEHINDAR (ZAMINDAR) One holding land as an actual proprietor but paying a fixed annual sum to the Government.

ZILA (ZILLA, ZILLAH) Division, District.

Index

A. Imam, 159-60

A.K. Fazlul Haq, 270

A.M. Khwaja, 273

Abbas Ali, character and antecedents 140-41

Abd/al-Rashid Quraishi, 221

Abdul Akbar, 236

Abdul Hasn Mirza, 123

Abdul Kalam Azad, 113, 146, 187, 261

Abdul Karim, 90

Abdul Latif, 270

Abdul Mughni, 174

Abdul Qadir, 89

Abdul Rauf, 88

Abdul Rehman, 89

Abdul Sattar, 89

Abdulla Nadimto, 122

Abdullah, 87, 96

Abdus Salam, 127

Abdus Samad, 128

Abu Bakr, 173-74

Abu Said Muhammad Hossain, 83

Abu Zafar Muhammad Tahir, 221

Achnera, 32, 185

Aden, 164

Afghans, 86, 90, 101

Afghanistan, 81, 88, 105, 126, 129, 235-36

Africa, 44 105, 150

Afridi, 87, 242-43

Afzal Haq, 113

Aga Khan, 66, 150

Agha Ghadnafar Ali Shah, 193-94

Agra, 25, 28, 32-7, 185-6; religious disturbances, 19-20, 33-5, 126, 133

Agror, 78

Ahmad Effendi, 87

Ahmadiyyah, *See* Ahmediya

Ahmed Ali, 96

Ahmed Faiz Beg, 132

Ahmed Ratib Pasha, 132-3

Ahmedabad, 201

Ahmediya, 105-6, 108, 186

Ahrar, 103 109-11, 113-4, 116, 118-9, 178, 199, 270; reject Congress formula, 110; criticism of government, 111; civil disobedience movement, 111-5; government's attitude towards, 113-5; relations with Hindus, 114-5; criticised, 115-8; comparison with Qadiani's, 118-9; conference, All India 117

Aitchison, Sir Charles, 82

Ajab Khan, 90

Ajit Singh, 27

Ajmer, 154, 156, 187

Ajodhya, disturbances, 2-3

Akali, 47, 181

Akbarpur, 156

Akola, 9; disturbances, 6-7; Hindu Sabha, 87

Al Azhar, 145

Al Ghazzal, 22

Alapur, 33

Ali, 164-5, 173

Ali Brothers *See* Muhammad Ali, Shaukat Ali

Ali Ghol, 44

Ali Husain, 128

Aligarh, 32, 81, 141, 156, 186, 202, 231, 259, 267; disturbances, 18; college, 140; university, 133

All India States Muslim League, constitution, 262-4; territorial zones, 263; object, 264; attitude towards war,